712.709 Joh
Johnson, Lauri Macmillan
Creating outdoor classrooms
: schoolyard habitats and
gardens for the Southwest
$39.95
CY ocn175217539
07/30/2008
1st ed.

Creating Outdoor Classrooms

WITHDRAWN
PRINT

Creating Outdoor Classrooms
Schoolyard Habitats and Gardens for the Southwest

Lauri Macmillan Johnson, with **Kim Duffek**: Drawings by **James Richards**

UNIVERSITY OF TEXAS PRESS, AUSTIN

Support for this book comes from an endowment for environmental studies made possible by generous contributions from Richard C. Bartlett, Susan Aspinall Block, and the National Endowment for the Humanities.

Copyright © 2008 by the University of Texas Press
Drawings copyright © 2008 by James Richards
All rights reserved
Printed in the United States of America
FIRST EDITION, 2008

Design by HOUSEdesign llc

Requests for permission to reproduce material from this work should be sent to:
   Permissions
   University of Texas Press
   P.O. Box 7819
   Austin, TX 78713-7819
   www.utexas.edu/utpress/about/bpermission.html
♾ The paper used in this book meets the minimum requirements of ANSI/NISO Z39.48-1992 (R1997) (Permanence of Paper).
Library of Congress Cataloging-in-Publication Data
Johnson, Lauri Macmillan.
   Creating outdoor classrooms : schoolyard habitats and gardens for the Southwest / by Lauri Macmillan Johnson ; with Kim Duffek ; drawings by James Richards. — 1st ed.
      p.   cm.
   Includes bibliographical references.
   ISBN 978-0-292-71746-6 (pbk. : alk. paper)
   1. School gardens—Southwestern States—Design. 2. Nature study—Southwestern States. 3. Outdoor learning laboratories—Southwestern States.
I. Duffek, Kim. II. Title. III. Title: Schoolyard habitats and gardens for the Southwest.
SB56.S68.J64   2008
712'.70979—dc22
                                      2007040760

First, this book is dedicated to Amy Rae and Steven M. Johnson and the many family nature outings with picnics and hikes as well as home gardening projects that created an essential fabric for our family.

Second, the book is dedicated to all the administrators, teachers, parents, and community members who make special efforts to connect children to the natural world.

CONTENTS

Preface, xi | Acknowledgments, xiii

KIM DUFFEK: Introduction

About This Book, xv
Making Outdoor Classrooms a Reality, xv
The Need for Wildlife Habitat and Native Gardens, xvi
Bioregions of the Arid Southwest, xvi

CHAPTER 1: Schoolyards

The Schoolyard as an Outdoor Classroom, 1
Overview of Schoolyard Environments, 2
    Introduction, 2
    History of Playground Design with Applications
      for Contemporary Playground Design, 2
    Nature and Play, 6
    Adult Memories of Valued Play Places, 8
    Implications for Design, 9
Learning and the Natural Outdoor Classroom, 10
Schoolyard Garden Types, 14
    Art Gardens, 14
    Cultural History Gardens, 16
    Ecological Gardens, 17
    Literacy Gardens, 18
    Vegetable Gardens, 20

CHAPTER 2: Design Theory

Introduction, 23
History of Garden Styles, 23
    Prehistoric "Gardens" (20,000–3300 BC), 24
    Ancient Egyptian Gardens (3300–500 BC), 24
    Ancient Mesopotamian (3500–538 BC), Sumerian (3500–900 BC),
        Assyrian (900–625 BC), and Neo-Babylonian (611–538 BC) Gardens, 25
    Ancient Persian Gardens (539–331 BC), 26
    Ancient Greek Gardens (700–136 BC), 26
    Ancient Roman Gardens (510 BC–AD 476), 27
    Ancient Chinese Gardens (1600 BC–AD 1279), 27
    Japanese Gardens (AD 575–1600), 28
    Medieval European Gardens (AD 476–1350), 29
    Islamic (Moorish) Gardens, Spain (AD 700s–1400s), 30
    Italian Renaissance Gardens (AD 1350–1765), 31
    French Grand-Style Gardens (AD 1495–1750), 32
    English Romantic Gardens (AD 1715–1840), 32
    Spanish Colonial Gardens (AD 1492–mid-1700s), 33
    Colonial and Early American Gardens (AD 1630–1840), 34
    American Romantic Gardens (AD 1830–1930), 35
    Victorian Gardens (AD 1820–1900), 36
    Classical Beaux-Arts Gardens (AD 1893–1930), 37
    Modern Gardens (AD 1930–late 1970s), 38
    Postmodern and Contemporary Gardens (AD mid-1970s–present), 39
Design Fundamentals, 40
    Design Principles, 40
    Design Elements, 43

CHAPTER 3: Beginning the Design Process

Introduction, 45
A Design Process for Planning Outdoor Classrooms, Wildlife Habitats,
   and Gardens, 47
    Identify Participants, 47
    Write a Design Program, 50
Conclusion, 71

CHAPTER 4: Site Research and Design Synthesis

Review and Evaluate Previous Steps, 73
Site Research, 73
    Site Selection, 73
    Site Inventory, 74
    Site Analysis, 77
Design Synthesis, 86
Conceptual Design, 87
    Zones, Spaces, Design Features, and Spatial Sequencing, 87
    Circulation Patterns, 87
    Testing Design Concepts, 88

Preliminary Design, 93
Final Design, 96

CHAPTER 5: Design Essentials

Introduction, 99
Project Funding, 99
    Grants and Cash Donations, 100
    In-kind Donations, 100
    Organization of the Fund-raising Process, 101
Design Features, 101
    Earthworks, 102
    Ponds, 102
    Plants, 104
    Shade Structures, 108
    Storage Areas, 110
    Pathways, 110
    Seating, 112
    Walls, 113
    Signs, 114
Maintenance, 115
    Weeding, 115
    Fertilization, 115
    Pruning, 116
    Bird Feeders and Bird Baths, 116
Accessibility, 116
    Requirements, 116
Safety, 117
Project Evaluation and Revision, 117
Outdoor Classroom and Schoolyard Habitat Assessment Criteria, 119

CHAPTER 6: Ecological Principles and Wildlife *by Kim Duffek*

Introduction to Wildlife Ecology, 123
Elements for Survival, 125
    Food Resources, 125
    Water Availability, 126
    Providing Shelter, 128
    Space to Survive, 129
Pollinator Gardens and Wild Visitors, 130
    Introduction, 130
    Hummingbird Gardens, 131
    Butterfly Gardens, 133
    Bee Gardens, 134
    Moth Gardens, 135
    Bat Gardens, 136
    Fly Gardens, 137
    Wildlife Gardens, 138
Completing the Web, 139
    Pest Control, 139

Decomposition, 141
Unwanted Visitors, 141
Seeds for Thought, 142
Words of Inspiration, 144

Appendix: Regional Plant Tables *by Kim Duffek*, 145
References and Additional Reading, 179

PREFACE

Natural environments are important for people of all ages, but especially for children. Wild places provide young people with opportunities to discover natural phenomena like those described by Mark Twain. Brilliant colors held within streams of sunlight; rainwater creating miniature drainageways in the mud; wind permanently bending trees; ant highways; and the endless sights, sounds, and tastes of the natural world are mysteries of life that have inspired civilizations throughout the ages.

This book is a general guide for the design and implementation of natural outdoor classrooms envisioned to include a variety of learning opportunities through the creation of wildlife habitats and other gardens, including art gardens, cultural history gardens, ecological gardens, vegetable gardens, and literacy gardens. As such, the text is intended as a sourcebook that includes sections on the history of garden styles, design fundamentals and processes, and information and ideas to provide readers with inspiration for their own unique garden creations. Focus is given to the Southwest—its natural and cultural history, arid land and climate, plants, and wildlife. But the content of this text can be applied in the creation of gardens for other regions, whether these focus on wildlife, art, culture or history, integrated learning, or simply delight and contemplation.

Because the parameters of all outdoor classrooms and other types of landscapes are unique, the design and implementation of any project will necessarily involve additional research and certainly modification of this information. Use this book as a touchstone reference and a point of departure, and be inspired to work collaboratively, particularly with children and youth, as their creative ideas are limitless. Be prepared to think of your garden project as a temporal place that will always evolve through time, as natural processes are dynamic and learning about the environment is interactive.

Now, far away in the woods a bird called; another answered; presently the hammering of a woodpecker was heard. Gradually the cool dim gray morning whitened, and as gradually sounds multiplied and life manifested itself. The marvel of Nature shaking off sleep and going to work unfolded itself to the musing boy. A little green worm came crawling over a dewy leaf, lifting two-thirds of his body into the air from time to time and "sniffing around," then proceeding again—for he was measuring . . .

MARK TWAIN, *The Adventures of Tom Sawyer*

ACKNOWLEDGMENTS

I would like first to acknowledge the Arizona Game and Fish Department, which funded a handbook and series of workshops on Schoolyard Habitat Design in 1999 that led to the development of this book. I would also like to acknowledge the contributions from the Arizona-Sonora Desert Museum.

Outdoor classroom teachers Mike Amundson, with Miles Exploratory Learning Center, Tucson, Arizona, and Renee Carstens, with Pueblo Gardens Elementary School, Tucson, Arizona, should be recognized for their creative teaching and exemplary outdoor classrooms that stand out as models for integrated and place-based learning. Photographs of their classrooms, over the span of several years, provided some of the examples seen in this book. Suzy Peacock and Stacey L. Hodge, with Real People, The Rainwater Environmental Alliance for Learning, and the REAL Schools Initiative, provided tours of their school projects in Fort Worth, Texas—some design features from these innovative outdoor classrooms are featured in this book.

Graduate students from the School of Landscape Architecture, The University of Arizona, who made contributions include Ariel Fisher, Jessie Maran, Laura Mielcarek, Gerardo Mayoral-Peña, Robin Jablonski, Mélisa Kennedy, Renee Schaefer, Janice Takessian, Robin Pinto, Julie Parizek, Helen Walthier, Fan Wang, and Hampton Uzzelle. Nancy Emptage, administrative staff at the University, provided technical support and encouragement. Ronald R. Stoltz, ASLA, FCELA, Director of the School of Landscape Architecture, provided critical direction on intellectual property rights. Margaret Livingston, Associate Professor of Landscape Architecture, made a number of content contributions, and her work with the Tucson Botanical Gardens as well as her ever-popular planting design studio at The University of Arizona demonstrates her expertise in desert ecology and urban wildlife. I wish to thank Kim Duffek, with the Arizona-Sonora Desert Museum, whose contributions in areas of wildlife ecology and desert plants have made this text a useful resource for southwestern gardeners. Finally, I am grateful for the generosity of James Richards, principal of TOWNSCAPE, Inc., who produced the drawings that activate our

LAURI MACMILLAN JOHNSON, Professor
School of Landscape Architecture
College of Architecture & Landscape Architecture
The University of Arizona

KIM DUFFEK, Horticulturist
Department of Botany
Arizona-Sonora Desert Museum

creative spirits; without his dedication to this project, it would have not been completed.

I am indebted to Steve Phillips, of the Arizona-Sonora Desert Museum, for having the faith in me to encourage me to tackle this project. Many thanks go to those who contributed their expertise in the compilation of the regional tables: Doug Larson, of the Arizona-Sonora Desert Museum; Michael Bostwick, of the Zoological Society of San Diego; Sally Isaacson, of the Santa Barbara Botanic Garden; Janica Jones, of the Los Angeles Zoo; Margaret Robison, of the Theodore Payne Foundation; Allison Shilling, of the California Native Plant Society; Daphne Richards, of the Texas Agricultural Extension Service; Peter Gerlach, of Spadefoot Nursery, Pearce, Arizona; Mike Bergan, of the Desert Water Agency, Palm Springs, California; Tim Gilliland, of Alice Byrne School, and Leigh Ann Hannan, horticulturist, both in Yuma, Arizona; Dave Heveron, of the Living Desert, Palm Desert, California; Shirley Waldrip, of Desert Garden Nursery, Yuma, Arizona; Peter Duncombe, of the Desert Demonstration Gardens, Las Vegas, Nevada; and Susan Jones, of the Landscape Architecture Program at the University of Nevada, Las Vegas. Although much of the original data has been shuffled and homogenized, without this expert help, my job would have been much more difficult.

The Botany Department at the Arizona-Sonora Desert Museum reviewed the tables for the appendix in several forms and, with their wonderful eyes for detail, kept me consistent and offered additional notes. These people are true coworkers: George Montgomery (Curator), John Wiens, Julie Emmett, Doug Larson, Kim Baker, Cory Martin, and Mark Sitter. Thanks to Barb Skye for supporting me in doing this project, and to Lauri Macmillan Johnson for conceiving this project.

KIM DUFFEK # Introduction

About This Book

This publication is intended to provide creative inspiration and guidance toward the implementation of successful outdoor classrooms for integrated learning. Designers of these spaces might consider art, mathematics, science, or, more specifically, native wildlife and plants as opportunities for learning. The text describes design processes and offers useful ideas for all garden types, particularly wildlife habitats and gardens of the Southwest. In recent years, much interest has arisen in obtaining information regarding the use of native plants to attract wildlife to backyards and schoolyards. Interaction with wildlife in a garden not only provides a venue for learning basic ecology but affords opportunity to study subjects as diverse as music and math. The need for a book such as this has arisen from a national movement in gardening with native plants. Thus the book, with its regional focus on the arid Southwest, is an essential tool for teachers in the Southwest who wish to initiate natural learning landscapes. Descriptive coverage of the subject also makes this text an ideal reference for landscape architecture students or home garden enthusiasts.

Making Outdoor Classrooms a Reality

The best outdoor classroom gardens are created with an overarching concept that is used toward the development of a schoolwide vision. This book contains ideas and necessary information for the design and implementation of successful outdoor classrooms. Several topics, including a history of playground design, nature and play, and learning in the natural outdoor classroom, provide a good overview. Other sections, such as schoolyard garden types and design theory, help designers develop strong design concepts, and information on site research and program development, with logical approaches to creating outdoor classrooms, will assist designers with approaches aimed at helping schools develop an individualized planning process for their unique goals. Special focus is given to ecological principles and garden requirements for pollinators and other wildlife of the Southwest, as these provide a good basis for integrated learning. Throughout the text are creative ideas on design features and materials, as well as thoughts on student activities that aid in the creation and utilization of outdoor classrooms. Sidebars, illustrations, photographs, and captions within the book can be used as helpful hints and overviews, with more detailed information contained within the main body of the text. The regional plant tables in the appendix provide a concentrated source of information useful in planning southwestern gardens of any type. Each table focuses on plants most suitable for a particular bioregion, with helpful comments, traits, and benefits for wildlife.

The Need for Wildlife Habitat and Native Gardens

With continued rapid growth of western cities, planning for the future needs of residents is reaching a critical stage. Every day, wild lands are removed to make way for human development. Habitat destruction creates an ever-increasing struggle for the wild creatures to survive and reproduce. Nevertheless, responsible planning could preserve our richest habitats and most critical wildlife corridors within cities and subdivisions. Schoolyard wildlife habitats might serve as design models for the community. Additionally, while some cities are already in a water crisis, others may have time for improvement. Cities such as Tucson, Arizona, have become exemplary models for desert living, as they have been successful in reducing residential water needs through the use of native and drought-tolerant plants. For some cities, however, there is room for improvement in the area of water conservation, particularly with regard to the ongoing implementation of high-water-use landscapes. Creating gardens and wildlife habitats with native plants is an important way to educate citizens and children alike about the necessity to conserve water. As they learn about the natural environment in general, they will also be exposed to specific information on regional ecology and natural resources. Within the context of desert environments, this will undoubtedly lead to better understanding about water resources. Therefore, contact with these outdoor classrooms will empower them to make a difference and become stewards of our environment throughout their adult lives.

Bioregions of the Arid Southwest

This book discusses creating outdoor classrooms and wildlife habitat gardens within the arid Southwest. A number of bioregions exist within this region, each with its own temperature and rainfall patterns, topography, and geologic history (see map in appendix). Each of these bioregions possesses attributes that differ from the others. This affects the types of plants that will grow or thrive there. From east to west and north to south, differences in temperature and rainfall patterns define many of the adaptations observed in wild communities regarding how they cope with conditions in their environment. Geology also influences these patterns greatly.

In the Southeast, high rainfall influenced by the Gulf of Mexico tapers off in the hill country west of Austin, Texas. To the west of that area, arid Desert Grasslands begin to reign. In the plains of Texas, sporadic surges of Gulf moisture bring primarily summer rain to the region, a region that extends in several bands from Texas through New Mexico to central Arizona. Characterized by bunch grasses, it also commonly contains yucca, agave, mesquite, and juniper species.

Southwestern Texas, southern New Mexico, and a small portion of southwestern Arizona are the northern limits of the Chihuahuan Desert. Rainfall in this bioregion is primarily in the late spring and late summer and is influenced by moisture from the Gulf of Mexico and the rain shadow effect of mountains. The Chihuahuan Desert bioregion occurs at higher elevations than the Desert Grasslands and is characterized by low shrubs and leaf succulents such as creosote, yucca, and ocotillo.

Abutting the western edge of the Desert Grasslands is the Arizona Uplands subdivision of the Sonoran Desert. Studded by iconic saguaros and leguminous trees, it is the wettest of southwestern deserts, with rain being distributed in both the summer, from the Gulf of Mexico, and the winter, from the Pacific Ocean. Most of the region is on slopes or sloping plains at lower elevations than the Desert Grasslands and the Chihuahuan Desert.

As the influences of summer rains diminish in southwestern Arizona and southeastern California, the Lower Colorado subdivision of the Sonoran Desert takes over. It is characterized by very wide, low-elevation valleys containing expanses of creosote and white bursage, with saguaros and small trees being limited to washes and low mountains.

To the north of the Lower Colorado lies the Mojave Desert, which receives only a small amount of rain during the winter. The wide plains and rugged mountains making up the Mojave share much of the flora and fauna with other North American deserts. It is hot in the summer and rather cold in winter. The Joshua tree is the hallmark plant of this region, and annual plants are abundant; other vegetation is sparse.

To the west of the Lower Colorado subdivision of the Sonoran Desert lies the Southern California Inland Valleys bioregion. Fire-adapted chaparral plants such as chamise constitute the native vegetation. Good rainfall occurs mostly in winter within this biologic community situated on mostly steep mountain slopes.

Nestled between the Southern California Inland Valleys and the Pacific Ocean is a narrow strip of land constituting the Southern California Coastal Edge bioregion. Although it receives less rainfall than the Inland Valleys in winter, it is influenced greatly by the ocean and benefits from higher humidity and almost no frost. Low-growing shrubs such as sage and buckwheat make up what little is left of the native vegetation.

In all cases, soils influence the performance of plants through their physical and chemical makeup. Particle size of the soil determines how quickly water drains through it and dictates the frequency of watering. A clay soil with small particle size will hold on to water much more than sand. Minerals within the soil can also influence plant growth.

The tables in the appendix address the characteristics of plants that tend to perform well within these diverse bioregions. Some of the same plants may have varying horticultural needs in different areas, and may be referred to with different common names in other parts of the country. The reader is invited to try plants from other regions if they seem to fit within the parameters of the garden site. None of the tables are all-inclusive, and although it can be difficult in some communities to find native plants, there are people who grow them. A great science activity for children might be an experiment in which they determine the best way to germinate and grow native plants. This could involve Internet research combined with hands-on activities. Commercial growers may lend their expertise and even benefit from the information. For example, the tables in this book are actually the work of many people who, over the years, have provided information on their plants to others.

Creating Outdoor Classrooms

CHAPTER 1 Schoolyards

The Schoolyard as an Outdoor Classroom

Schoolyards can be developed as outdoor classrooms that are spirited and interactive places for integrated and place-based learning. Children can play a major role in the design and implementation of the place. Characterized by natural, cultural, and artistic features, schoolyard outdoor classrooms can be dynamic and evolve through time as children and their leaders make design adjustments and create and re-create the place.

Heidi Vasiloff (1998, 6), of the Arizona Game and Fish Department, promotes the use of a portion of the schoolyard for development of wildlife habi-

tats, and she defines these environments as "places where young people and wildlife connect. Built and planted with native vegetation to provide a home for wildlife, they serve as outdoor classrooms where students learn about our natural environments. Schoolyard habitats are rooted in communities: in students, teachers, parents, and businesspeople. They require work and commitment, and they establish a lifelong connection with wildlife." Through hands-on activities in schoolyard projects, students can explore and learn about the deep connections between themselves, other people, nature, and the world at large.

Traditionally, school natural areas have had a botanical or wildlife focus, but they are now being used across the curriculum for active learning in all subject

(far left) A schoolyard outdoor classroom can be designed as a natural area for hands-on learning and should be allowed to change over time as new users make refinements and additions. This approach will keep students interested in the place for years to come. (center and far right) This schoolyard has evolved through the years, and it always offers something new to learn. Mike Amundson, outdoor teacher at Miles Exploratory Learning Center, Tucson, Arizona, should be commended for his innovation in teaching outdoors.

areas. They often have themes that include not only wildlife areas, which recreate natural habitats, but also a variety of other garden types. Pollinator gardens and wildlife gardens are expanded upon in Chapter 6, "Ecological Principles and Wildlife," but some of the specifically themed gardens, such as *art gardens,* designed to cultivate art literacy and appreciation; *cultural history gardens,* which explore traditions used by native cultures; *ecology gardens,* which aim to promote environmental protection; *literacy gardens,* created to stimulate avid reading; and *vegetable gardens,* which encourage healthful nutritional choices, are discussed in this chapter in the "Schoolyard Garden Types" section below. These garden types and others are being created within school environments as outdoor laboratories for research, learning, and student enjoyment.

Overview of Schoolyard Environments

Introduction

Schoolyards have typically been thought of as spaces that provide students with opportunities to "let off steam" through structured physical fitness and free play. This concept has been realized through the construction of athletic fields and playgrounds, which help students develop physical, social, cognitive, and emotional skills. However, natural outdoor areas within schoolyards have historically been overlooked and even ignored as places for play and learning. "A typical pattern wherever schools and child care centers are built is to destroy the natural features—trees, grass, topsoil . . . and leave a barren, lifeless area where children are expected to play" (Frost and Wortham 1988, 24).

History of Playground Design with Applications for Contemporary Playground Design

During the nineteenth century, Frederick Law Olmsted promoted the transcendentalist belief that natural parks could humanize and heal ill-natured and socially distressed urban dwellers, particularly those living in crowded slums. The Olmsted and Calvert Vaux 1857 plan for what became New York City's Central Park included active play areas for children, with boat rides on the lake and open fields for fun and frolic. Social reform movements of the late nineteenth century, responding to the Industrial Revolution, removed children from factory labor and helped to launch the American playground movement. In 1885, Boston created large wooden sandboxes, or *sand gardens,* based on play areas developed in Berlin, Germany. According to Aase Eriksen (1985), playground equipment was developed as early as 1891, and Philip Pregill and Nancy Volkman (1999, 569) note that during this same period athletic programs within schools began to promote physical fitness to encourage and demonstrate the Puritan "values of hard work and self-reliance" to immigrant children. As World War I approached, school athletic programs, such as organized baseball, football, and gymnastics, prepared youth for possible military engagements.

This interest in active sports and school exercise programs gained momentum under John F. Kennedy's administration through the establishment of the National Council on Youth Fitness in 1961 (Weston 1962). Playground equipment from this period included swings, monkey bars, flying rings, slides, and other climbing apparatuses that were developed to improve large motor skills. Composed of a collection of isolated metal structures set upon a flat paved sur-

Many schools lack natural features for play and learning—playgrounds are often empty paved areas that look much like parking lots.

Frederick Law Olmsted designed several Romantic American parks to provide the experience of nature within the city, and in this way these great spaces serve as healing gardens for park users.

Metal playground equipment from the 1960s was used to promote physical fitness, but, unfortunately, the design layout of these playgrounds often resembled that of prison yards.

face, however, play yards from this period evoke visions of prison yards. These environments reflected the stark industrial image typical of Modern machine-age design. Today there is a movement to remove and discard some of the old 1960s playground equipment from public parks and playgrounds. Although redesign of these play areas is warranted, the apparatuses from this period can be reused in creative new ways. For example, monkey bars could be sited along a sandy hillside with shade trees planted tightly around the base of the structure. This arrangement would create a new identity and purpose for the metal structure, which now becomes an enclosure; children might imagine a fort, a house, or a boat. Small hiding spots where children can "see without being seen," in accordance with Jay Appleton's *prospect-refuge theory* (1996), are important places for children. Branches, cardboard, rope, and other collected materials could be used for ongoing creative adaptations. Swing sets from this period (1960s) provide places to sit, swing, and watch and are enjoyed by all ages as wonderful additions in playgrounds today.

As a reaction to the austere playgrounds from the Kennedy era, a second playground movement occurred in the late 1960s and 1970s. Partially informed by John Dewey's (1938) theories in education centered on childhood interactive learning and environmental manipulation, innovations in playground design arose. Richard Dattner (1969, 137) wrote:

> Play is the way that children learn about themselves and the world they live in. In the process of mastering familiar situations and learning to cope with new ones, their intelligence and personality grow, as well as their bodies. The environment for play must be rich in experience, and it must be, to a significant extent, under the control of the child.

It was suggested that the places that children create for themselves have the power to evoke high levels of satisfaction and learning. Adventure playgrounds (Allen 1968) were cited as a prototype for fulfilling children's natural desire to learn through *arousal-seeking* behavior—in other words, play (Ellis 1973). In an approach developed in Denmark in 1943, vacant lots were made into play areas

Consider small spaces for children. "Over time I have come to realize that a few intimate places mean more to my children, and to others, than all the glorious panoramas I could ever show them. Because I sense their comfort there, their tiny hand-shaped shelter has come to epitomize true intimacy for me. When my children are not staying with me, I often walk near their hide-away within the hackberry canopy, and imagine that they are simply nested within it, not far away" (Nabhan 1994, 7).

This tree house made by children is a good example of creative play—an engaging, exciting activity through which children learn and grow. Photograph by Steven M. Johnson.

by the children themselves under the safe supervision of an adult *play leader* who coordinated the construction and regulated safety. Lady Allen of Hurtwood (1968) was an advocate of these innovative places, and she wrote: "At its best, *play is a kind of research,* and like all research at the adult level, it should be an adventure and an experiment that is greatly enjoyed" (as quoted from Bork 1983, 68; italics added).

Play was linked to social, emotional, and cognitive development, and it was suggested that play equipment and playground design strive to promote healthful childhood development through imagination and problem solving. Research called for complex equipment choices and indicated that "realistic" equipment, such as rocking horses, replicas of Cinderella's carriage, or rocket ships, limited creativity, as children were not likely to invent new uses for the forms. In response, designers created amorphous playground layouts and connected climbing structures with each other in linked complex patterns within a variety of settings intended to promote inventive play. Design features included wooden climbing structures, cobblestone-covered earthen mounds, tire swings, cable bridges, and soft ground surfaces such as gravel, sand, and rubberized safety surfaces. Children could pretend to climb mountains, row across rivers, and live in tree houses. *Loose parts,* a term used by Simon Nicholson (1976) to describe recycled household objects such as cardboard boxes and milk cartons, were often added to the play setting to facilitate the child's manipulation of the environment. As research progressed in this area, natural features such as earth, water, and trees were credited as important play stimuli that held long-term satisfaction (Hart 1979; Moore and Wong 1997; and Nabhan and Trimble 1994).

Robin C. Moore suggests that the loose parts, or *play props,* favored by children are natural materials such as twigs, berries, and nuts. In his book *Plants for Play,* an account of one girl's experience is a wonderful testimony to this idea: "'The flowers are magic,' a girl says very matter-of-factly, 'especially these.' She bends down and picks some scarlet flax. 'They'll make your hands magic, then everything you touch'll be magic. Pens will write magic, glasses will see magic. Everything'll be magic'" (Moore 1993, 4).

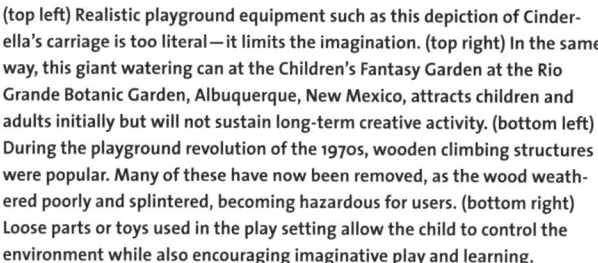

(top left) Realistic playground equipment such as this depiction of Cinderella's carriage is too literal—it limits the imagination. (top right) In the same way, this giant watering can at the Children's Fantasy Garden at the Rio Grande Botanic Garden, Albuquerque, New Mexico, attracts children and adults initially but will not sustain long-term creative activity. (bottom left) During the playground revolution of the 1970s, wooden climbing structures were popular. Many of these have now been removed, as the wood weathered poorly and splintered, becoming hazardous for users. (bottom right) Loose parts or toys used in the play setting allow the child to control the environment while also encouraging imaginative play and learning.

This child is pretending the snapdragon can talk. Natural materials are play props favored by children and are often used in imaginative ways.

Although the research indicates benefits for children through manipulation of the environment in play, American communities have not been able to fully or accurately embrace the implications of this research for public playground design, and the spirit of childhood adventure is often missing in contemporary outdoor environments for children. Brightly colored, glossy enameled catalog-selected play structures now dominate the play setting within manicured landscapes that do not permit manipulation of the environment. Trees are not climbable, and children are not allowed to make forts, build tunnels, play with mud, or find secret hiding places in these public play spaces. Yet as urban children are increasingly removed from these activities in their home environments, public design for children must accommodate these primordial needs—allow children to create artifacts, even messy ones, and allow direct contact with nature.

As playgrounds and schoolyards in America adhere to safety guidelines in an attempt to prevent injuries and reduce lawsuits, places for children have developed into spaces that lack the complexity needed to challenge them and sustain their interest. Children often seek adventure in these "sanitized" places by climbing across the tops of swing sets, crashing their bikes into climbing structures, or vandalizing furnishings. By designing these environments to be "safe," complex play interactions are discouraged, and some children find deviant ways to satisfy their need for adventure. They use equipment in unsafe ways and seek alternative play spaces such as drainage culverts, trash Dumpsters, or construction sites where they can manipulate scrap wood, tree branches, rocks, used tires, discarded mattresses, and other found materials.

Nature and Play

Nature has been cited as a valuable component in children's play and learning environments (Cooper-Marcus 2001; Francis 1995; Hart 1979; Moore and Wong 1997; Sebba 1991; Wilson 1997). As Roger Hart, who has spent many years observing children at play, explained in an article in *Natural History* (1973, 69):

American playgrounds, such as this one in Tucson, Arizona, frequently consist of climbing structures selected from playground equipment manufacturing companies. Play environments are often static and unused.

(above) Although there is a playground nearby, this child from an urban neighborhood chooses to play in a trash Dumpster.

(left) This unplanted tomato garden in a private backyard was spontaneously converted into a mud bath—children prefer to manipulate natural materials in play.

"The natural environment offers a wealth of play potential for young children, with trees and small patches of water the most valued elements. One tree can engage a child for days at a time or, periodically, over a span of years. Manufacturers of playground equipment have found it impossible to re-create such richness." An early example of a nature-centered playground was the Washington Environmental Yard (Moore and Wong 1997), an elementary school playground in Berkeley, California. The design, by Robin C. Moore and Herb H. Wong, transformed an asphalt playground into an ecological garden for play and learning. Roger Hart (1973, 69) recorded another school situation in which children spontaneously built "dams, bridges, tunnels, islands, and waterfalls . . . [within] elaborate stream systems." These pioneering school examples use natural elements—trees, hills, water, and dirt—in design concepts that encourage children to manipulate the environment. Unfortunately, places such as these are the exception and not the standard.

Children place high value on natural places for play and personal investigation, as was revealed by Lisa Schicker (1987), who observed children playing. Within her sample, 50 percent of all activity involved direct contact and experimentation with natural materials, including animals and insects. She suggested that their least favorite play spots were, in fact, traditional playgrounds. Children seem drawn to unkempt landscapes—ones that include piles of dirt

Children in a housing project in Loveland, Colorado, were asked to show the design/research team their favorite play places: these included natural drainage ways and piles of dirt that were manipulated with twigs, pieces of lumber, and other construction materials.

or sand, discarded materials, and overgrown plants. According to Roger Hart, "Children will not manipulate or modify an overtly cared for and guarded landscape. Manicured lawns, miniature trimmed trees, and the absence of dirt piles, surface water, and large trees all convey a strong message to a child—do not touch" (1973, 67). In a study by the author (Johnson 1988), children living in a housing development in Loveland, Colorado, were asked to show the design/research team their favorite play places. Results indicated that natural drainage ways and construction sites with piles of dirt and discarded materials were their preferred sites. These nondesigned places seem to attract children because they make them feel freer to manipulate the environment in ways that parks and playgrounds often prohibit.

Adult Memories of Valued Play Places

In several studies by the author, various groups of adults were asked to explore childhood memories of play places and experiences. The questions asked were: (1) Where did you play as a child? and (2) What were your most memorable play activities or experiences? Participants wrote short descriptions about their childhood play places and play experiences and, in some cases, included hand drawings or photographs of the actual places where they played. Selected writings below describe the tenor of the results:

> A narrow swath of feeble trees and shrubs bordered our yard, into which my mother carved a few "campsite" clearings. There was a narrow "jungle path" along the center of the band of trees which connected the open areas. This clump of brush, raspberry bushes, and thin trees was alternately a woodland camp for tree houses, a South Pacific World War II jungle island for foxholes, or a haunted forest theme park at Halloween. (Barry Morse, cited from Johnson 2004)

. . .

> I grew up in northern Florida. As a child, I climbed trees, rode bikes, and played "spy." As a young girl, I had as many scraped knees as my older

brother. One of my most favorite places to play was a forest-swamp area. Cattails and occasionally snakes were in my backyard. I loved the ditches, the trees, the meadowlike fields—I liked the dirt. We made an underground fort that almost killed us . . . my mom pointed out that not only should fires not be lit underground; . . . [she] also pointed out the obvious—that our structure could have caved in on us. There is something so exciting and calming about nature . . . Every sense is awakened and soothed simultaneously. My mother and father let me play—encouraging me to get "dirty." Aside from gnats and mosquitoes, I loved being outside. Now if I could only get my office windows to open. (Anonymous school principal, cited from Johnson 2003)

. . .

The school had a wash next to it, and at one end the wash went under a road. The tunnels that allowed for water flow were the most interesting places to play around. Only a few times did we actually go in the tubes, but they were always interesting places to hide, meet and talk . . . I think the lure of the unknown is what hooked us in. The tunnels are dark and spooky, so they were perfect. It seems we were always interested in little "fort"-like areas that could protect us [and where] we could hold our "business." (Anonymous student, cited from Johnson 2002)

Responses, in some cases, were categorized into: (1) play settings, (2) play activities, (3) play objects, and (4) feelings associated with the play experience. Play settings were divided into two subcategories: (a) public parks and playgrounds and (b) less structured places that included trails, riparian areas, private yards, tall-grass meadows, parking lots, culverts, and streets. Results indicated that approximately 25 percent of the responses mentioned public parks and playgrounds as their places for play, whereas approximately 75 percent of the responses reported the use of less structured spaces. Regardless of the setting, play activities largely included interaction with natural materials, such as digging in earth or sand; gathering sticks, grass, or other materials for construction; and exploring a variety of insects and small animals. Predominant play objects included dirt, sand, mud, grass, rocks, and plant parts such as branches, twigs, and pine cones, with less mention of manufactured objects such as toys. Feelings associated with play centered on imaginative play and included descriptions with words such as "dangerous," "adventurous," "magical," "mysterious," "private," "no adults," and "forbidden."

Implications for Design

American playgrounds are in need of design reform. Some of the considerations for success might include community involvement, adult supervision (hired play leaders/teachers), and provision for ongoing physical change—particularly environmental modifications by children. Attitudes regarding how playgrounds and schoolyards are supposed to look (pristine and well manicured) versus how they might look if children were more actively manipulating the environment will play a role in reform as well as issues regarding liability concerns. The method of asking adults to recall favorite childhood play places could be used as a component in design process and development. This technique could be adapted to public meetings with parents and municipal administrators as a means toward playground reform. It seems when adults are asked to remember where they played as children they more clearly identify with what children need. It is then that adults begin to realize that most playgrounds are static and not really places where children can engage in manipulation of the environment—an important component of play.

Learning and the Natural Outdoor Classroom

When children explore natural places, they gain a better understanding of the connections between humans, natural systems, and the world and universe at large. They develop self-confidence as they meet challenges such as hiking through the desert over mountains and hills, climbing rocks, or wading across streams, and they have an instinctive need to interact with the environment. "Research . . . suggests that children seem to have a special affinity, or connection, to the natural world—that they experience a type of 'primal seeing' which, for most people, diminishes with age. . . . This primal seeing allows children to 'experience the natural world in a deep and direct manner, not as a background for events, but rather, as a factor and stimulation'" (R. Sebba, quoted in Wilson 1995, 31–32).

Young people who experience the natural environment may develop sensitivity toward natural systems, wildlife, and habitat protection as they grow older.

This natural outdoor classroom includes native vegetation, a stream, curved pathways, and plenty of shade and seating. These students take pride in showing the wildlife that live in their outdoor classroom.

Schoolyard natural outdoor classrooms, including wildlife habitats and other gardens, provide an ideal setting for environmental programs. This text offers discussion on a variety of natural school environments, and the terms *outdoor classroom, wildlife habitat,* and *gardens* are interchanged as needed to illustrate various points. Although a focus on habitat creation is reflected throughout this book, school groups should feel free to formulate their own concepts for the outdoor classroom.

Through the planning, creation, and care of these natural outdoor classrooms, young people can observe firsthand the environmental issues that affect our lives. For many students, these places provide the catalyst to inspire their budding curiosity and creative spirit. Several schools throughout the country have developed and implemented programs that integrate environmental education into the general curriculum. In these programs, students develop an increased awareness of, and appreciation for, the importance of environmental protection. A number of writers stress "the moral and cultural aspects of [ecological] restoration in generating healthy relationships between people and the land" (Grant and Littlejohn 2001, 10).

As students learn more about the natural world, they may come to respect it and, in doing so, perhaps begin to develop the belief that people must live in balance with nature. In *The Backyard Naturalist* (1993, 63), Craig Tufts, chief naturalist at the National Wildlife Federation, observed: "Suburban children benefit substantially from growing up in a rich natural environment. Through play in natural environments, kids develop ecological values early in life. They are far more apt than other children to become environmentally sensitive adults— with wonderful childhood memories, like yours and mine." As more people are living in urban environments with diminished access to natural areas, he has suggested that our schools and learning centers might strive to better expose our youth to direct contact with nature and the natural world. Additionally, Thomas Lickona (1995, 8) sees "a clear and urgent need" for schools to "get back in the business of moral education." He reminds us, "Young people are increasingly hurting themselves and others, and decreasingly concerned about contributing to the welfare of their fellow human beings. In this they reflect the ills of our society in need of spiritual and moral renewal."

Natural outdoor classrooms offer an opportunity to introduce ethics and values into the public school atmosphere. A spiritual awakening and sensitivity toward living creatures, including other people, can be cultivated through learning experiences within the schoolyard and the natural world at large. It is critical that these opportunities be made available to our youth, and especially to those living in cities who are largely removed from daily contact with nature.

Today, the inclusion of natural areas within school campuses has become an increasingly popular concept, and a variety of these natural classrooms have emerged throughout the country. Recently, with an increase in childhood obesity, these natural areas are being explored for potential health benefits. It is expected that with the addition of natural outdoor classrooms and play areas, including trails and other circulation systems, children's physical activity will increase as they play outside more often.

Howard Gardner offers the notion that individuals possess multiple intelligences: (1) linguistic—exhibited by poets; (2) logical/mathematical—indicative of ability in math and science; (3) spatial—possessed by artists and designers; (4) musical—"Leonard Bernstein had lots of it; Mozart, presumably,

Shown here is one teacher's inventive way of helping children learn state capitals through kinesthetic learning. Children clutch miniature cars while they crawl on hands and knees, driving the toys across this tile map of the United States on pretend road trips. When they get to a new state boundary, the teacher requires that they name that state's capital before they are allowed to cross the line. If they do not know the capital, they can return to the classroom to find the information on the Internet or in books. In this way, the outdoor environment facilitates Howard Gardner's theory of multiple intelligence learning.

had even more" (1993, 9); (5) bodily-kinesthetic—needed for surgeons, dancers, and craftspeople; (6) interpersonal—the ability to understand others; and (7) intrapersonal—the capacity to understand oneself. Gardner's research suggests that in-depth learning occurs when children are actively engaged in multidisciplinary perspectives that span several of these at once. This approach facilitates cognitive connections between real life and the integration of skills in a cross-curricular context. More recently, Gardner (2000) added another intelligence that relates directly with the natural outdoor classroom: (8) naturalist—the ability to see natural cycles and processes. Additionally, Gardner considers three other intelligences with more complex interpretations—spiritual, existential, and moral.

Gerald A. Lieberman and Linda L. Hoody (1998) take the concept of integrated learning another step when they list five pedagogical objectives of the "environment as the integrating context for learning." These are:

- To transcend traditional boundaries between disciplines
- To provide hands-on learning experiences, often through problem-solving and project-based activities
- To incorporate team teaching
- To adapt to individual students and their unique skills and abilities
- To develop knowledge, understanding, and appreciation for the community and natural environment

This student is designing her schoolyard environment, based on stories she read in language arts class. Outdoor classrooms are places for active learning across the curriculum—all classes should be involved in their creation, implementation, and use.

The physical design of an outdoor classroom and the activities that take place within it can be used as educational themes to foster endless opportunities for the types of integrated and multiple-intelligence learning described by Gardner, Lieberman, and Hoody. Natural areas and gardens are universally described as spiritual, emotional, and intellectual places. Used as outdoor classrooms, they present possibilities for active learning and the integration of the arts, sciences, and cultural studies through scientific experiments, math exercises, design and planning, poetry writing, storytelling, plays and skits, environmental art, dance and music performances, horticulture, history, archaeology, oral histories, and even more. Integrated learning helps students excel in making topical connections across broad contextual frameworks. Student enthusiasm for school and learning often increases with this interactive and hands-on teaching approach.

In their 1993 book, *Integrated Studies in the Middle Grades,* Judy F. Carr and

Chris Stevenson illustrate how educational themes can be selected as a foundation for comprehensive integrated curriculum frameworks. A visual diagram, or *web*, is made to represent the curriculum structure, placing the theme at the center, with various subjects (science, art, music) radiating outward from it. They cite natural places, such as rivers or mountains, as possible curriculum themes. Children learn to write, prepare science projects, and become engaged in creative artworks that focus on the central theme. This educational approach is termed *place-based learning*, and it focuses on regional history, culture, and the natural environment as the central themes for education.

The schoolyard natural classroom is a dynamic living system that is an ideal theme for integrated and place-based learning. Nature has a direct tie to the sciences, and it also inspires and serves as a great stage for the arts. The habitat environment facilitates scientific experiments and math exercises; inspires nature writing, drawing, and mural making; and provides the setting for storytelling and dance performances. Students and teachers flourish in the schoolyard garden, where wonder and intellectual and spiritual growth may be found under mesquite trees or sitting at the side of a pond.

The diagram of a curriculum web shown here places the schoolyard habitat or outdoor classroom at the center as a theme for integrated learning. Many schools hire curriculum specialists to assist with the planning and creation of schoolyard projects; these experts write curricula and work with teachers to develop specific lesson plans for ongoing use of the outdoor classroom. Without such forward planning, the habitat project may not be incorporated into the curriculum, and there is a good chance it could fail. The lesson here is that everyone should be a part of the planning process to determine how the place will be used, what it will look like, how it will be maintained, and how it will change over time to accommodate new ideas and users.

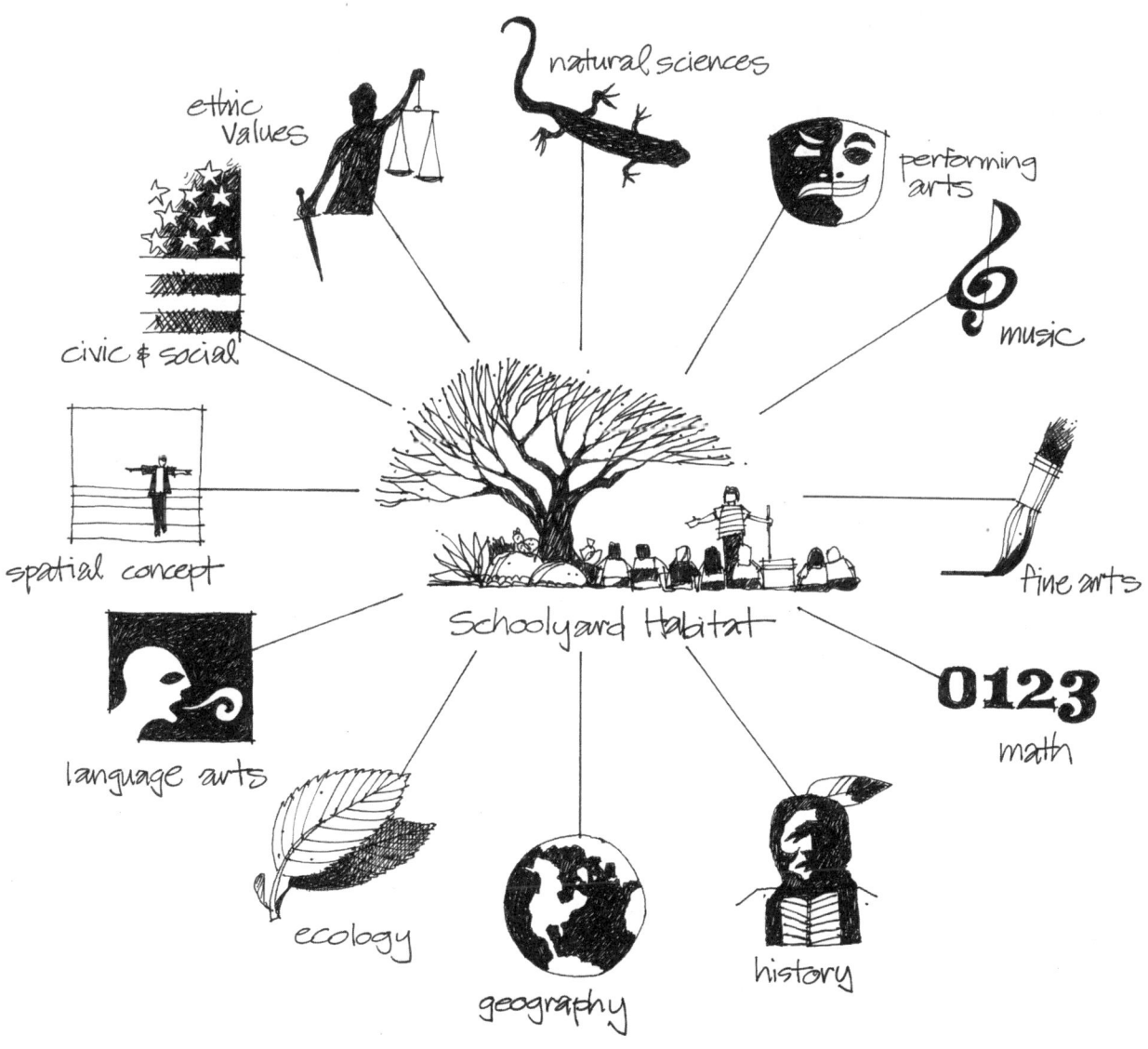

Schoolyard Garden Types

The schoolyard setting provides many opportunities to create and implement a wide variety of themed garden types for learning, pleasure, and even free play. A few garden types are briefly described in this section, and more can be found in Chapter 6, "Ecological Principles and Wildlife." Most of these garden types are conceived as outdoor classrooms for integrated learning approaches within the curriculum, and many of the ideas central to these garden types look far beyond wildlife study for ways to support integrated learning and foster an appreciation for nature. In fact, it is possible that garden creators will integrate several of these garden themes into the outdoor classroom.

Art Gardens

An art garden should not be thought of as merely a sculpture garden for the display of isolated art projects. Although displays of art are an important component used in most garden types, a wider definition is warranted for a garden whose central theme is art. When art is the basis for the creation of a garden, it affects all aspects of design and planning. The artist's method of creation revolves around problem-seeking, not just problem-solving, activities. Art is an open-ended process, a highly subjective activity that is created primarily through inductive reasoning. A more linear, closed-ended process, following scientific methods that use deductive reasoning exhibited by hypothesis testing, a narrowing of scope, and control over variables, is not a typical approach taken by artists. More often, the artist's process is dynamic and multifaceted, highly intuitive, with art outcomes that can be expressed and understood in many ways. Ansel Adams wrote in 1975: "It is not what the artist *has* done but what he *can* do for the great cause of the environment that should command our attention . . . Art always has been, and definitely is, a variable and unpredictable force . . . Many well-meaning individuals concerned with the environment are rather factual minded in that they do not initiate or respond to the 'magical' elements of experience which relate to art" (1975, 4).

Artwork in the schoolyard can take many forms. This sundial at Gasworks Park in Seattle, Washington, for example, is an artwork created with white cement and colored sands and gravels, with an assortment of bronze, stone, tile, and glass inlays. The playful shapes and colorful composition might inspire art for schoolyards.

In this type of garden, art literacy and appreciation play an important role in learning. Natural features such as earthworks and structural features such as benches or birdhouses provide opportunities for artistic expression. Various styles of art such as cubist, pop, and environmental or land art might provide avenues for interpretation and discussion, while regional field trips to art museums, galleries, and local artists' studios can offer information and inspiration. Projects can explore environmental issues such as water and air pollution, or local interests such as regional history. Projects can be functional, such as wind structures, or more ethereal, such as wind harps. Many schools tie environmental issues and recycling programs to art projects.

This pattern, based on a cubist painting, could be used as inspiration for a garden layout. Some of the forms could be turned into planters, while other shapes might be reflected in the pathway design. It is important, however, that the shapes be adjusted to accommodate specific site requirements such as sun patterns and pedestrian circulation.

Specific art themes can be used to create the garden layout. For example, one school created a garden based on Claude Monet's garden in Giverny, France. As part of this project, children conducted research to understand Monet's paintings and found information and images of his garden to use as a basis for design. This was a fun and successful hands-on research project. Another art-themed option might be to fashion a garden based on the layout of an abstract painting, a method used in 1920s Paris to create cubist gardens. Geometric abstract patterns were created with a colorful palette of plants and laid out according to the principles of cubist art. Children and teachers might have fun generating

These artworks were created out of discarded materials. Recycling programs are often coordinated with school art projects.

ideas for the garden's layout if they think of it as a living painting with seasonal changes.

Art programs have been eliminated from many public schools, and the idea of creating an art garden as presented here is not a common theme among schools. An art garden project might be best coordinated with an artist as the leader of the creative process, with the whole site conceived as the *art* or the canvas for expression. In problem-seeking projects—which involve research, self-discovery, and environmental manipulation—inductive reasoning will become the focus for learning.

Cultural History Gardens

There is now greater public awareness than ever regarding the importance of the history and culture of past inhabitants of our land. Cultural and historic landscapes have received attention from Congress and the National Park Service, and by implementing cultural history gardens, schools can play an exciting role in expanding cultural landscape literacy and fostering a greater appreciation for our heritage.

The Southwest is a culturally rich environment that has a particularly deep landscape history. Schoolyard gardens in the region may draw from the area's past residents, such as the Pueblo cultures (Mogollon, Hohokam, Patayan, and Anasazi), which used pit-style houses and grew corn as the dominant agricultural crop. The Hohokam and Anasazi are known for their water-conservation techniques and sophisticated irrigation systems that involved land terracing, check dams, headgates, and waffle fields. These and other historic features could be incorporated for use in the schoolyard cultural history garden.

Ocotillo "living fences," created by the Tohono O'odham (formerly Papago) Indians, are still used today to create naturally attractive screens. Care must be taken to ensure that natural desert habitats are not destroyed in the production of these fences.

A Chiricahua Apache *wikiup*

Topics for potential application within the schoolyard include cultural traditions, land-use patterns (trails, the arrangement of dwellings), and agricultural and architectural artifacts, such as the Tohono O'odham (formerly Papago) Indians' living fences. To create these live barriers, the Papago wove together ocotillo (*Fouquieria splendens*) branches into a screen that, when placed on top of the soil, would set out roots and become a wall of established living plants. Landscape features like this or the Chiricahua Apache *wikiup* (home) are relatively easy to duplicate, and they help students connect with the history of their landscape. Involve the descendants of these Native American cultures, if possible, as they may provide valuable information and insight on design and construction of such projects. This type of cultural exploration is most effective if it includes the many layers of history within a school region, from prehistoric to modern culture. As students gain knowledge about local cultural heritage, they can begin to apply it to the schoolyard environment.

Other areas of historical research may involve literature, folklore, stories, legends, local craft traditions, and other forms of art, including music and dance. Aspects of local history such as these can be incorporated into a standards-based school curriculum. Exercises might incorporate important local resources such as libraries, historical museums, state historical societies, public and private archives, state and federal agencies, artisans, storytellers, and parents. Students might also learn to draw from firsthand sources like historical recorded interviews, biographies and autobiographies, military records, historical summaries, and academic theses for information about cultural and environmental events.

The National Park Service method for determining historical significance

(left) History murals like this one can be created for display in the schoolyard.

(right) Created by students, this mural memorializes a maintenance staff member whom students dubbed "Farmer" Sean because he took care of plants in the schoolyard. This project, although not a typical history lesson, is a personalized reflection of local culture—a unique and thoughtful expression that offers hope and meaning to students.

(below) An ecological garden might include demonstrations of natural plant communities or life zones. This schoolyard ecological garden has demonstration areas representing riparian, grassland, and aspen forest communities.

is a particular theme that could be modified for use in school curricula. Their research focuses on the preparation of cultural landscape inventory reports, archaeological surveys, and ethnographic reports. For more information on these topics, refer to *A Guide to Cultural Landscape Reports: Contents, Process, and Techniques* (Page, Gilbert, and Dolan 1998). Another helpful reference, *Living Traditions, A Teacher's Guide: Teaching Local History Using State and National Learning Standards* (Skelding, Kemple, and Kiefer 2001), outlines potential curriculum activity ideas.

Ecological Gardens

Ecological gardens focus on land stewardship and the connections between natural and cultural heritage. Their primary concern is ecological literacy, so ecological issues and principles, such as the preservation and restoration of native habitats within the region, will provide a basis for research and design. Ethical issues revolve around human harmony with natural systems, and important environmental concerns include population growth, water shortage, biodiversity loss,

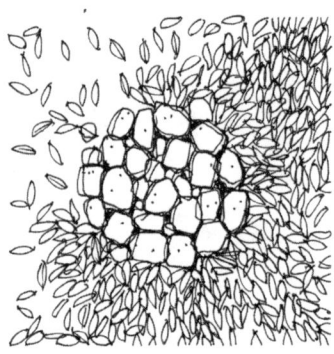

These are depictions of Andy Goldsworthy's natural art. Children are inspired by his work with natural materials and enjoy imitating his creations.

erosion of fertile soil, and suburban sprawl. Principles from landscape ecology as presented by Dramstad, Olson, and Forman (1996) include four categories of conditions—*patches, edges/boundaries, corridors/connectivity,* and *mosaics*—that could provide helpful ideas for application in the ecological garden.

Ecological gardens often are demonstration gardens of local plant communities or life-zone simulations. Outside field trips and guest lectures could provide additional information for students in the preparation and use of these demonstration gardens. Some potential activities for integrated learning include nature writing, descriptive observations, plant pressing, and art projects involving nature studies. For example, children are attracted to Andy Goldsworthy's photographs of his compositions made with leaves, stones, and twigs. Once they have observed Goldsworthy's art, they are ready to make similar creations of their own based on his philosophy, as stated here: "I have become aware of how nature is in a state of change, and that change is the key to understanding. I want my art to be sensitive and alert to changes in material, season, and weather. A rock is not independent of its surroundings. The way it sits tells how it came to be there" (Goldsworthy, as quoted in Beardsley 1984, 134).

Within the context of subject matter involving nature/biology and human/cultural systems, the work of many artists evolved from gallery art installation to the creation of public outdoor environments that employ cross-disciplinary approaches. The term *ecological art* (ecoart) arose in the late 1990s as a classification of art that explores the infinite connections between human and ecological systems. Complex interrelationships between physical, biological, cultural, political, and historical aspects of ecosystems and human communities became the forum for exploration (Rosenthal 2003). Ecoartists interpret environmental and cultural histories, reveal environmental problems and solutions, and restore damaged ecosystems. Primarily concerned with site-specific interventions and ecological function, ecoartists are involved in the reclamation of degraded landfill sites, brownfield mitigation, wetland restoration, and water-purification projects. Addressing concerns for biodiversity, urban infrastructure, and environmental law, many ecoartists work with local community groups to instill a greater awareness and concern for ecological health. For example, environmental artist Lynne Hull has created a series of *Raptor Roosts* in the United States, England, Kenya, Mexico, and Northern Ireland. Her sculptures are described as art created for animals ("trans-species art"—her words). These artistic perches are for hawks and eagles, but they are also intended to draw attention to ongoing habitat destruction.

Literacy Gardens

All schoolyard gardens may be thought of as literacy gardens: all gardens have that power. Literacy gardens are places where words and language arts are connected to the outdoor environment. Diane Ackerman's book *Cultivating Delight: A Natural History of My Garden* (2001) tells often-personal anecdotes of her garden observations. Because Ackerman writes from the heart, her book presents a writing style that might inspire children. She writes, "As I do my garden rounds, I can feel the weight of an oatmeal raisin cookie in my pocket, so I pause beneath an apple tree to chew a few mouthfuls while surveying the shade garden. I see the deer have paused here, too, and chomped off hosta flowers. The slugs stopped here to eat holes in the hosta leaves. I wonder what makes the hostas so tasty to deer and slugs" (Ackerman 2001, 137).

This drawing of a girl reading under the trees was produced in a workshop in which students designed a literacy garden for their school.

An archetypal tree represents all trees from literature—one day it is from Christopher Robin's Hundred Acre Wood and the next day it is Silverstein's "giving tree."

In this literacy garden, children demonstrate how the kindergarten students learn their ABCs by jumping to the appropriate tile when the teacher calls out a letter.

Language arts programs are moving outside to explore active teaching techniques, and they have begun to use literacy gardens to inspire reading and writing. Young children can learn ABCs kinesthetically by jumping from one alphabet tile paving stone to another: the teacher calls out, "Jump to an A"—the child does so—then another call, "Jump to a B," and so on. Older students enjoy research and journal-writing assignments.

Students involved in school vegetable gardens sometimes sell their produce at farmers' markets. This provides revenue to support the garden and raises student self-esteem.

Many literacy gardens include plant representations derived from books, such as bean plants to initiate conversation about the ever-popular *Jack and the Beanstalk,* or a willow tree to represent the "whomping" willow in J. K. Rowling's Harry Potter chronicles. These literal textual representations, of course, have serious limitations, and because reading activates the imagination, a more open-ended approach may be more productive. For instance, the willow tree could also represent an archetypal *tree* from multiple literary sources—one from Sleeping Beauty's Enchanted Forest or from Christopher Robin's Hundred Acre Wood. It could be a tree from Maurice Sendak's *Where the Wild Things Are* or Shel Silverstein's *The Giving Tree.* The tree could be thought of as an actor to appear in a wide range of roles, including stories that students create themselves.

Because a garden setting makes an ideal reading area, another way a literacy garden might be used is for quiet reading. Often located near school libraries, these small spaces should provide shady spots with comfortable seating options. Japanese-style Zen gardens might offer inspiration for the design of reading areas, since their central focus is on meditation, contemplation, and intellectual enlightenment.

Vegetable Gardens

Vegetable, herb, and flower gardens are popular at many schools across the country. In fact, most other garden types incorporate some form of gardening for food production. Students almost universally seem to gain self-esteem and motivation when they become involved in planting and caring for a vege-

A checkerboard pattern similar to this depiction could be created as a replication of ancient cultivation patterns.

Schoolyard vegetable and flower gardens can be coordinated with outside community support and involvement—this facilitates the potential for year-round gardening and creates many shared activities among the school's members and neighbors.

table garden, and it is thought that children who grow, harvest, and eat their own food become more likely to make healthful nutritional choices. Vegetable gardens are often created in conjunction with nutritional programs or lessons in composting for soil enrichment, with class discussions related to foods for healthful diets and proper nutrition. Garden food plants are usually grown organically; water-harvesting and composting programs can add important benefits to the effort.

Schoolyard vegetable gardens reflect our agricultural heritage and can often be successfully linked to the neighborhood or community if coordinated with national or local organizations such as youth gardening programs, the Master Gardener Program, and the National Gardening Association. Planned events and festivals, such as fall harvesting, as well as culinary arts programs, offer additional opportunities to connect with the community. Harvests from the garden might be sold by the students at farmers' markets or donated to local food banks.

Vegetable gardens can have a cultural theme based on ancient gardening techniques, such as the waffle fields or gardens used by Navajo and Pueblo cultures: fields were divided into a checkerboard pattern of squares that would alternate between planted and unplanted plots. The planted squares would receive organic matter and water retained by small earthen dams, while the unplanted areas would be for circulation and access. Vegetable gardens can also be ethnic—Italian or Chinese, for example. Ethnic gardens, which usually involve ethnic cooking and celebrations, are good ways to celebrate cultural diversity.

Vegetable gardens are activity-based, integrated learning environments that are usually most successful with community collaboration. Some specific potential activities include intergenerational classes, ethnobotanical demonstrations, performances by children, harvest dinners, cooking and baking, storytelling, planting ceremonies, sign creation, composting, and journaling on garden ecology and plant life cycles.

CHAPTER 2 Design Theory

Introduction

Theories of design in visual art, architecture, and garden design developed as a reflection of the natural conditions of the environment, cultural influences, and artistic interpretations of the time. This theoretical information is presented to help designers generate strong concepts and alternative layouts as they create their natural outdoor classrooms, wildlife habitats, and gardens. These ideas have broad application to landscape design, and within the context of this book, the terms *outdoor classroom, wildlife habitat,* and *garden* are interchanged in various applications. Keep in mind that this background information is an overview of styles and visual fundamentals (principles and elements) of design that must be used in conjunction with a good understanding of the specific needs of the school and the opportunities and constraints of the site.

History of Garden Styles

Since the earliest times, humankind has been concerned with the design of gardens and outdoor places for the purposes of function, pleasure, and beauty. Garden design and landscape architecture have progressed through the ages in a number of identifiable styles, which are presented here in overview to offer inspiration for the design of outdoor classrooms. These various garden styles, including the Japanese, Italian, French, and Modern, to name a few, could be modified for use in the layout of any outdoor classroom. For example, the principles of Japanese garden design might prove useful, since children are often drawn to the Japanese garden's intimate hidden spaces, use of rocks with water features, elements of surprise, and delicate plant textures.

The concepts obtained from an understanding of historic garden styles may also provide many avenues for integrated learning. Questions about the cultural backgrounds of past garden creators, their relationships with the natural environment, and their artistic landscape expressions provide many opportunities for research. History classes can conduct projects related to these various periods of time on specific topics such as historic plant use, plant symbolism, irrigation techniques, and architectural forms. Math classes could even explore the spatial geometries of historic garden configurations.

It should be understood that design solutions must be ecologically sustainable. For example, several of the historic garden styles presented here were created in lush environments where water use was not restricted. These styles will need to be modified with sensitivity toward water conservation by using appropriate southwestern plants. The plants listed among some of the styles presented herein are identified by Nancy A. Leszczynski (1999) as those used in the respective regions and periods in history. Those plants that are not native to the arid Southwest should not be planted, but they can be represented through other creative means. Other garden styles presented in this chapter were created in dry environments and will hold particular interest for garden designers of the arid Southwest, who may glean important lessons from historic water-harvesting techniques, cultivation practices, and garden cooling effects.

Prehistoric "Gardens" (20,000–3300 BC)

Early humans, as hunters and gatherers, had a very strong connection to the earth and their natural surroundings. We know little about their gardens, but we are aware of ceremonial and religious landscapes created during this time, such as the cave paintings of Lascaux, France. These very realistic, lifelike paintings of bison and other animals were probably created as a part of religious hunting rituals and produced through community gatherings over an extended period of time. Other early significant landscape artifacts include artificial hills, earth carvings, and stone arrangements. Specific examples include the Celtic earth carved art such as the White Horse of Uffington and the monolithic stone statues of Easter Island created for ancestral worship. The stone structures of Stonehenge probably used for burial, sacrifice, and astronomical observation continue to intrigue us about the past.

Ancient Egyptian Gardens (3300–500 BC)

The ancient Egyptians were one of the earliest gardening cultures. The environment of Egypt is hot and arid, but these desert lands have continually been subjected to annual flooding, a phenomenon that created a fertile region within

Today, certain landscape artists produce large topographic landforms, or earth art, similar to prehistoric manifestations like the White Horse of Uffington. Examples of these contemporary works of art include abstract forms but also realistic depictions, such as Michael Heizer's landfill concepts in Illinois for a giant water spider, catfish, turtle, snake, and frog. This depiction of the White Horse of Uffington could become a pattern on a wall or the basis for a paving pattern that provides interest as well as a history lesson.

The garden of Amenhotep III, as interpreted from a tomb painting, is the best depiction of an ancient Egyptian garden. The painting shows a walled, symmetrical garden with pavilions, rectangular pools stocked with fish, and a variety of plants. It illustrates the Egyptian love for gardens and plants, which was often expressed in decorative arts.

the Nile Valley. Well-developed methods of irrigation were used to harvest the Nile waters for cities, agriculture, and the pleasure gardens within elaborate government complexes and residential estate gardens.

The Egyptian garden, created for the gods, was a refuge from the harsh conditions of the desert. It was enclosed within walls for protection from the heat and winds, and garden designers used a main axis to organize garden elements along either side in a bilateral symmetrical layout. Design features included rectilinear or T-shaped pools stocked with fish. These pools were connected to irrigation canals that were used to transport water to adjacent areas. Sometimes the water features were even small lakes large enough to accommodate rowboats. Early Egyptian gardens also included tree-lined *allées,* or wide boulevards; vine-covered trellises and arbors; pergolas (covered walkways); garden pavilions; exotic birds and habitats; a variety of plants; and decorative art.

Some of the plants used included: *Chamaerops humilis,* palmetto; *Cyperus papyrus,* papyrus; *Ficus sycamorus,* sycamore fig; *Nymphaea caerulea,* lotus; *Phoenix dactylifera,* date palm; and *Punica granatum,* pomegranate.

Ancient Mesopotamian (3500–538 BC), Sumerian (3500–900 BC), Assyrian (900–625 BC), and Neo-Babylonian (611–538 BC) Gardens

This time and these locations are characterized by a temperate climate and the broad floodplain known as the Fertile Crescent, which lies between the Tigris and Euphrates Rivers. Many people lived in populated, urban, walled cities that were often organic in form. Individual residential houses were constructed of sun-baked brick and featured interior courtyards to provide open-air ventilation and separation from the harsh, noisy public streets. Elite members of society had royal hunting parks, which were large, enclosed areas for imported game animals. Design features included artificial mounds, ziggurats (pyramid-shaped towers), temples, palaces, and exotic plant materials. The legendary Hanging Gardens of Babylon (605 BC), created for the wife of King Nebuchadnezzar, was a seven-story palace with lush gardens planted on each level. This great monument was thought to have included a sophisticated irrigation system within each level of the palace gardens.

The elements of the ancient Persian garden include a walled enclosure, a central fountain, and a variety of plants used to create a cool relief from the summer heat. These elements are particularly welcome additions to schoolyard gardens in the arid Southwest.

Ancient Persian Gardens (539–331 BC)

The Persian Indus River Valley is hot and arid. The people who settled in this area were a synthesis of Assyrian, Egyptian, and Ionic Greek cultures, with a religion based on mysticism. Figurative art was banned, a circumstance that led to abstract geometric patterns in art and architecture. Religious activities were held outdoors in highly structured and beautiful outdoor spaces.

Irrigation methods used *qanat*s, or tunnels, that transported water from an aquifer to agricultural land. The Persian culture is the origin of the Islamic (Moorish) style. For beauty and pleasure, they created *chahar bagh* (paradise) gardens, symbolic of heaven on earth. These gardens were built in geometric patterns, with four water channels flowing from a central point in a quadrilateral, symmetrical fashion. Enclosed within walls, the gardens included a variety of beautiful fountains and lush plant materials for shade, cooling effects, and fragrance, while flowering and fruiting plants carried symbolic meaning. Reference to the paradise garden appears in all major religions. In Christianity, the paradise garden, or Garden of Eden, was described by water flowing and parting into four heads.

Ancient Greek Gardens (700–136 BC)

Ancient Greece was rugged and mountainous, with numerous peninsulas and islands. The culture was based on the quest for pure reason and truth as derived through scientific evidence. As a result, the culture believed in a basic order and idealized harmonies of forms. Rules of proportion, developed through ratios found in nature, were used in architecture, art, city planning, and garden design. Design theories and philosophies based on these ratios are variously referred to as the *golden mean, golden section,* or *golden rectangle* and were used as guidelines for design. The many sacred places in ancient Greek culture include the acropolis, the agora, and the sacred grove, which was a natural setting for the academy and a place to develop the body and the mind.

Plant symbolism played an important role in Greek culture and mythology. The Adonis garden was created by children and women who propagated herbs and flowers in pots placed on rooftops, windowsills, and balconies. These fast-

Plant symbolism played an important role in Greek culture and mythology, and could be used interpretatively in the design of the schoolyard garden. Language arts classes, for example, could conduct research about plant symbolism found in Greek literature.

growing plants symbolized Adonis, whose short life was compared to the seasonal cycle of annual plants. The laurel tree was another important symbol to the ancient Greeks. Based on the myth about Apollo and Daphne, its aromatic scent represented purification, peace, and victory.

Many modern design concepts are derived from the ancient Greeks, such as *atrium* (courtyard), *colonnade* (row of columns), *portico* (porch), and *amphitheater*. Some of the plants used by the Ancient Greeks included *Acanthus spinosus,* acanthus; *Crocus sativus,* saffron; *Hedera helix,* English ivy; *Laurus nobilis,* bay or laurel; *Myrtus communis,* myrtle; *Olea europaea,* common olive; *Platanus orientalis,* Oriental plane; *Punica granatum,* pomegranate; and *Taxus baccata,* English yew.

Ancient Roman Gardens (510 BC–AD 476)

Ancient Roman civilization originated in the hot, arid central Italian peninsula, in the city of Rome (510 BC). It expanded westward to Spain, north to Scotland, eastward to the Persian Gulf, and south to northern Africa. The Roman Republic (510–29 BC) was based on Greek democracy and religion. The Romans made great design advances and achievements in the areas of engineering and technology, most notably in their roads, bridges, aqueducts, and triumphal arches.

Important country villas, *villas rusticas,* evolved as high officials sought the benefits of rural life. Pliny the Younger had a villa at Laurentinum (AD 100), while Hadrian had one at Tivoli (AD 117–138). Hadrian's villa was inspired by the Egyptian estate gardens; it was designed as a luxurious retreat from public and city life and exemplified Emperor Hadrian's love for art, architecture, and gardens. The 750-acre complex of buildings and carefully choreographed spaces was designed to fit the topography and to blend architectural axes with irregular angles. The villa included meeting and conference structures, residences, pools, terraces, and recreational areas. This design became the inspiration for the Renaissance estate gardens that would follow.

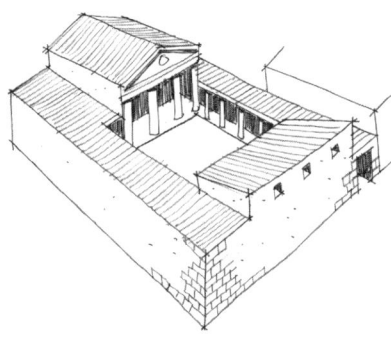

Roman atria open-air *peristyle* courtyards would be good additions to the schoolyard environment in the arid Southwest.

Smaller residential buildings had atria or open-air *peristyle* courtyards to provide fresh air, sunlight, and privacy. Some of the plants cultivated for use in Ancient Roman gardens included *Acanthus spinosus,* acanthus; *Buxus* spp., boxwood; *Citrus* spp., lemon; *Cupressus sempervirens,* Italian cypress; *Hedera helix,* English ivy; *Laurus nobilis,* bay or laurel; *Lavandula* spp., lavender; *Mentha* spp., mint; *Myrtus communis,* myrtle; *Olea europaea,* common olive; *Pinus pinea,* Italian stone pine; *Platanus orientalis,* Oriental plane; *Prunus* spp., apricot, cherry, plum; and *Thymus* spp., thyme.

Ancient Chinese Gardens (1600 BC–AD 1279)

Ancient Chinese gardens, influenced by Taoist philosophy, were built for reflection and meditation, guided by a strong desire to achieve harmony with nature. The Tao, "the Way," suggests a flow or natural process in which humans are subordinate to the whole. Through meditation, the ancient Chinese believed, the ideals of Taoist philosophy would be understood. Garden design was the premier art form in the expression of these ideals. Educated in philosophy, poetry, calligraphy, landscape painting, and geomancy, garden designers were poets and scholars skilled in all the arts and sciences of the period.

The scholar's garden was a spiritual retreat and a place to nourish the heart, inspire creativity and fantasy, or simply be captivated by beauty. Gardens repre-

The ancient Chinese believed that the garden was a place of great beauty for spiritual and intellectual enlightenment.

sented paradise; they housed immortals with magic secrets that held the key to longevity. The two dominant features in Chinese gardens were mountains and lakes, which were symbolically represented in smaller gardens. Symbolism played an important role in garden design: rocks, pools, flowers, and trees all had meaning, and transformations of nature were often represented. Latticework, for example, symbolized the cracking of ice. Ancient Chinese gardens were highly controlled, yet informal and organic, with *occult* balance that creates a feeling of harmony without symmetry.

Selected plants used in Chinese gardens include *Bambusa* spp., bamboo; *Camellia* spp., camellia; *Chrysanthemum* spp., chrysanthemum; *Ginkgo biloba*, ginkgo; *Morus alba*, white mulberry; *Nelumbo nucifera*, Chinese lotus; *Nymphaea* spp., water lily; Orchidaceae, orchid family; and *Paeonia suffruticosa*, tree peony; *Rhododendron* spp., azalea.

Japanese Gardens (AD 575–1600)

Japanese gardens evolved from Chinese gardens, with one important difference: as an island, Japan developed an inward focus, physically and perhaps culturally as well. Their garden compositions were originally based on the ancient Shinto worship of nature. Forces of the natural world held religious and sacred value and were represented through rock placement and the creation of lakes, ponds, waterfalls, islands, and shorelines within the garden. One of the most famous examples is the palace estate gardens of the Katsura Imperial Villa in Kyoto, built in 1620.

Small garden types, usually set within a larger garden, are many and include the *moss garden,* the *pond garden,* and the *dry garden.* As Zen Buddhism came into focus, gardens were associated with meditation and enlightenment (such as the famous Ryoanjidry garden in Kyoto, Japan). Dry gardens reduced nature to its most simple elements—sand, rocks, and moss. Hidden order and harmony in the universe, discovered slowly through meditation, were used as the basis for the creation of landscapes whose scenes opened sequentially as one strolled through the garden. Much like the scroll paintings that unravel to expose a picture little by little, Japanese stroll gardens were designed to conceal and reveal views. The sixteenth-century text *The Book of Tea* led to the tea ceremony, which was developed in conjunction with the stroll garden. Tea houses were placed in the garden as a retreat from the problems of the outside world.

Children are attracted to Japanese-style gardens because of the intimate small spaces and use of tactile materials. Garden features such as stepping stones, groups of stones, and ponds make good additions to the schoolyard wildlife habitat. A Chinese or Japanese moon gate is a circular window in a wall for viewing the scenery behind it. This helpful device would make a good wildlife screen—offering protection for the animals while allowing children to watch unobtrusively.

Japanese gardens are characterized by an in-depth understanding of design principles (unity, balance, variety) and elements (texture, light, form). Designers of these gardens used occult balance, with rocks and plants placed in obtuse triangular patterns that used odd numbers. They followed a grid as the basis for layout but avoided symmetrical patterns. They used overlapping techniques in the placement of plants as well as diagonal lines to create an optical illusion of greater depth. The *shaffei* (borrowed scenery) incorporated adjacent (off-site) views within the garden. Other features included translucent movable *shojis* (screens) to allow the garden to become a part of the house, moon gates for framing views, stepping stones and stone groupings, ponds, streams and waterfalls, bridges, stone lanterns, *shishi odoshi* (deer scares), and *tsukubai* (water basins). Small stones were used in place of water to make a dry landscape, or *kare sansui*.

Create the feeling of flowing water with the Japanese design technique used in *kare sansui*: Stones are carefully placed in a dry streambed to appear as if they were moved by water currents. This effect is useful in dry climates where water conservation is mandatory.

Selected plants used in Japanese gardens include *Acer palmatum,* Japanese maple; *Bambusa* spp., bamboo; *Camellia japonica,* Japanese camellia; *Cercidiphyllum japonica,* katsura tree; *Iris ensata,* Japanese iris; *Pinus densiflora,* Japanese red pine; *Pinus thunbergiana,* Japanese black pine; and *Prunus serrulata,* Japanese flowering cherry; *Rhododendron* spp., azalea.

Medieval European Gardens (AD 476–1350)

After the collapse of the Roman Empire, numerous small, walled kingdoms developed in Western European countries. These city-states were often at war with one another and managed to destroy many of the preceding classical works. Monasteries grew in power to become important institutions that struggled to preserve Greco-Roman knowledge. These monasteries were self-sufficient complexes, arranged in an orderly design that included a central open space, or cloister. The cloister was an outdoor room or garden called a *physic,* which was designed with the paradise garden–style quadrangle fourfold layout. Physics included medicinal plants and contained a water feature (well, pool, or baptismal font) joined by four gravel walks.

Foreign travel during the Crusades led to the adoption of more lushly planted paradise gardens. Important landscape features included the use of wildflowers, fruit and flowering trees, walls, carpenter's work (lattice fences), earthen seats, fountains, topiary, viewing mounts, sundials, stone figurines, mazes and laby-

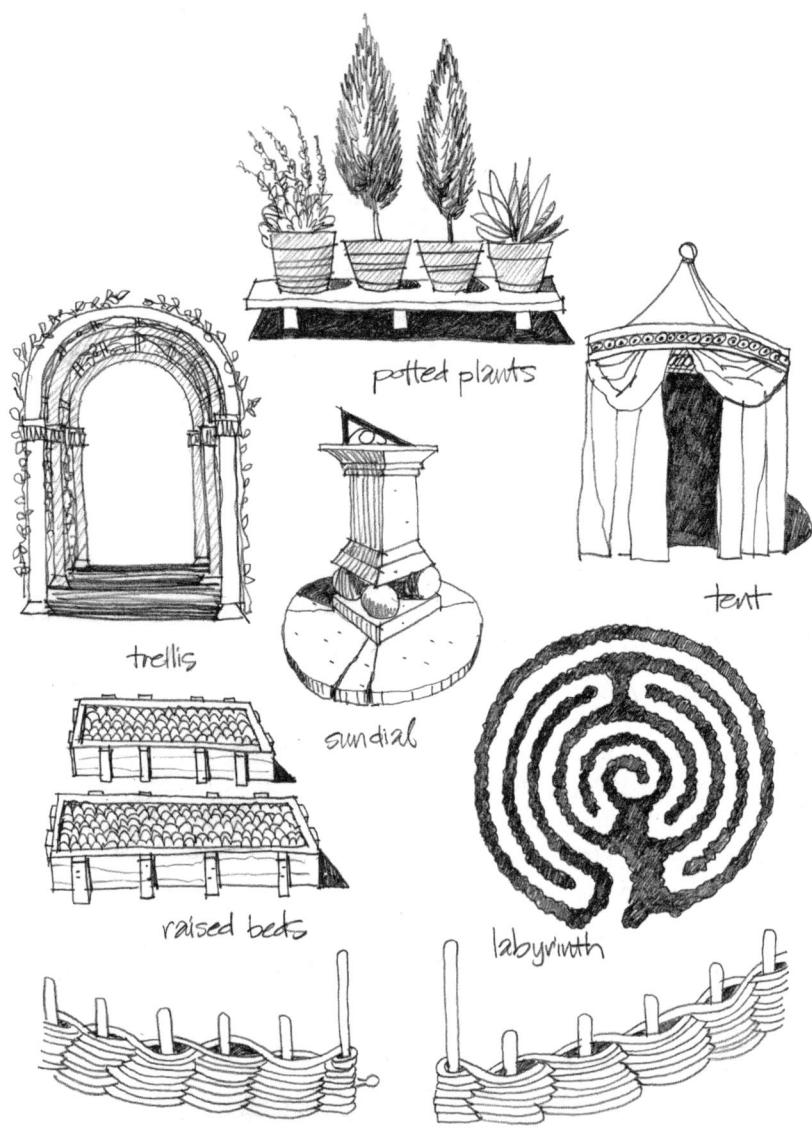

Garden features used in the Middle Ages include sundials, aromatic benches, labyrinths, and latticework—all of which would be ideal additions to the schoolyard garden.

rinths, knot gardens, kitchen gardens, and bowling greens. Stone benches had openings for herb plantings such as chamomile that released a soothing aroma when one sat on the bench.

Plants used in this period include *Artemisia abrotanum,* southernwood; *Foeniculum vulgare,* common fennel; *Helleborus niger,* Christmas rose; *Lilium candidum,* madonna lily; *Morus alba,* white mulberry; *Prunus persica,* peach; *Quercus* spp., oak; *Rosa* spp., rose; *Ruta graveolens,* rue; and *Salvia* spp., sage.

Islamic (Moorish) Gardens, Spain (AD 700s–1400s)

Between the eighth and fifteenth centuries, the Moorish people of hot, dry Granada, Spain, created stunning paradise gardens for religious reflection and military protection (the people of Spain were called Moors because they had migrated from Morocco). The religion of Islam was the basis for their culture, and their gardens were intended to prepare one for the afterlife in heaven.

Religious and palatial courtyards were enclosed within high, often decorative walls, and the geometric layout of the *chahar bagh* pattern was used. This fourfold garden was symbolic of the four quarters of the universe (milk, water, honey, and wine). Equilateral parts were divided by four pathways that joined at a central water fountain. Plants were arranged in straight rows along irrigation channels, often in sunken planting beds for better water conservation. Ablution tanks were used for religious cleansing, as reflection pools, and to provide cooling effects. Other design features included irrigation channels, terraces, and fruit and flowering trees.

The palace grounds at the Alhambra, including the Court of the Myrtles, the Court of the Lions, and the Generalife Gardens, serve as key examples. Selected plants used at these and other sites include *Cinnamomum camphora*, camphor; *Citrus* spp., orange, lemon; *Coriandrum sativum*, coriander; *Cuminum cyminum*, cumin; *Cupressus sempervirens*, Italian cypress; *Ficus carica*, edible fig; and *Rosa* spp., rose (white and yellow).

Italian Renaissance Gardens (AD 1350–1765)

The Italian landscape is varied: it includes peninsulas, flat and mountainous land, and climates ranging from hot-dry to cool-lush. Italy's independent republics, often at war with each other, went through a great rebirth of artistic expression during the period from 1350 to 1765. Humanism replaced mysticism as the accepted philosophical outlook. During the Renaissance, classical art was rediscovered and garden design became a primary art form and statement of wealth and power. Advances in garden design led to the development of the philosopher's garden, designed for pleasure, entertaining, and artistic innovation. Villa landscapes were enclosed with walls and included elongated hillside terraces that were often used for strolling.

Fountains, cascades, pools, and other water effects played an important role in villa landscapes. Fountains at the Villa d'Este, in Tivoli (1549), had sound effects like rainfall, chirping birds, or cannon shots. Water channels began uphill in a *bosco,* or group of trees, with the symbolic water source coming from a *grotto,* or cave. The villa house and landscape were highly integrated, with connections between indoor and outdoor rooms. Predominately axial in layout, garden spaces included the use of evergreen trees, ornate statues, stone furniture, steps, and intricate ornamentation such as knot gardens.

The Villa d'Este, Tivoli (1549); the Boboli Gardens of Pitti Palace, Florence

The *chahar bagh* pattern, or fourfold garden, is an enclosed courtyard with a central fountain divided by four pathways. Along the pathways, planting beds were often sunken for water conservation. These lowered planted areas created a cool lush effect.

The schoolyard wildlife habitat or outdoor classroom could include reference to Italian Renaissance gardens through the design of rectangular terraces for outdoor rooms; the creation of a *bosco,* or group of trees; and the implementation of a symbolic water source coming from a grotto, or cave. These references might inspire a greater appreciation for history and origins.

(1550); the Villa Lante, Bagnoia (1566); and the Villa Farnese, Caporolla (1573), are typical of this period. Selected plants used in such gardens include *Arbutus unedo,* strawberry tree; *Castanea sativa,* Spanish chestnut; *Citrus* spp., lemon, orange; *Cupressus sempervirens,* Italian cypress; *Lavandula* spp., lavender; *Olea europaea,* common olive; *Pinus pinea,* Italian stone pine; *Platanus acerifolia,* London plane tree; *Punica granatum,* pomegranate; *Quercus ilex,* holly oak; *Rosemarinus officinalis,* rosemary; and *Viburnum tinus,* laurustinus.

French Grand-Style Gardens (AD 1495–1750)

The Baroque style of France emerged from the snowy winters, sunny summers, and rich agricultural productivity of central Europe, whose varied landscape includes the Alps, flat marshes, rolling hills, river valleys, and floodplains. Chateau gardens of the seventeenth century are expressions of the power of the absolute monarchy. The Grand Style emphasizes axial vistas and optical illusions in an exaggeration of depth, particularly in the central vista.

> The mathematical formulas and geometries of René Descartes and Blaise Pascal formed the basis for the Grand Style plans of French gardens. Along these lines, math classes could develop geometric patterns for use in the layout of schoolyard gardens.

These formal gardens are symmetrical in layout and highly ordered, with geometrical patterns such as radial avenues; cross axes; and straight, tree-lined *allées* (boulevards). Spatial order was derived from mathematical theorists René Descartes and Blaise Pascal. Other features include linear grand canals, elaborate parterres, and topiary work.

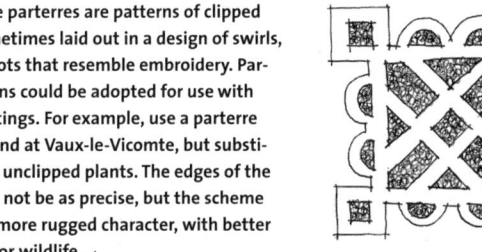

> French-style parterres are patterns of clipped shrubs, sometimes laid out in a design of swirls, lines, and dots that resemble embroidery. Parterre patterns could be adopted for use with native plantings. For example, use a parterre like one found at Vaux-le-Vicomte, but substitute native, unclipped plants. The edges of the pattern will not be as precise, but the scheme will have a more rugged character, with better provisions for wildlife.

The best examples from this period include garden designer Andre Le Notré's Vaux le Vicomte (1656–1661) and Versailles (1661–1662).

Selected plants for this type of formal garden include *Acer pseudoplatanus,* sycamore maple; *Anemone* spp., windflower; *Aquilegia vulgarus,* European columbine; *Buxus sempervirens,* English boxwood; *Carpinus betulus,* European hornbeam; *Fritillaria imperialis,* crown imperial; *Lilium* spp., lily; *Polianthes tuberosa,* tuberose; *Taxus baccata,* English yew; and *Tilia platyphyllos,* broad-leaved linden.

English Romantic Gardens (AD 1715–1840)

The English island environment includes subtle landscape variations, from rocky coasts through rolling land to flatlands. Rich agricultural lands are abundant, and the moist climate supports diverse plants. The eighteenth-century English Romantic style was based on art and literature, with a central theme of the beautiful and sublime qualities of nature. William Hogarth's *Analysis of Beauty* (1753) introduced the theory that beauty is achieved through the geometry of the serpentine line. Scenic landscapes were composed as works of art with pastoral views, irregularly shaped lakes, and rolling topography. These picturesque landscapes imitated the natural scenes depicted by French Romantic painters

The English Romantic technique of "clump-and-gap" planting is an approach that simulates nature by grouping plants together in dense clumps and leaving open areas or gaps. Planting plans that employ this technique will have a natural appearance that creates opportunities for surprise.

such as Claude Lorraine, Nicolas Poussin, and Salvator Rosa. Design features in Romantic gardens included Greek temples, pagodas, meadows, ponds, and hidden *ha-ha* walls that keep cattle and wildlife away from the kitchen gardens but within the picturesque view. Plants were not clipped into topiary, and *clump-and-gap* planting arrangements were used to achieve a more natural appearance. In this method, plants are grouped or clumped together to form masses in certain locations, with other spots left as open areas, or gaps. *Follies,* or *eye catchers,* were usually nonfunctional buildings erected to draw the eye across the landscape to a prominent position or focal point. They were intended to give the appearance of age and were added for amusement.

Useful examples of this type of garden include Stowe by Charles Bridgeman (1713), redesigned by William Kent (1740) and later Lancelot Brown (1750); Stourhead by Henry Hoare (1741); Blenheim (1761); and Chatsworth (1760) by Brown. Lancelot "Capability" Brown (1716–1783) was nicknamed Capability because he once said he could see the "capabilities" of a site. He perfected the creation of naturalistic gardens.

Selected plants used in this style include *Cedrus deodora,* deodar cedar; *Leptospermum scoparium,* New Zealand tea tree; *Liriodendron tulipifera,* tulip tree; *Magnolia grandiflora,* southern magnolia; *Philadelphus coronarius,* sweet mock orange; *Syringa vulgarus,* common lilac; and *Ulmus americana,* American elm.

Spanish Colonial Gardens (AD 1492–mid-1700s)

Spanish settlement throughout Mexico and portions of the southwestern United States began as a feudal system featuring rural, self-sufficient farms called haciendas. The main buildings of the hacienda were designed as a series of interconnected, functional courtyard enclosures that were in close proximity to agricultural lands. Later settlements included three types: the presidio (military fortress), the mission, and the pueblo (village).

Mission compounds were composed of a series of interconnected courtyards enclosed by buildings. The courtyards were simple rectangular or square spaces with pathways that divided the space into four equal parts, crossing at the midpoint, which was the location of a well or fountain. An arcaded or colonnade-covered walkway surrounded the courtyard, making its perimeter a cooler, shaded, comfortable area within the harsh conditions of the arid Southwest.

Adopt the philosophy of the Spanish or Mexican lifestyle to create a courtyard that is a comfortable multipurpose space for work, festivities, relaxation, or contemplation. Include plenty of shade, movable seating, and places to enjoy food in the garden. Vegetable and flowering plants and garden art make these spaces ideal for schoolyard gardens or classrooms. Shown here from the Tucson Botanical Gardens is Nuestro Jardín, the *barrio garden* designed by Margaret Livingston. Inspired by Tucson Mexican American gardens, the space includes adobe walls, a shrine, a birdbath, fruit, flowers, herbs, and delightful backyard and household objects like coffee-can flower holders, an old washtub, and tire planters.

During early mission life, the courtyards served as outdoor work spaces where livestock were held temporarily and cooking occurred. The multifunctional space also served for church festivals and school gatherings. These utility spaces may have included vegetable plots and a few trees, but they were not initially particularly ornamental. In the early part of the twentieth century, however, according to the records of Prentice Duell (1919), a trader who visited several missions in the Southwest in the early 1900s, many of these courtyards with their surrounding cloisters had become beautiful gardens used by the missionaries as places of respite and meditation. Missions used extensive irrigation systems with acequias (canals) and aqueducts to divert water from streams to the mission farmlands.

The pueblo settlements were organized according to design guidelines set by the Law of the Indies, issued by King Phillip II in 1573. The king's criteria for selection of a town site included good climate, clear sky, fertile land for agriculture, and grassland for livestock. The town plaza was the central public square for fiestas and other public gatherings (sometimes plazas temporarily held livestock). Residential homes had an inward focus, and although they were sited very close to the street without a front yard, they were largely isolated from that public arena. These private residences, as the center of everyday life, had internal courtyards surrounded by various rooms within the home. The courtyards were the places for cooking, family gatherings, and relaxation, and over time they evolved into beautiful gardens with potted plants, tile work, ornamental paving, central fountains, vines, large shade trees, and furniture.

Colonial and Early American Gardens (AD 1630–1840)

Colonial gardens were fashioned from the Renaissance prototypes, reflecting the specific cultural backgrounds of the settlers. Spanish-style gardens, created in residential courtyards within the home complex, often used the *chahar bagh* pattern typical of Islamic gardens of Spain and the Middle East. The French and Dutch colonial gardens emphasized geometric order and topiary. They used, as did the English, ornamental parterres or knot gardens. English colonial gardens were usually simple, functional plots that included herbs, medicinal plants, and

The informal, natural style of the cottage gardens from England and colonial America was often associated with small residences as a way to satisfy the homeowners' interest in plant collecting and gardening. The comfortable feel offered by these modest gardens would be a good style for interpretation within the school environment, provided plant selections are native to the region.

flowers. The garden layout was often symmetrical, with rectangular and occasionally circular forms. Located near the house, kitchen gardens were typically enclosed with wooden fences, stone walls, or low clipped hedges.

In New England, small dooryard gardens were developed adjacent to the front door of the house. These small, fenced gardens held plant collections valued by the settlers. Colonists obtained specimens for their gardens through plant trade and the importation of plants from Europe. Dooryard gardens later evolved into cottage gardens, which became popular ornamental displays of irregular plantings of shrubs, annuals, and perennials.

In contrast, larger colonial residences with extensive agricultural lands had elegant formal pleasure gardens. Southern gardens, associated with plantation estates, were magnificent displays of wealth and power. As self-sufficient farms, plantations relied on slave labor for the production of the three cash crops: tobacco, rice, and cotton. Houses were grand, and gardens were primarily symmetrical, using geometric patterns, long vistas, and showy collections of indigenous and exotic trees and shrubs. This early American style is characterized in the homes of two U.S. presidents, George Washington (1732–1799) and Thomas Jefferson (1743–1826).

American Romantic Gardens (AD 1830–1930)

The American nurseryman André Parmentier (1780–1830) was one of the first, in the mid-1820s, to introduce the English Romantic garden style to the United States through his nursery operation in Brooklyn, New York. The importation of North American plants to Europe by horticulturists such as Parmentier made the "American Garden" (a collection of indigenous American plants) popular.

American horticulturist Andrew Jackson Downing (1815–1852) promoted the naturalistic landscape style for specific application in the United States. His theories, based on the English Romantic garden style, emphasized asymmetri-

It was thought in the mid-1800s that Romantic landscapes, based on an artistic interpretation of natural landscapes, could heal emotionally distressed city dwellers by offering them fresh air and beautiful scenery. In this way, New York's Central Park was perhaps one of the first "healing gardens"—a contemplative garden created to promote health. Adaptations of the Romantic style for schoolyard garden design in the arid Southwest could prove useful if the scale of the project, particularly landforms and water bodies, is reduced and the use of turf grass is eliminated. Additionally, native or desert-adapted plants would be warranted without compromising this style.

cal plant arrangements with undulating paths and an exaggerated imitation of nature. As an architect, horticulturist, and nurseryman, Downing understood the need to integrate the cottage villa with the garden in artistic harmony. He promoted ideas for suburban living, which became one of the visionary premises for the "Country Place Era" in the late nineteenth century. Living along the Hudson River Valley, Downing, who was associated with the Hudson River School of intellectuals, applied theories of Romantic beauty to residential gardens in suburban communities.

Central Park (1858–1863, 1865–1878), designed by Frederic Law Olmsted (1822–1903) and English architect Calvert Vaux (1824–1895), became the first Romantic park in the United States. Romantic American landscapes have their roots in the English natural style, with Victorian architectural influences that provide formal elements (e.g., buildings, bridges, steps) as works of art within the landscape setting. Curved land forms and water bodies with naturalistic plant compositions were used to create vistas and spatial sequences that provide beautiful scenery and recreational opportunities as a repreive from city life. Transcendentalists, at the time, believed parks would improve humanity and alleviate the social problems caused by urban industrialization. This utopian idea was reflected in Romantic landscape paintings and writings such as those by Ralph Waldo Emerson (1803–1882) and Henry David Thoreau (1817–1862), who promoted values related to simple living and land stewardship.

Victorian Gardens (AD 1820–1900)

The Victorian period was the transition between Romantic design and the classical Renaissance-inspired design of the early twentieth century. Victorian garden design was an eclectic medley of foreign styles. Horticultural variety and specimen plant displays—particularly rose gardens—were popular, and exotic plants in tropical or alpine gardens and lily ponds were fashionable.

Garden features, often isolated within the landscape, included stone lanterns, Japanese pagodas, and French Renaissance parterres. Mass-produced ornate garden objects such as cast-iron cornstalk or grapevine fencing, decorative gnomes, and Italian classical figures became commonly repeated motifs.

Although the Victorian style is often criticized as an eclectic medley—even a hodgepodge—of historic styles, in principle it could provide a useful model for schoolyard garden design. The schoolyard is one public arena that offers designers the opportunity to explore a variety of styles and materials as they relate to learning across the curriculum. If a Victorian approach is used, care should be taken to make adjustments to accommodate the climate and natural conditions of the school's region and site. For example, geometric beds, carpet bedding, and French Renaissance parterres could be homes for wildlife, but these as well as other specialty gardens must use a pallet of native plants, and lily ponds might be discarded in favor of riparian areas and ponds with native rushes, sedges, cattails, and horsetails.

Turf was used as a living carpet and background for these freestanding garden objects. Geometric beds in the shape of circles, diamonds, and stars were set as focal points within the lawn. This *bedding out* of herbaceous plants also took the form of *carpet bedding,* which placed annuals and perennials in ornate layouts to create the shapes of fleurs-de-lis, family crests, dogs, boats, and signs of the zodiac.

The Victorian period was one of enthusiasm for residential gardens in both modest suburban homes and expensive country estates. Gardens were used for weddings, poetry readings, and recreational activities (e.g., croquet, tennis, softball, and badminton). Gardening during this period became a "home-based" hobby, reflecting the new humanism characterized by modern social reform movements, including women's suffrage, children's rights, and temperance movements.

Classical Beaux-Arts Gardens (AD 1893–1930)

The World's Columbian Exposition (Chicago World's Fair) of 1893 was a commemoration of the four hundredth anniversary of Columbus's "discovery" of America. The fair presented the "classical ideal" as prescribed by the École des Beaux-Arts. This resulted in the City Beautiful movement (1893–1940), which encouraged classical revival architecture and planning, and led to the establishment of the American Academy in Rome (1894). Pierre L'Enfant's 1791 Versailles-inspired design for Washington, D.C., epitomizes the use of classical city planning, with axial and cross-axial geometries, magnificent vistas, parks, and promenades.

The École des Beaux-Arts tradition emphasized symmetrical layout patterns: mirror-image repetition along an axis to create unmistakable balance. Designers built radial symmetrical patterns with identical elements: for example,

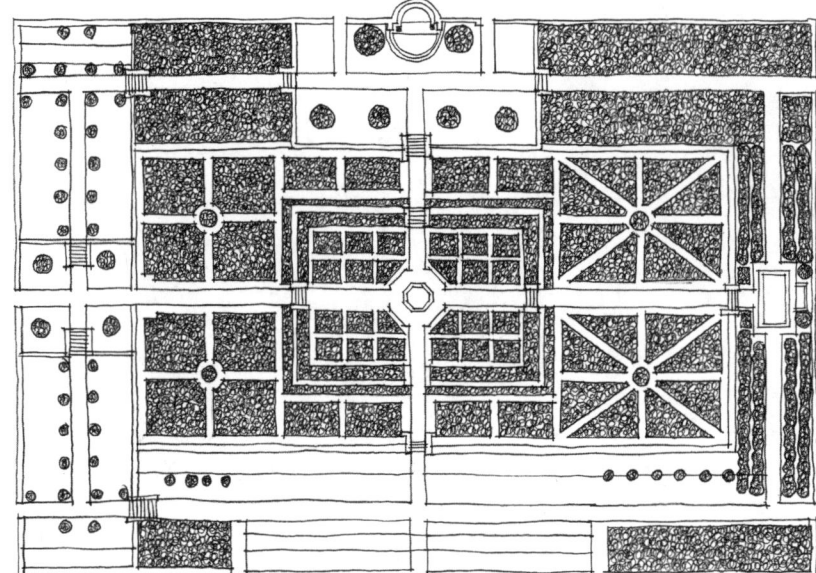

A classical Beaux-Arts garden layout, as depicted in this plan, is a formal and symmetrical design that could prove useful for a portion of the outdoor classroom. As the plan shows a strong sense of geometry, it could work well in coordination with math exercises.

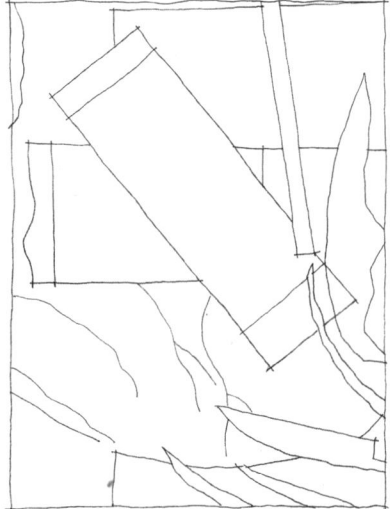

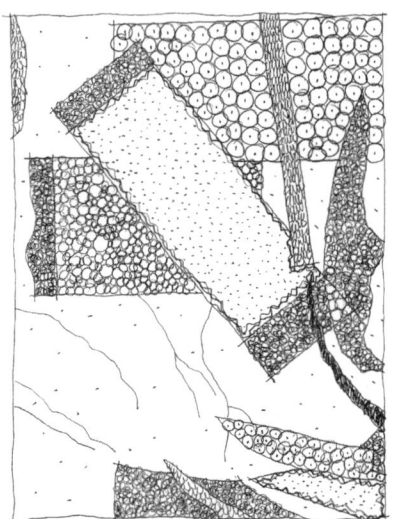

A fun assignment for students would be to adapt the forms in a painting by abstract expressionists for the layout of an outdoor classroom or garden.

pathways placed at even intervals around a central focal point that often was a decorative fountain.

Modern Gardens (AD 1930–late 1970s)

Artists at the turn of the twentieth century introduced a variety of new styles of art, which were generally characterized by freedom of expression across a wide range of subject matter and media. Modern garden plans from this period began to resemble nonobjective or abstract art, such as paintings and sculpture by Piet Mondrian, Wassily Kandinsky, Jean Arp, Joan Miró, Alexander Calder, László Moholy-Nagy, and Pablo Picasso; these gardens are often referred to as abstract or cubist gardens.

Landscape architects such as Thomas Dolliver Church, Garrett Eckbo, Daniel Urban Kiley, and James Rose paid attention to human scale, spatial sequence, and simplicity in color, line, and form. They considered ease of maintenance and appropriate plant selection and paid particular attention to innovative use of new materials. Their asymmetrical gardens with multiple sight lines were a departure from the classical symmetrical Beaux-Arts style. Client needs were emphasized as well as design integration with existing site conditions.

Modern landscape architecture in the United States was influenced by Brazilian landscape architect Roberto Burle Marx (1909–1994) and Mexican architect Luis Barragán (1902–1988). A horticulturist and plant collector, Burle Marx promoted ecological biodiversity and rainforest protection before the environmental trend became popular. He approached garden design as a fine art, and created landscape compositions that resembled three-dimensional paintings made with earth, water, sky, and plants. His garden layouts typically blended a series of fluid curves with geometric angles, and he, as well as other Modern garden designers, created garden rooms for outdoor living.

During the late Modern period, the environmental movement (1960s and 1970s) brought ecological design into focus. Ian McHarg's popular book *Design with Nature* (1969) influenced the enactment of the 1969 National Environmental Policy Act (NEPA). McHarg's innovative planning technique, termed the *overlay system,* is a process of recording site-specific data (soil, vegetation, slope, and other site conditions) on individual maps, then layering these upon each other to create a composite map. This technique is discussed further in the site analysis section of Chapter 4, "Site Research and Design Synthesis."

Postmodern and Contemporary Gardens (AD mid-1970s–present)

Postmodernism was a step toward even greater freedom in design. Characterized by "freestyle" classical forms with personal interpretations, Postmodern design was largely artistic experimentation that referenced historic styles. Environmental artists Isamu Noguchi, Robert Smithson, Walter De Maria, Nancy Holt, and Christo Javacheff, to name a few, inspired garden design during this period.

Early Postmodern landscape architectural projects demonstrated that landscape architects could explore artistic and humorous directions. Martha Schwartz's Bagel Garden, Cambridge, Massachusetts (1979), perhaps created for its shock value, was a temporary parterre of lacquered pumpernickel bagels

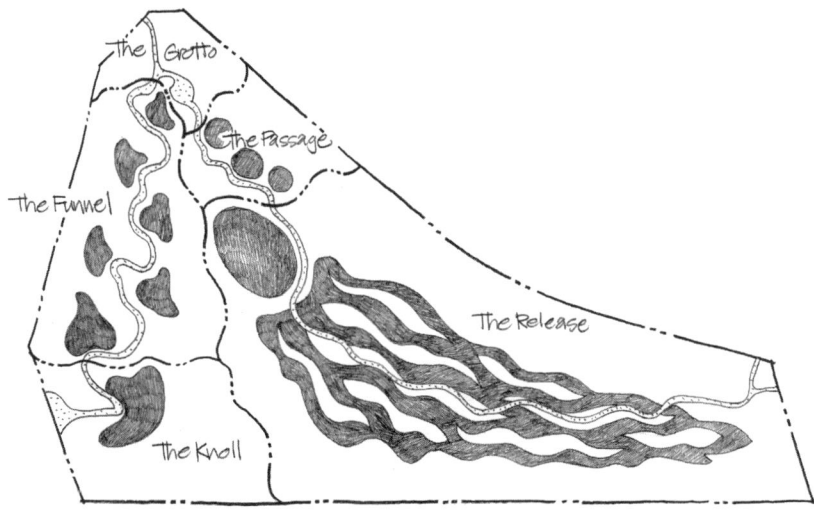

Waterworks Gardens (1996), located in Renton, Washington, and created by Seattle-based artist Lorna Jordan, is a park designed to cleanse stormwater through a series of ponds and wetlands that filter and remove sediment, oil, and grease from vehicles, as well as suspended metals and fecal coliform from bird populations. This process parallels the visitor's perambulatory experience through five garden rooms—the Knoll, the Funnel, the Grotto, the Passage, and the Release—which were created to tell the story of water filtration through ecological processes. Inspired by shapes found in plants, her plan for the park envisioned the landscape as a living metaphor for the hydrologic cycle. On foot, visitors follow the journey of polluted water through various spaces that represent specific parts of the plant, as a way to reinforce the important role plants play in the natural purification processes.

Habitat gardens for wildlife observation will probably draw inspiration from informal natural garden styles, but designers should feel comfortable adopting (with modification) any of these historical styles. Most small wildlife will not be affected by stylistic choices if there is plenty of native vegetation and water. For example, it would probably be unusual to create a schoolyard wildlife habitat based on a French chateaux garden, but it would be possible, and perhaps interesting, as these formal gardens also incorporated natural areas with dense vegetation—ideal habitats for wildlife.

arranged on a bed of purple aquarium gravel. George Hargreaves's Harlequin Plaza, Greenwood Village, Colorado (1982), was a surrealistic courtyard that showcased several large harlequin statues set on black and white, distorted, diamond-shaped paving and surrounded by red and purple walls of diminishing heights, all of which created false perspective and spatial illusion. Personal expression within the designer's frame of reference became accepted practice, and classical historic garden forms became popular again.

This new style continues to evolve, and with it the design aesthetic that searches for deep understanding of the complexities of site, region, and community. Contemporary designers now strive for a more complete integration of sustainable ecological design, regional history and culture, and landscape as art.

Design Fundamentals

Schoolyard gardens should be both visually exciting compositions and unified, harmonious places well suited for both wildlife and people. They can be an explosion of colors, forms, and textures that change over time and through the seasons as natural features grow and evolve. Human-made features can also be used for function and visual interest. These, too, could change over time as new students and teachers make creative adaptations to existing spaces.

Contemporary garden design theories have evolved to include sustainable ecology, historical and cultural interpretation, and art. What follows are some of the concerns related primarily to visual aspects of design. These concepts were presented by the author (2001) in the *Encyclopedia of Gardens: History and Design*. The visual design fundamentals described in this section (usually termed the principles and elements of design) offer a few specific suggestions for application in schoolyard garden design. Designers will also want to investigate other design concerns such as function and use, site parameters, and economic considerations. The following chapters will address these topics.

Design Principles

Design principles are the organizational precepts or theories of visual art that determine the site design layout. Designers use principles (e.g., unity, balance, and proportion) in the placement of elements (e.g., forms, textures, and colors) as they build two- and three-dimensional compositions. In garden design, the assemblage of earth, water, plants, bricks, and stone has function, meaning, and visual attraction. The principles and elements presented here provide a universal vocabulary for the visual aspects of place design. As Sylvia Crowe argues in her classic book *Garden Design* (1958, 81), "Through all the variations, due to climate, country, history and the natural idiosyncrasy of man, which have appeared in the evolution of the garden through successive civilizations, certain principles remain constant however much their application may change."

Balance is an ordering of elements in the design, which implies stability and equilibrium. The École des Beaux-Arts tradition emphasized symmetrical layout patterns: mirror-image repetition along an axis to create indisputable balance. Radial symmetrical patterns consist of identical elements placed around a central point. Asymmetrical or occult balance, on the other hand, gives a sense of order without bilateral or identical duplication. The schoolyard wildlife habi-

Balance

Contrast

tat will probably be derived from natural landscapes, which are asymmetrically balanced. Planting groupings of odd numbers and clump-and-gap planting plans described previously will help achieve this effect.

Contrast implies opposition or difference within the elements of design and is used to create variety through the lightness and darkness of objects. Contrasting forms, colors, shapes, and textures will enhance the visual quality of the environment. For instance, a flowering shrub will be accented if it is placed against a wall of a contrasting color.

Diminishing detail

Diminishing detail is a means of creating the appearance of depth in the garden through the variation of detail. In this type of design phenomenon, nearby objects will show detail clearly, whereas objects in the distance will have less definition as their form disappears into an outline. This principle can be used to exaggerate the viewer's sense of perspective by changing the size of objects to make views appear shorter or longer. For example, repeat an object along a sight line, but as the distance from the viewer increases, repeatedly decrease the size of the objects. This optical trick will make the overall distance appear longer.

Direction

Direction suggests movement. Some forms, such as the circle, are static and do not alone suggest direction; a linear or triangular shape, however, will suggest direction by implying movement. A ground-plane grid pattern (perhaps a paving pattern) placed on a diagonal will imply visual direction and movement.

Emphasis, attraction, or **focal points** within the garden are accent points that will engage viewers. They are distinctive places within the garden composition, which may be areas that are brightly colored or that include dynamic works of art. They may possess unusual materials or other contrasting expressions of tone, texture, or shape. They could hold symbolic meaning and provide places for contemplation. Water features have historically been common focal points in the garden.

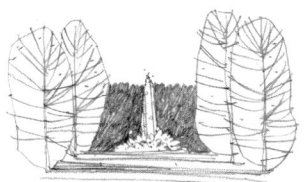

Emphasis

Figure–ground relationships within a composition provide dialogue between the figure or object and its background, or neutral contextual setting. In garden design, figures such as trees, walls, and sculptures could be showcased against a contrasting background.

Figure–ground

Movement can be objective (an actual change in the visual field or environment) or subjective (the perception of change). In landscape design, movement is a critical component that applies both to what viewers see in the garden and to how they walk through the outdoor spaces. The designer orchestrates both in the creation of the garden layout. Views will be directed through sight lines and framing devices or screening techniques that draw the viewer's eye. Also, circulation pathways are built to direct the physical movement of visitors through a series of spaces designed to offer them a variety of visual and physical experiences. In reality, these two types of movement work together as people walk and "see what they can see."

Movement

Overlapping is a layering of objects to create depth and visual interest. In garden design, layering is often accomplished with plant compositions but also with walls, trellises, and artwork. For example, large evergreen trees could be

Overlapping

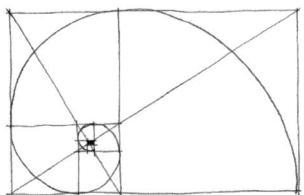

Proportion

Repetition

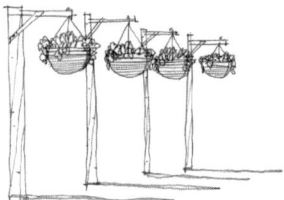

Rhythm

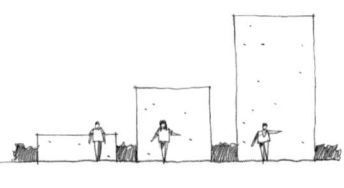

Scale

Transparency

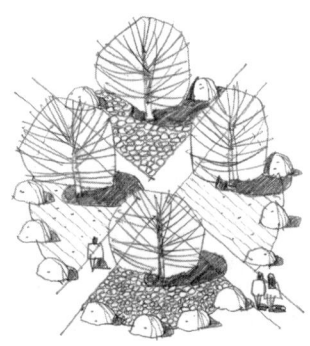

Unity

planted as the background for smaller flowering deciduous trees and shrubs, and colorful walls could be used to separate space and create interest. This overlapping effect creates a greater sense of depth, adds visual curiosity, and provides pockets and protection for wildlife.

Proportion refers to the mathematical relationships exhibited in the various dimensions of an object or space. Often, a ratio or comparison between objects is used to describe the relationship of one object, mass, or material to another. The *golden mean,* or *golden section,* is a mathematical proportion used by the ancient Greeks that was represented through a rectangular or logarithmic spiral that could grow or subdivide indefinitely, with magnifications or divisions retaining the same proportional properties as the original shape. The creators of the Parthenon, for example, used this tool of proportional order in their design. It was believed that key numerical relationships within the golden mean disclosed the harmony of the universe. These proportions are best described in the work of mathematician Leonardo of Pisa, also called Fibonacci. His treatise *Liber abaci* (1202) describes the number sequences that have come to be called Fibonacci numbers.

Repetition is a pattern created by multiple applications of the same or a similar form or object. A repetitive pattern can have radial balance or a more irregular, occult progression. Music and art teachers understand how repetition is used to create continuity. Their input in the design of the schoolyard garden could offer greater understanding of this and other design fundamentals.

Rhythm involves movement often marked by expected recurrence. The repetition of similar forms and colors creates visual rhythm. Rhythm relates to proportion and is understood as ratios and organic forms in nature. Visual rhythm can repeat in predictable recurrences or be more spontaneous and create unpredictable patterns, which in turn can potentially offer greater interest.

Scale refers to how we perceive the size of an element or space relative to ourselves—to the dimensions and proportions of the human body often referred to as human scale. Spaces can be created in a wide range of sizes, from monumental football-field-sized spaces to tiny child-sized places. Landscape spaces should be designed with consideration for the scale appropriateness of the proposed activity. The outdoor classroom should include a variety of space sizes and scales. Small spaces are often ignored in public place design, but these will be especially attractive to children and small wildlife.

Transparency is used to create depth and accent. Used in coordination with overlapping techniques, transparency can control views by framing vistas for enhancement or illusion. For example, tree branches or fences with strategic transparent openings, when placed in the foreground, frame the *borrowed* landscape of the distance.

Unity is a cohesiveness that is attained when all the elements of a garden—colors, textures, and forms—are perceived as parts of a whole, harmonious system. Unity is the *glue* of design. It can be achieved through a spatial layout of repeated forms or materials (such as plant species), or through other ordering devices, such as balance, rhythm, and proportion.

Variety refers to the variation and contrast within the composition. Changes in color, texture, and form create interest within the garden. This visual interest, or liveliness, is similar to dissonance in music; it is the *spice* of design. Variety in the landscape can be attained through differences in the sizes of spaces, spatial sequences, and plant species. While some variety creates interest, too much variation will be visually chaotic and confusing. Good designers incorporate variety with unity to ensure that their site is lively without being disorganized. Designers of schoolyard gardens should consider variety in many ways, including plant species, activity settings, artworks, and materials.

Variety

Design Elements

Design elements, the building blocks of design, interact with one another in degrees of harmony or discord. Designers manipulate the elements through a series of study sketches until a final resolution or equilibrium is attained between all factors (visual, artistic, functional, ecological, and cultural).

Color

Color is the visual effect of light upon matter, often referred to as the hue or pigment of an object. Full-spectrum light rays fall upon a surface, and that surface absorbs some rays and reflects others. The reflected rays are seen by the eye as color: when an object absorbs all other colors in the light spectrum and reflects red, the color red is seen. Flower color can be used in the schoolyard wildlife habitat to attract various types of wildlife and create visual interest.

Forms are defined by the total mass of an object or space. The visual properties of forms include shape, size, color, texture, and direction. Forms can be natural and organic (informal), or they can be symmetrical and highly ordered (formal). The schoolyard garden will probably consist mainly of organic forms derived from nature. Refer to a topographic map for natural shapes that can become the basis for forms within the habitat project, as it is hard to replicate natural forms from memory without them tending to look artificial.

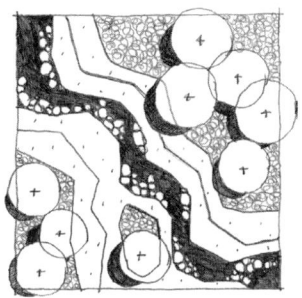

Form

Light from the sun during the day and other stars at night as well as artificial lighting sources can contribute dramatically to the feeling and experience of a place. In the arid Southwest, light is perhaps harsh but always dramatic. As sunlight moves and changes intensity during the day and throughout the seasons, it will affect the visual and physical qualities of the site. The schoolyard garden designer might try to interpret, enhance, or mitigate sun patterns through the use of sundials, shadow patterns, and certainly shade devices as needed.

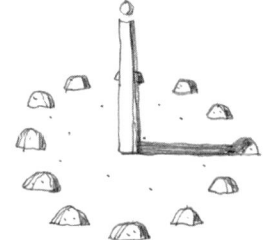

Light

Lines within the garden define edges or boundaries, suggest movement, and add interest. Lines are articulated through changes in material, texture, color, or shape. For example, paving materials can be used to define lines along the ground plane. Less obvious lines in the landscape include lines of sight that direct and frame views through the configuration of plants or other features.

Lines

Masses are forms that are perceived as solid volumes. In architecture and landscape architecture, mass is evaluated largely by proportion, context, and scale. Plant massing is a term used to describe a grouping of plants, usually of similar species, used to define and unify space as well as to provide visual interest. Plant masses within the schoolyard wildlife habitat will be used to screen views and noise, define spaces, and provide specific habitat zones.

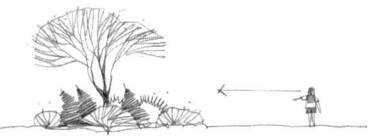

Masses

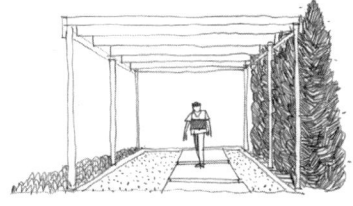
Planes

Points

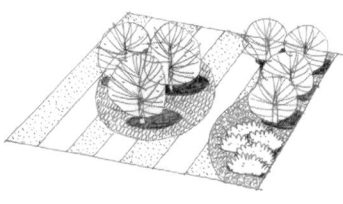
Shapes

Texture

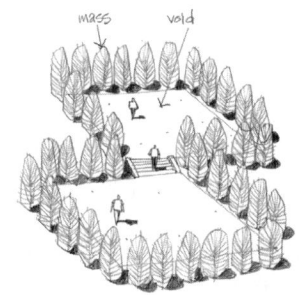
Volumes

Planes (ground, vertical, and overhead) are the "floors," "walls," and "roofs" used to define spaces within the garden. Planes may be created with architectural structures or natural features. Ground planes can be hard, paved surfaces or soft, natural materials, depending on their intended purpose. The ground plane offers designers a canvas of opportunity for expression in color, form, texture, and line, including topographical contour and patterns of flowers, grasses, stones, tiles, and paint. Vertical planes are spatial dividers and can be earthen forms, plant masses, solid walls, lattice or open-air structures, or single vertical elements such as trees. Variations in texture, form, color, and size are central to the creation of vertical planes. Overhead planes are the *roofs* of landscape spaces, which are used to protect and create various degrees of enclosure. The most dramatic overhead plane is the open sky, but for functional reasons, more tangible materials, such as tree canopies, ramadas, and solid architectural structures, are important additions to the schoolyard garden. But unlike building architecture, the figurative walls used in outdoor environments have a much wider range of option and expression—they do not have to be level; they can have peep holes in them, they can slope or even be concave or convex, or they might even pivot or swivel.

Points in compositions are static, directionless positions in space; they imply stability. Within three-dimensional places, these elements are best regarded as focal points, spots where the eye or person is directed. Focal points within the schoolyard wildlife habitat are special areas or elements of interest or surprise that attract the attention of both wildlife and people. Examples include unique wildlife features such as ponds or special birdhouses, artworks like sundials, and even functional features like colorful pathways or drinking fountains.

Shapes are two-dimensional patterns. Within the garden, they are lines and edges of spaces often seen in the ground plane. Shapes could be amorphous and natural or may be geometric in nature (circles, squares, rectangles, and triangles).

Texture refers to the surface characteristics of forms, which affect both the tactile and light-reflective qualities of the surface. Texture occurs in objects such as plants, rocks, water, and walls. The schoolyard garden should be rich with diverse textures, both natural and human-made. Texture ranges in plant foliage will provide needed cover for wildlife.

Volumes of spaces are created through human-made and natural materials. The volume of an outdoor space is the form and mass of the objects within the garden, as well as the open air or voids made by the configuration of masses (vegetation, walls, etc.). Variations in the spatial volumes of the landscape spaces will create visual interest and functional variety.

The information presented in this chapter serves as an overview of the history of garden design, which can be used as inspiration for concept development. Care should be taken not to mimic or reproduce a style but to extract useful applications with unique interpretations. Additionally, visual design fundamentals (design principles and elements) must be used as tools to guide garden composition. Application of this information should be incorporated in design concepts that strive to create meaningful narrations and experiences for children. The sequential steps presented in the next two chapters create methods that help communities realize this goal.

CHAPTER 3 Beginning the Design Process

Introduction

In designing school campuses, it is important to equally consider all of the indoor and outdoor spaces that will be part of the architecture and landscape architecture of the school, including classrooms, roads, athletic fields, and schoolyard gardens. These should be designed as a whole and harmonious system laid upon a foundation of ecological principles, cultural factors, artistic influences, and economic and functional requirements. However, as the buildings take priority in school construction projects, they are often designed in isolation, without regard for existing site conditions or possible outdoor functions. Schoolyard natural areas and many other outdoor spaces are consequently eliminated from the *design programming* phase of school architectural proposals, and the design and construction of these "less important" places occur after the building is constructed, if at all. When school communities decide to add outdoor spaces later, they are sometimes implemented one at a time, without the benefit of an overall campus master plan. This piecemeal process and lack of planning create serious problems, as outdoor spaces can be incorrectly sited, and the physical relationships between one space and another, as well as related activities, may be in conflict with one another. Of course, the array of potential problems common in poor planning practices—including soil erosion, vehicular and pedestrian conflicts, and scorching hot play areas—can be avoided through the development of a campus master plan.

The term *master plan,* as used in this book, is defined as an overall design scheme for the entire campus. A campus master plan locates all outdoor spaces and activities, and can be implemented in a phased manner over an extended period of time. The term *site plan* is used to describe the more detailed and specific design scheme of the schoolyard project, which implies a smaller area within the campus master plan. The process and methods described relate specifically to the design of natural outdoor classrooms, but these concepts can be applied to all site design or master planning projects. Both master plans

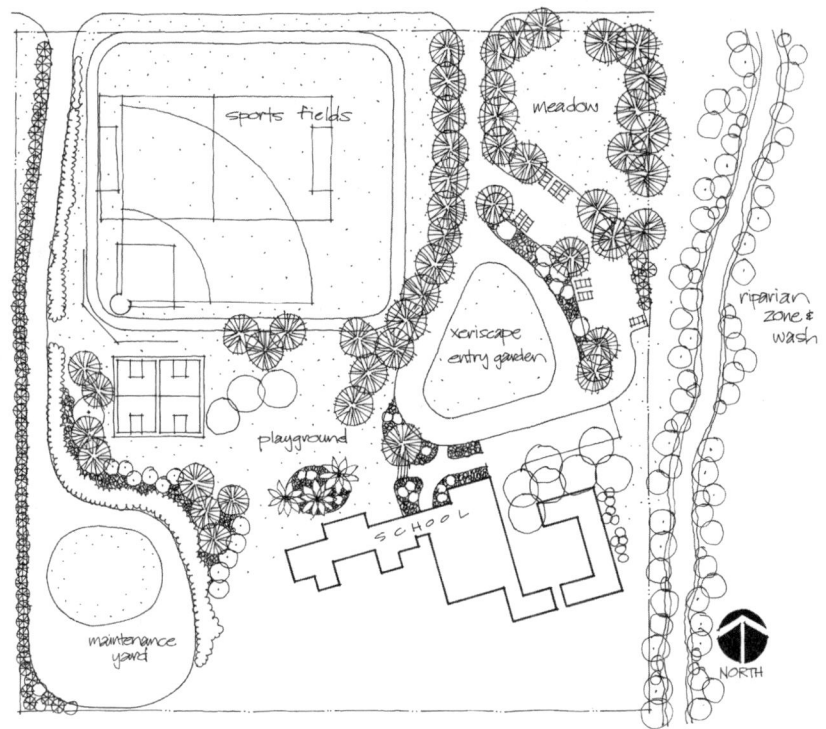

This master plan drawing for an elementary school, based on the work of Arizona architect Les Wallach, shows the building footprint and locations for outdoor functions, including the sports field, maintenance yard, playground, xeriscape entry garden, meadow, and wildlife habitat garden. It is ideal when all the various school functions are planned at the same time and presented in the form of a final master plan. However, the outdoor classroom is often created after the school is built and many of the outdoor functions have already been designated.

As schools prepare site plans, it is important for them to realize that even the smallest natural area may have a positive impact on the development of participating children.

Outdoor classroom designers will follow several steps to arrive at a final design solution. This process involves background research related to the site conditions and the intended use of the outdoor classroom or garden. This research is critical to the success of the project and provides good opportunities for student involvement and learning.

and site plans become a record of the collective vision of all the participants. Design solutions for the schoolyard gardens are represented through plan, section, elevation, and perspective drawings, and also through three-dimensional models. These are usually colorfully rendered to clearly show zones, spaces, pathways, design features, and materials such as paving and specific plants. This display becomes an indispensable communication tool for fund-raising and construction.

Site design methods or design processes are described by authors Kevin Lynch and Gary Hack (1984), Albert Rutledge (1971), and John Simonds (1983) to help landscape architects create beautiful, satisfying, and appropriate design solutions. Their various approaches involve a series of similar sequential steps that guide these designers and community groups in the creation of outdoor places. In the spirit of these authors, the information contained in this section is presented as a step-by-step method that includes background research, site selection, site inventory and analysis, and design generation. In reality, the steps may not follow a perfectly linear path, as later steps may affect and alter decisions made earlier. In these cases, designers will have to go back to repeat earlier steps. *Stay flexible, and your goals will be realized.*

Legal construction drawings—or "working drawings," as they are often called—are very detailed drawings used in the construction of most public projects. If a project will be subject to the construction bidding process, these drawings may be needed. In this case, it is advisable that the design committee contact a licensed landscape architect for advice regarding the preparation of construction drawings. However, many outdoor classrooms, wildlife habitats, or garden projects are implemented through community volunteer efforts and can avoid the necessity of the public bidding process and the hiring of licensed contractors. For these projects, illustrative site-plan drawings and models could

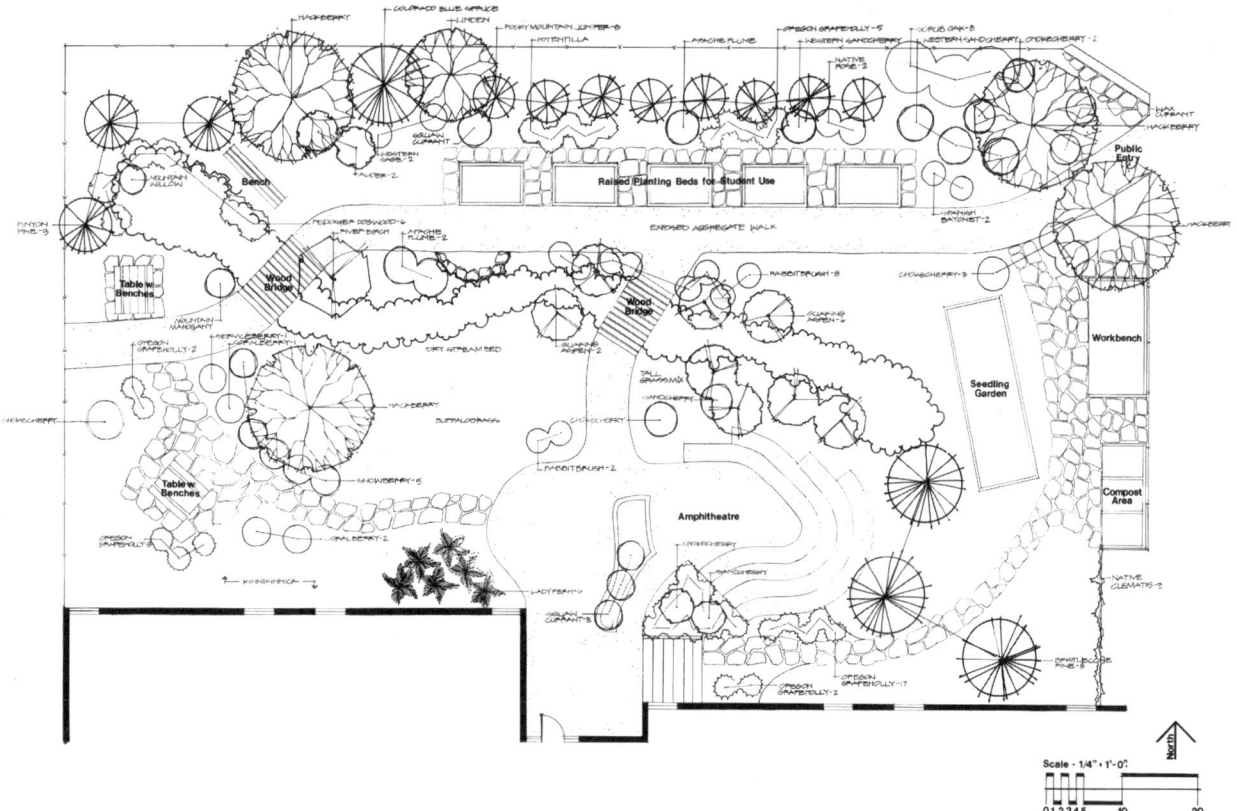

This final site-plan drawing, though not a legal construction drawing, was detailed enough to use as a guide for construction. Small design adjustments were made during the building process, since the drawing did not perfectly match the site conditions.

suffice. Keep in mind that even after the completion of site plans for the schoolyard, design adjustments will occur during construction.

The following design approach can be used in the development of several types of landscapes. In this text, focus is on outdoor learning in the schoolyard, and thus the terms *outdoor classrooms, wildlife habitats,* and *gardens* are again interchanged throughout, as the process applies broadly. Students can participate in these steps, especially if they are developed into classroom exercises within the curriculum. It is important to note that this process should be modified to fit the specific parameters and goals of a particular project.

A Design Process for Planning Outdoor Classrooms, Wildlife Habitats, and Gardens

Identify Participants

Outdoor classrooms are typically created through the collaborative efforts of many volunteers (referred to within this text as "participants" or "designers"). Group involvement in the project will encourage a sense of community ownership and pride and help ensure the longevity of the project. The most successful school gardens will involve school administrators, teachers, maintenance staff, students, parents, community members, landscape architects and landscape designers, artists, and a variety of outside professionals. The contributions of individuals with these diverse points of view will help to create a dynamic schoolyard project. In fact, everyone connected with the school should be invited and encouraged to participate.

School principals and school boards must be involved in the design process, as they are responsible for physical changes to the campus. Sometimes school administrators prefer to let teachers and parents implement the project. However, all types of outdoor classrooms, habitats, and gardens will have a better chance of being built and used within the curriculum if they are developed under the guidance and support provided by these administrators.

Teachers work hard managing the educational atmosphere of their indoor classrooms. Sometimes the process of planning and constructing an outdoor classroom creates an overload in a teacher's work schedule, making it difficult to get fully involved. Administrators should consider creating incentives, such as reduced workloads, for those teachers participating actively in the planning process. Of course, for many teachers, the incentive often comes solely from the idea that they can be better teachers if they have outdoor classrooms.

Maintenance is sure to increase with the implementation of a wildlife habitat. This should be addressed at the onset of the project by involving the maintenance staff and developing a clear maintenance plan.

ADMINISTRATORS

It is essential to involve administrators such as the school superintendent, principals, and school board members in the planning process. Schoolyard projects will not be approved for construction without the support of these key individuals.

TEACHERS

Try to represent teachers from various specializations and grade levels in the planning process. If the schoolyard is to be used by students of all ages and become a part of a schoolwide theme for integrated studies, representatives from all disciplines must feel invested in the project. When these outdoor classrooms are created by only a few teachers, the use of these places tends to become limited to the needs and desires of those individuals, and they run the risk of eventually becoming neglected as those teachers leave the school or lose interest in the project.

MAINTENANCE PERSONNEL

The expertise of the school's maintenance staff will greatly benefit the project. These individuals have a comprehensive knowledge of the existing conditions of the school grounds and are invaluable in the process of site inventory and analysis. Maintenance staff may be understandably concerned about the potential for an increase in overall maintenance as a result of the development of the outdoor classroom, as new features—plants, ponds, shade structures, and bridges—would require additional ongoing maintenance. It is important that designers address maintenance concerns early in the planning process and include maintenance tasks in the curriculum as lessons and, perhaps, daily activities for students. A final maintenance plan should be developed as a written guide for the care of the schoolyard.

STUDENTS

Because the main goal of the outdoor classroom is learning, students of all ages should be involved as much as possible in the planning and design of the project. Many of the tasks outlined in this section could be developed into special projects or areas of study for students. A visiting artist, landscape architect, biologist, or interested teacher or parent might be willing to lead students through a series of lessons and workshops to generate research and design ideas for the project. As a result of their creative efforts, students will develop a sense of pride and ownership in the project—it will become a meaningful place for students, and the risk of vandalism and neglect will be reduced. As children are guided through design methods and processes, important lessons to be gained might include site ecology or regional history, and as the design is implemented, even construction techniques will offer many teaching scenarios. It could prove useful to hire a curriculum consultant to assist administrators and teachers in developing specific lessons related to design and planning efforts as well as outdoor classroom activities.

The outdoor classroom, wildlife habitat, and other gardens should not be thought of as fixed, rigid, and manicured landscapes. Rather, they should evolve over time and be modified by new teachers, parents, and children to better reflect the needs of the current school population. New artworks should be added, plants moved, and pathways adjusted in order to challenge children and improve the learning environment. Changes and updates will make the place

These students have been asked to develop ideas for their ideal schoolyard in a workshop aimed at determining what students really want. Students will often begin the session with a list of features they think the adults "want them to want." It is as if they are searching for the right answers to a test. Usually, in time, and after they are assured they have real latitude to be creative, they develop their own unique ideas.

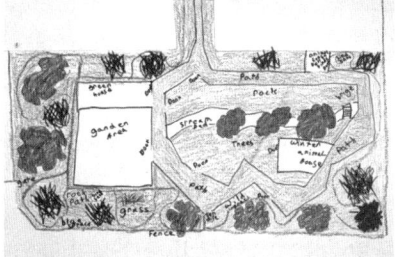
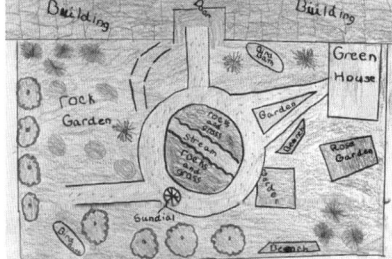
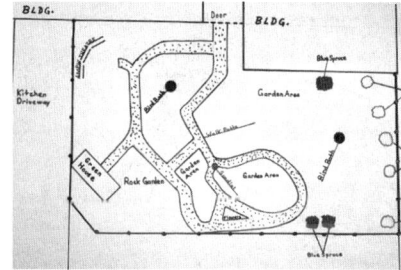

These four workable plans were developed by students.

meaningful for new users as they participate in the additions or revisions. This process of evolution will also help to sustain students' interest as they get older and progress through the grade levels. It is interaction with the environment that will create deep meaning.

PARENTS AND COMMUNITY MEMBERS

The assistance of parents and community members in the design effort will be diverse, often including strengths in fund-raising, design, and construction. Local special-interest groups such as garden clubs, scouts, and 4-H might welcome the opportunity to participate in this community project.

LANDSCAPE ARCHITECTS, LANDSCAPE DESIGNERS, AND ARTISTS

Landscape architects, landscape designers, and artists can play an important role in the facilitation of design and the preparation of conceptual, preliminary, and final site plans for the schoolyard project. A landscape architect or landscape designer from the community might be willing to volunteer time; alternatively,

It is important to involve the school community in the design process, as everyone should have a voice.

Schools begin the process by sharing ideas and writing a design program. Consider the following useful brainstorming categories: goals and objectives, requirements, activities and activity settings, design features, and curriculum ideas.

college or university programs in landscape architecture or landscape design are often willing to help. The American Society of Landscape Architects (ASLA) provides useful information regarding the selection of these professionals.

OUTSIDE PROFESSIONALS

Outside professionals from various agencies, including the USDA Forest Service, National Park Service, U.S. Department of Agriculture Natural Resources Conservation Service (formerly the U.S. Soil Conservation Service), wildlife departments, and cooperative extension programs can be contacted for specialized input as needed. Local businesses from the construction industry, if involved in the project, will be valuable and appreciated participants.

Write a Design Program

INTRODUCTION

A *design program* is a written and graphic expression of the parameters for design, including the school participants' goals and objectives, requirements, activities and activity settings, design features, and curriculum ideas for the design. The program should be explicit and detailed, but also open-ended; it should be thought of as the story or *script* for the design of the project. If handled in this manner, the program will direct the planning effort in a fashion that allows flexibility as the design progresses.

In the creation of a design program, there are many ways to involve the project's various participants. In some cases, designers might form a steering committee to develop a system of participation that would include classroom projects, subcommittee research groups, open-ended brainstorming sessions, and task-oriented workshops, thereby involving everyone in the process. In any event, no one should be left out, creative thinking should be a priority, lines of communication should be kept open, and individual participants should be assigned specific roles with clear charges or objectives.

A brainstorming method that can be used in this early stage of design was developed by architect William W. Caudill (1973), of Caudill, Rowlett, and Scott (CRS Inc.) in Houston, Texas. The *analysis card technique,* as it is called, is a way to discuss, record, and organize ideas in a forum of open community participation. All ideas and thoughts about the project are expressed verbally, and designated recorders write down these suggestions on a 5″ × 7″ piece of paper or card as a short phrase, with a fast sketch or diagram to accompany the written text. The cards are placed on a wall in a collage where everyone can see them. As developed by CRS, these cards are typically organized within three categories: *goals* (statements of vision), *facts* (known problems, concerns, or parameters), and *concepts* (solutions or design ideas). School participants should identify their own categories and modify these headings; for example, goals, needs, and ideas are groupings that simplify the CRS units and work successfully.

An even simpler idea-generating option is to just allow people to say whatever comes to their minds. Later, the collection of thoughts and ideas can be organized into a structure that makes sense, and this information will become the basis for the written design program. Of course, not all the ideas generated in brainstorming sessions can be used in the schoolyard project. Eventually, ideas will have to be ranked, which can be achieved by requesting individual participants to select and discuss their most important concerns. Sometimes a voting system can help facilitate the establishment of priorities. As priorities are

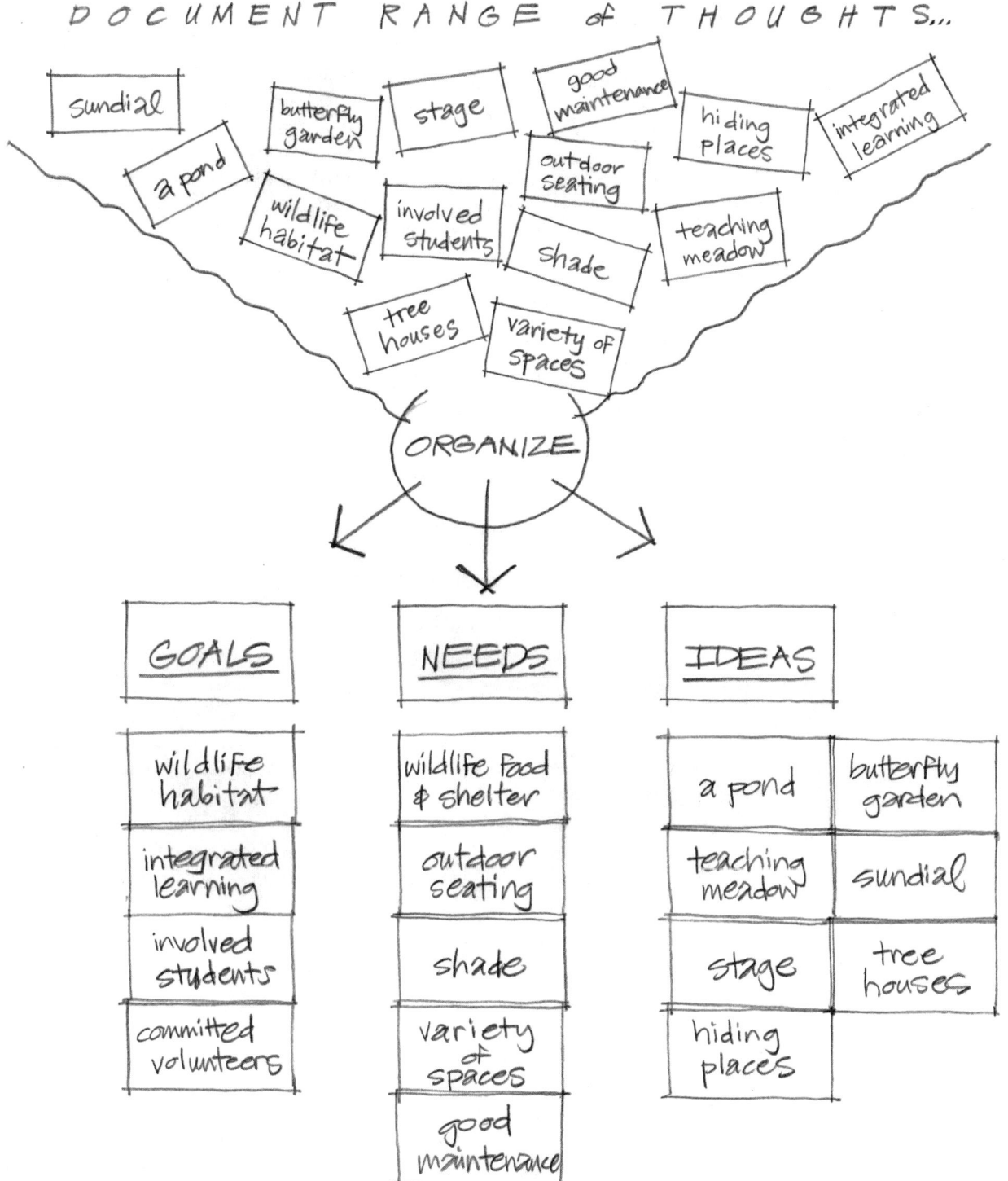

established, ongoing open dialogue will help everyone keep in mind the many unique points of view that should be represented within the outdoor classroom, wildlife habitat, or garden.

As the planning process progresses, a tool often employed in design generation is the creation of a *storyboard* of design possibilities. These examples help to clarify and refine the design ideas put forward in the design program. Photographs or sketches of design possibilities cut from magazines or other sources

The analysis card technique, used in planning workshops, was modified here to gather information that could eventually be expanded and organized into a guide or program for the design.

A *storyboard* of design possibilities—photographs, sketches, and ideas cut from magazines—could be put together in a display at the school. Sometimes children are given disposable or digital cameras so they can photograph specific design features or favorite places that might inspire design ideas for their schoolyard.

are collected from students, teachers, and parents and displayed in a large montage format. This mural of gardens, fountains, wind chimes, plants, and other ideas becomes the inspiration for design. A wall within the school could be used for this evolution of ideas as participants add images on a regular and ongoing basis. As the design progresses, it could prove useful to actually measure and map a prototype of an existing natural space. This could provide inspiration for design, although modification will certainly be necessary.

CREATE A DESIGN FRAMEWORK WITH MEANING

From the onset of the project, it is important that designers establish an overarching conceptual framework. In the case of outdoor classrooms, wildlife habitats, and thematic gardens, this framework may be derived from a synthesis of ecological factors, cultural conditions, site history, and artistic principles. At this early stage in design, it is important to think broadly and idealistically. Discussion about ecology, culture, and art as they relate to the project will provide ongoing inspiration for design ideas and solutions.

Economic and functional parameters will also play an important role in design, but they should not be allowed to dominate the project's ideal goals. Functional aspects of design—including safety, accessibility, and ease in movement—will be some of the easiest to identify. Overall function will be explored frequently throughout this discussion.

Nearly every schoolyard project will have economic limitations, but as these are usually surmountable, they should not be emphasized greatly at the beginning stages of design. When communities temporarily disregard cost to develop strong concepts and ideal site plans, they are usually able to find funding sources based on their energy and optimism. Strong, good design is easy to support. If design ideas are compromised at the onset, a great design plan will never be realized. Outside donors are more likely to provide resources when they see a well-articulated design plan and enthusiastic community members. Project phasing is another possible way to resolve budget limitations. Chapter 5, "Design Essentials," provides more details on how designers can expand their construction budgets.

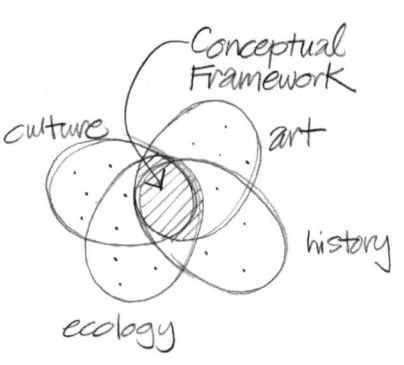

The framework for design is a synthesis of ecology, culture, history, and art.

Art

Human-made landscapes and gardens throughout history have long been thought of as forms of fine art. Brazilian landscape architect Roberto Burle Marx employed modern abstract curved patterns in his landscape works of art to create dynamic combinations of color and texture in three-dimensional compositions. He has compared his artistic manipulation of plants, water, pavement, and other materials to an artist's application of paint on canvas: "I decided to use natural topography as a field of work and the elements of nature, mineral, and vegetable, as materials for the plastic construction, as the other artists worked on canvas with paint and brush" (quoted in The Garden Conservancy 1996, unpaginated).

The outdoor classroom should be thought of as a work of art. If the garden is to be pleasing to the senses and evoke powerful emotions of delight, it must be created with an understanding of the visual fundamentals of design (principles such as unity, balance, and proportion, and elements including forms, textures,

Too much concern about limited budgets may greatly inhibit the process of generating innovative ideas. The scheme shown here represents an "ideal" plan that shows generous boundaries for various activities, including play, wildlife observation, and outdoor classes. This plan could be used to generate outside funds, and the construction could be phased over time, if needed. The small observation area with native plants might be the first phase, later the wildlife habitat could be added, and eventually the outdoor classroom and stage/amphitheater could be constructed. If the school did not have an overall vision, as represented in this plan, the end result could be chaotic.

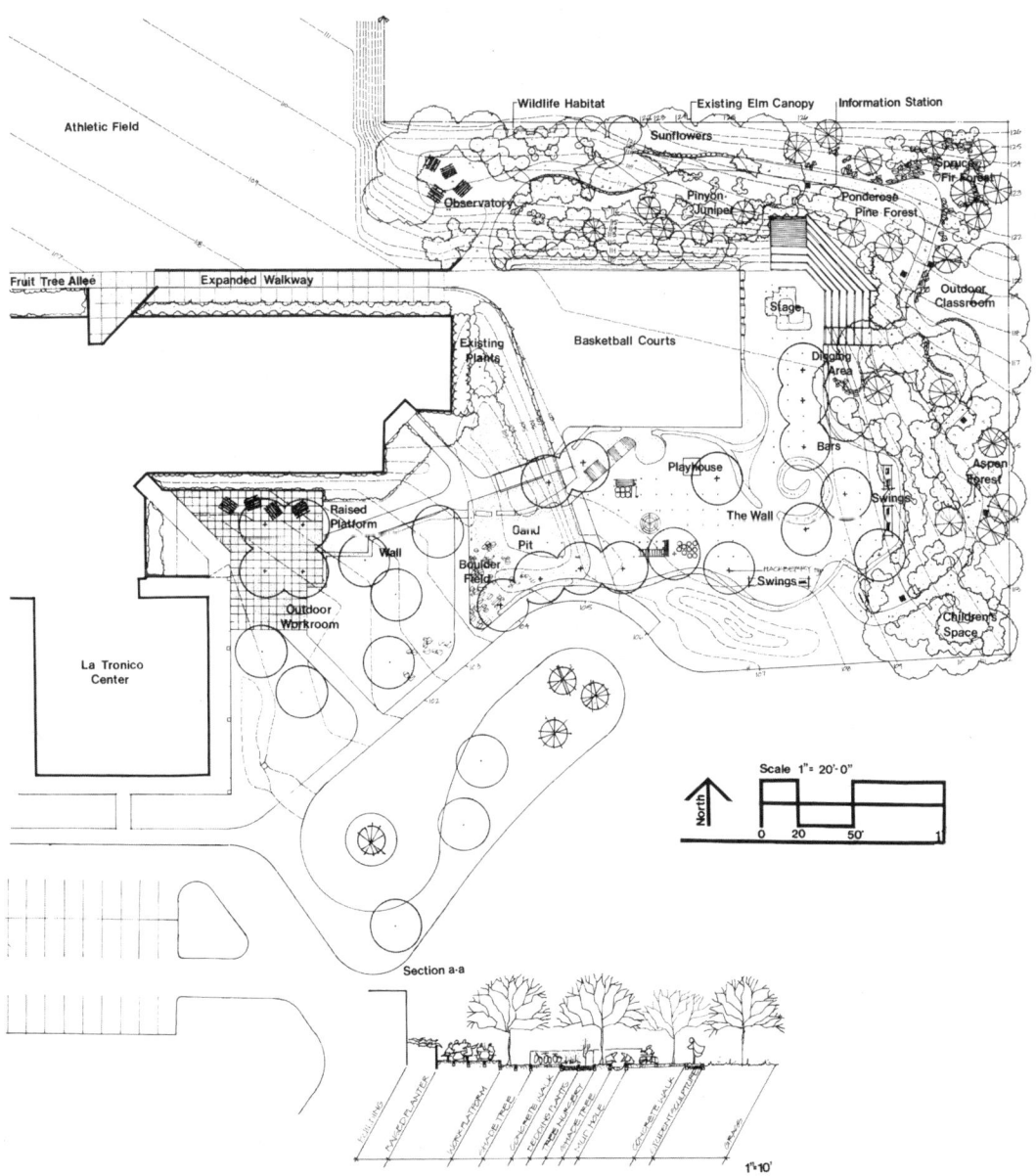

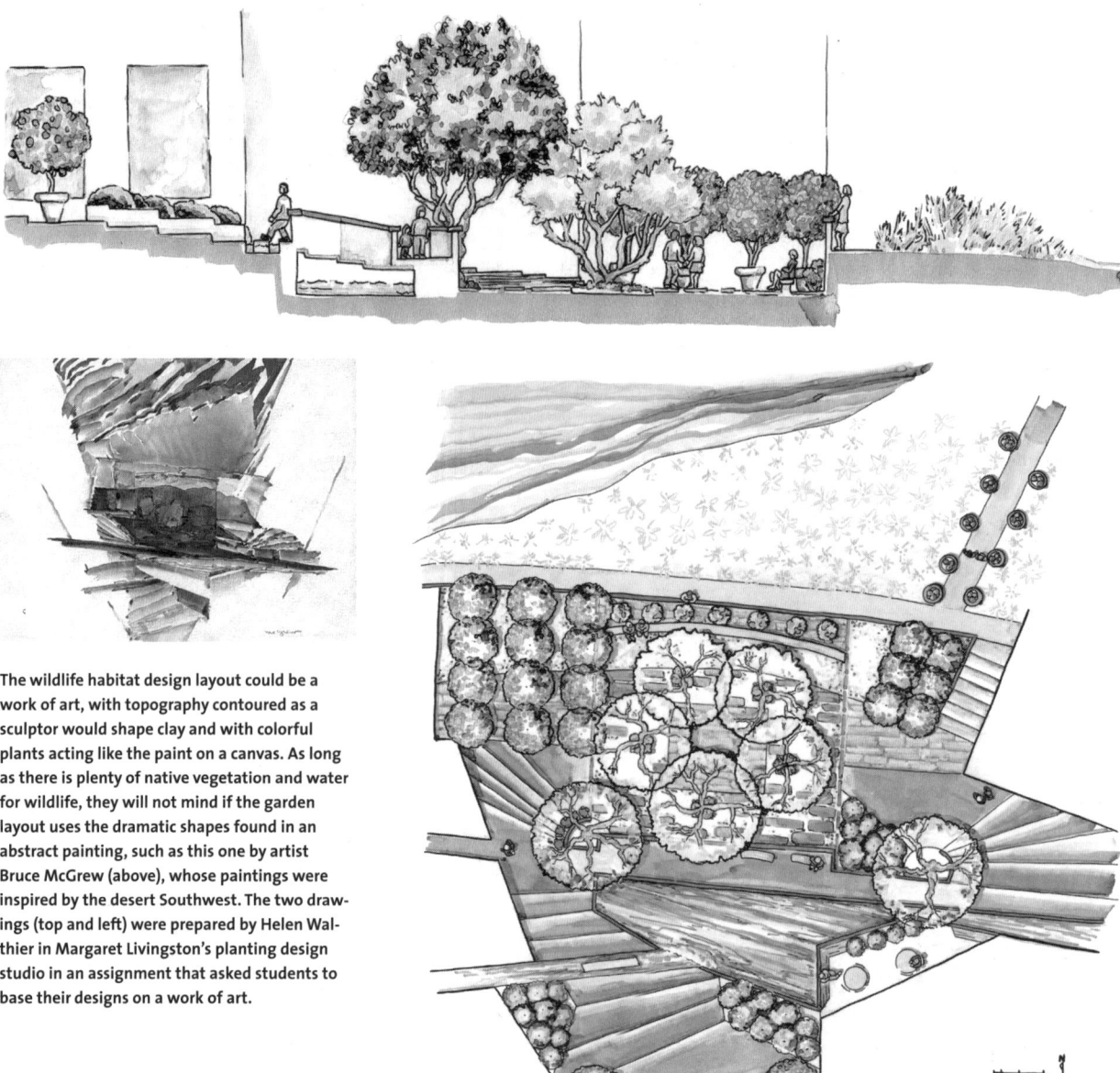

The wildlife habitat design layout could be a work of art, with topography contoured as a sculptor would shape clay and with colorful plants acting like the paint on a canvas. As long as there is plenty of native vegetation and water for wildlife, they will not mind if the garden layout uses the dramatic shapes found in an abstract painting, such as this one by artist Bruce McGrew (above), whose paintings were inspired by the desert Southwest. The two drawings (top and left) were prepared by Helen Walthier in Margaret Livingston's planting design studio in an assignment that asked students to base their designs on a work of art.

and colors) discussed in Chapter 2, "Design Theory." These concepts, used by artists and other designers, interact to form the three-dimensional layout of the garden. As a work of art, the outdoor classroom may play an important role in art literacy and appreciation.

As was described earlier, Claude Monet's garden in Giverny or the French cubist gardens of the 1920s could become the inspiration for the interconnected spaces within the outdoor classroom or wildlife habitat. For example, an abstract painting or graphic design might be used, with modification, for the garden layout; geometric patterns found in these artworks could, for example, inspire the shapes in planting beds for a butterfly garden.

Sculpture and artwork made by children and placed within the landscape might be another approach that would provide artistic interest. Wind harps, murals, sculpted earthworks, benches, ramps, walls, and other elements could provide opportunities for artistic invention. Additionally, art projects often require interdisciplinary research, so students might explore environmental issues such as water harvesting, use of recycled materials, or history for the interpretation of historic garden styles. In general, however, the creation of the outdoor classroom, wildlife habitat, or other garden should be an artistic journey.

Culture/History

Cultural conditions can be divided into two main categories.

First, the basic needs and desires of the current school population must be identified, with sensitivity to the preferences, beliefs, and specific backgrounds of the individual families of the school.

Second, understanding the larger cultural and historical context of the region requires research and interpretation regarding the historic cultures who once occupied the region.

The cultural landscape, according to the National Park Service (Page, Gilbert, and Dolan 1998), is a significant geographic area described within one or more of the following four categories: (1) *historic site*—associated with an important historic event, activity, or person; (2) *historic designed landscape*—significant as a masterful work of art, architecture, or landscape architecture; (3) *historic vernacular landscape*—reflecting the customs and lives of endemic traditions and customs of everyday people; and (4) *ethnographic landscape*—exhibiting qualities that reflect natural and cultural resources defined as heritage resources, such as prehistoric dwellings, monumental geological formations, or conditions of cultural value such as ethnic American settlements. This challenging concept is something to consider in the design of the schoolyard, since important lessons about the history of the site or region could be applicable.

Students examine the tile mosaic art they made for use in the schoolyard.

The cultural groups that could be explored, depending on the location of the school, include past and current Native Americans, early pioneers, ranchers, miners, or even more recent cultural groups living in the region. Students could research postwar (World War I or II) populations, or time periods such as the 1950s or 1960s. Even more recent decades, like the 1980s or 1990s, have historical interest for children and youth. Topics for discussion could range from multigenerational ethnographies to the expansion of technology, overconsumption, pollution, and waste. Specific areas of research on the various cultural groups who may have inhabited the current school grounds, including their cultural heritage and artifacts, may provide design inspiration for the project.

The history of the cultures who once occupied the region should be researched for potential interpretation and learning.

An understanding of site history and the many cultures that lived in the area may set the stage for discoveries related to human relationships with the land. Landscape narratives and stories, such as the following from Leslie Marmon Silko (1995, 156) may offer great insights in this discussion: "The creators of petroglyphs never conceived of removing themselves from the earth and sky. So long as the human consciousness remains *within* the hills, canyons, cliffs, and the plants, clouds, and sky, the term *landscape,* as it has entered the English language, is misleading. 'A portion of territory the eye can comprehend in a single view' does not correctly describe the relationship between the human being and his or her surroundings. This assumes the viewer is somehow outside or separate from the territory she or he surveys. Viewers are as much a part of the landscape as the boulders they stand on."

Other stories, perhaps of survival, quests for territory, searches for food and water, hunting practices, plant cultivation techniques, diseases, wars, and travel

The "circle of life" motif used throughout this park, designed by Christy Ten Eyck, portrays the Native American message of never-ending life and offers hope for the future. Words and poetry of past and current tribes have been etched in seatwalls and walkways as subtle representations that offer enlightenment and understanding to all cultures.

advances, could offer further inspiration for research and discussion within the learning environment of the schoolyard. For example, students may discover that past cultures used water-harvesting techniques that could prove useful in schoolyard water conservation. The historic use of wild and domesticated animals could be demonstrated through murals or informational signage, and native plants used for food, medicine, spiritual benefit, and manufacturing could become yet another source of research and expression. The site history might be manifested through organized events like performances, storytelling, or other forms of interpretation.

As school communities make discoveries about history and culture, they sometimes feel compelled to re-create cultural artifacts within the site. While this could provide a good learning basis for the outdoor classroom, the mimicking of cultural forms can sometimes look artificial and even trite. It is better to learn the principles from past cultures and not re-create them but abstract them or incorporate them into new forms of expression. Take care to use historic forms as a way to pay tribute to our past, celebrate those who walked before us, and acknowledge our culture's triumphs and failures as gentle reminders of another time.

Ecology

As one of the purposes of a wildlife habitat is to provide a home for wildlife, the ecological factors of the site and region will probably become the main context for design. These factors are so important that Chapter 6, "Ecological Principles and Wildlife," has been devoted to this topic.

To attract wildlife to the schoolyard, the habitat must offer the four elements that are essential for survival: *food, water, shelter,* and *space*. All of these must be provided to sustain wildlife. Food and water are critical on a daily basis, and shelter and space offer long-term benefits. The wildlife habitat should provide densely planted areas for protection and security, as wildlife fear predation and will not expose themselves to open areas for long periods of time. Some birds, for example, will not nest if human activities nearby threaten their security. Therefore, the wildlife habitat should provide secluded areas that include water sources and a diverse collection of plant species in a variety of sizes, shapes, and textures, including trees, shrubs, and grasses. In short, the success of the

At least a portion of the schoolyard should be a natural environment. In cases where the existing habitat was destroyed, natural areas will have to be reconstructed or re-created.

wildlife habitat in attracting wildlife is largely dependent upon how well the site or portion of the site can re-create a natural environment.

IDENTIFY GOALS AND OBJECTIVES

The overarching framework for design—a mixture of ecology, nature, history, culture, and art—usually takes the form of a written statement of vision, which guides the design for the project. This should include a listing of goals and objectives. *Goals* are broad, comprehensive end results. They are the project's aims, ideals, and intentions—its theme for design. *Objectives* are specific and particular: the short-term attainable means to the goals. What actions are to take place by whom and with what purpose? Objectives should be planned in coordination with a work timeline that schedules aspects of the planning and design process. An example of goals and objectives might be as follows:

Project Goals
- To create an ecologically sustainable wildlife habitat for small mammals, birds, lizards, and insects.
- To use this habitat project as a theme for integrated learning, involving cultural and artistic aspects of design.

Project Objectives
- To form a planning committee with subcommittee special interest groups.
- To develop a site plan using native plant communities.
- To actively involve teachers, students, and parents in planning and design processes.
- To implement phase one of the site plan in conjunction with a planting festival and neighborhood barbecue.

DETERMINE PROJECT REQUIREMENTS

The project requirements are basic physical needs of wildlife, students, teachers, administrators, and community users. Specific needs will vary from school to school and should be developed through a series of planning or design workshops. The specific wildlife needs for a particular region will also require additional research. The following list shows how designers might begin to organize and address the various needs of wildlife, students, teachers, and ad-

What do we need in our natural outdoor classroom or garden? Planning workshops must allow students, teachers, parents, and administrators to list all the needs and desires for the project. Eventually, the most important requirements will take precedence in the design development phase.

Wildlife need safe places such as this one provided in a schoolyard habitat.

Natural areas in schoolyards make ideal classrooms.

(below) Children need natural settings for play and learning.
(center and far right) Teachers and administrators need volunteers to help maintain and construct the schoolyard project.

ministrators. This information represents only a start in the development of the garden.

Wildlife Needs

Food (feeding stations, native plants)
Water (ponds, drippers, birdbaths, streams)
Shelter (brush piles, bat houses, snags, nest boxes)
Space (safe places for wildlife to raise their young, connected open space corridors)

Students' Needs

Natural areas for play and learning
A variety of learning activities (science projects, artworks, exploring, and journal writing)
A variety of types of spaces (private spaces, eating areas, trails/paths, active areas)
A variety of places to sit (benches, retaining walls, seats under trees)
Shade (large trees, structures such as ramadas and arbors)

Teachers' Needs

Inspiring places to teach
Learning stations
Curriculum support
A variety of outdoor seating (flexible chair arrangements, an amphitheater)
Site visibility
Storage of teaching materials
Noise control
Financial support for special projects

Administrators' Needs

Means to inspire and facilitate teachers
Good management and maintenance of the outdoor classroom
Workable budgets
Liability issues addressed
Community/Volunteer support

PLAN ACTIVITIES AND ACTIVITY SETTINGS

Students must be nurtured and inspired by the people and places in their daily lives. As our schools are the places where students spend much of their time, it is important that they provide young people with a variety of structured and unstructured activities in appropriate activity settings. A school activity setting is a place designed for a specific type of behavior, such as reading, playing ball, sitting, running, or listening. The physical characteristics of the place should match the expected or planned activities. The following pages provide a few examples.

Activities and Activity Settings

Activity: **Being quiet and alone.**
Activity Setting: **Place enclosed with vegetation (teachers can see over or under plants), or temporary houses made out of fabric.**

Activity: **Composting.**
Activity Setting: **Areas with easy access but screened and located away from other activities, perhaps near storage areas.**

Activity: Performing.
Activity Setting: Multiuse stage area; open meadow where chairs can be set up, away from sensitive wildlife areas.

Activity: Group discussions.
Activity Setting: Tables and benches in a shaded area.

Activity: Class lesson.
Activity Setting: Outdoor group seating/amphitheater.

Activity: Observing wildlife.
Activity Setting: Wildlife viewing blinds—these can be works of art.

Activity: Exploring.
Activity Setting: A real *wild* place within the schoolyard; field trips.

INTEGRATE DESIGN FEATURES

This step is another way to gather and organize design ideas. Design features imply a list of desires or wishes. To come up with a list of design features, school communities should simply ask, "What do we want in our outdoor classroom or wildlife habitat?" Creative ideas for different features typically come to mind throughout the research and design process. An *idea wall* at the school could be the repository for these creative thoughts; additionally, students and teachers could keep design journals. As mentioned earlier, not all the ideas generated will be used in the project, but it is important to keep a record of all of them. *Early rejection of creative ideas could restrict future avenues for innovation and discovery.*

The images on pages 62–69 demonstrate possible design features for use in the schoolyard.

Natural Features

(top) Pond

(center left and right) Wildflower meadow

(below left and right) Sacred grove of trees (described in Greek mythology)

(left) Lookout tower

(right) Riparian area

Wildlife Features

Birdhouses

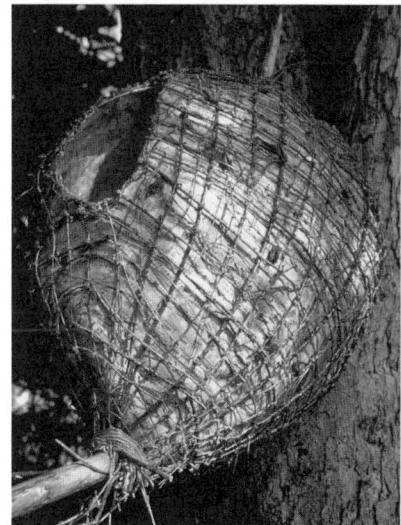

Butterfly garden

Rock garden for attracting reptiles

(above) Brush and litter piles for wildlife shelter

(left) Diverse plant species

Cultural Features

(far left) Garden plots using Native American seeds

(left) Educational trails with cultural themes

(below left) Archaeological dig site

(below right) Demonstration area for historic pioneer and ranching heritage

Art Features

(above) Mural composition depicting cultural features

(right) Examples of tile art

Bench art

Fence art

Wall art

(above) Sundial

(right) Focal totem

(above) Stone slate or concrete for chalk art

(far left) Wind chimes

(left) Water feature

Functional Features

Amphitheater

Greenhouse

Structures for protection from sun, wind, and rain

Signs

Weather station

DEVELOP CURRICULUM IDEAS

The educational goals and related curricular activities for the outdoor spaces within the schoolyard must be discussed at the onset of the design process. Schoolyard projects can be designed and built, but if they are not used for specific teaching purposes, they will probably become neglected places of limited value. Participant designers should encourage all teachers to explore how their educational goals could be enhanced through the development of outdoor classrooms, wildlife habitat areas, or other garden types.

Schoolyards, as mentioned earlier, can be developed into ideal places for integrated learning. Several guides could serve as useful starting points in the development of curricula for outdoor classrooms, for example, Joseph Kiefer and Martin Kemple's *Digging Deeper: Integrating Youth Gardens into Schools and Communities* (1998). This text in particular offers extensive practical information for teachers.

Possible Curriculum Ideas

NATURAL SCIENCES—ECOLOGY
During the Design Process: Examine the site prior to construction: What plants and wildlife are currently in the schoolyard? This inventory of existing conditions will help designers make informed design decisions.
After Construction: See what new life exists in the outdoor classroom. Learn about butterflies and moths, for example: What stages of life can be observed? Within the schoolyard habitat, examine ecological concepts such as photosynthesis, effects of human actions on ecosystems, and energy exchange. Start a herbarium at school.

MATH
During the Design Process: Measure the slope of the land to calculate slope percentages. Measure and record onto maps the size and location of all existing structures such as buildings and sidewalks. This important step in site inventory involves hands-on math experience.
After Construction: Take various measurements over time, such as pond water levels, plant growth, and wildlife numbers. Make a new sitting area for the outdoor classroom—spatial geometries would need to be determined.

LANGUAGE ARTS
During the Design Process: Write a description of the existing schoolyard. This might be used in the site inventory phase of the design process. Write to local businesses and seed companies for potential donations.
After Construction: Write nature poetry and literature; keep a wildlife or nature journal. Write stories about future ideas and plans for the schoolyard.

FINE ARTS
During the Design Process: Develop design ideas and drawings for the new outdoor classroom. Produce a video of all stages of the project. Make birdhouses, sundials, and benches that can be used in the various locations within the schoolyard gardens.
After Construction: Continue to add new artworks even after the project is built. The art could be anything from sundials or sun structures to bridges and tunnels; even riparian areas offer ways to be artistically expressive. Draw and photograph wildlife in the schoolyard.

HISTORY
During the Design Process: Learn about the past. What was the site like before there was a school there? Try to find old photographs of the site and neighborhood from libraries and historical societies. Interview family members and local residents who remember what things were like "way back when."
After Construction: Continue to design and develop different gardens and spaces—perhaps some of these will be inspired by Native American gardening traditions; others might be fantastic futuristic schemes.

PERFORMING ARTS—MUSIC
During the Design Process: Create and perform a play about all the creatures that might find a home in the new habitat garden.
After Construction: Use the outdoor classroom as a place for drama, music, and discussions. Discover interrelationships between all classes, both in natural sciences and in the arts.

SOCIAL AND COMMUNITY OUTREACH — ETHICAL VALUES

During the Design Process: Make contact with local businesses, professionals, and community members who might provide assistance and even become mentors.

After Construction: Form environmental clubs or other community-based groups and conduct field trips that reinforce lessons learned in the outdoor classroom. Sell plants and seeds to community members as a way to promote native planting practices. Invite community members to participate in special events and ongoing design projects.

Conclusion

As participants go through the tasks discussed in this chapter, they will begin to formulate and clarify community desires that will be documented in a written program—a statement of goals and objectives, a detailed list of requirements, proposed activities, activity settings, desired design features, and curriculum ideas. These important first steps will shape how the design evolves. As the design progression continues through stages of research (Chapter 4, "Site Research and Design Synthesis"), which involve the selection of a site, the documentation and mapping of existing site conditions (site inventory), and the evaluation of these conditions (site analysis), designers prepare themselves for design synthesis.

CHAPTER 4 # Site Research and Design Synthesis

Review and Evaluate Previous Steps

Chapter 3, "Beginning the Design Process," led designers through a process aimed at writing a design program, which includes a statement of goals and objectives, a detailed list of requirements, proposed activities, activity settings, desired design features, and curriculum ideas. Continuing through the process, this chapter demonstrates how site research used in the selection of a site, the documentation and mapping of existing site conditions (site inventory), and the evaluation of these conditions (site analysis) continue to help designers prepare for design synthesis.

Site Research

Site Selection

The selection of a site for the outdoor classroom is most rewarding when it is coordinated with the development of an overall campus master plan that designates the location, size, and shape of all outdoor activity areas. In reality, site selection for habitat areas and other outdoor classrooms and gardens often happens by default and is limited to the leftover spaces that have not been claimed for sports facilities, parking, and portable classrooms. However, the absence of prime landscape can eventually be mitigated if designers include in their design the creation of landforms and the addition of trees, water, rocks, and other natural materials. This is a more expensive and labor-intensive solution to good master planning, but it can produce a good effect in the end.

In general, designers should consider site ecology, sun exposure, and site size and shape as they select a site. Ecological interest is an important factor: look for topographic changes (hills and valleys), plant diversity, and washes or drainageways. If the site is to be welcoming to humans as well as to wildlife, the wildlife habitat should have some protection from harsh weather conditions such as the

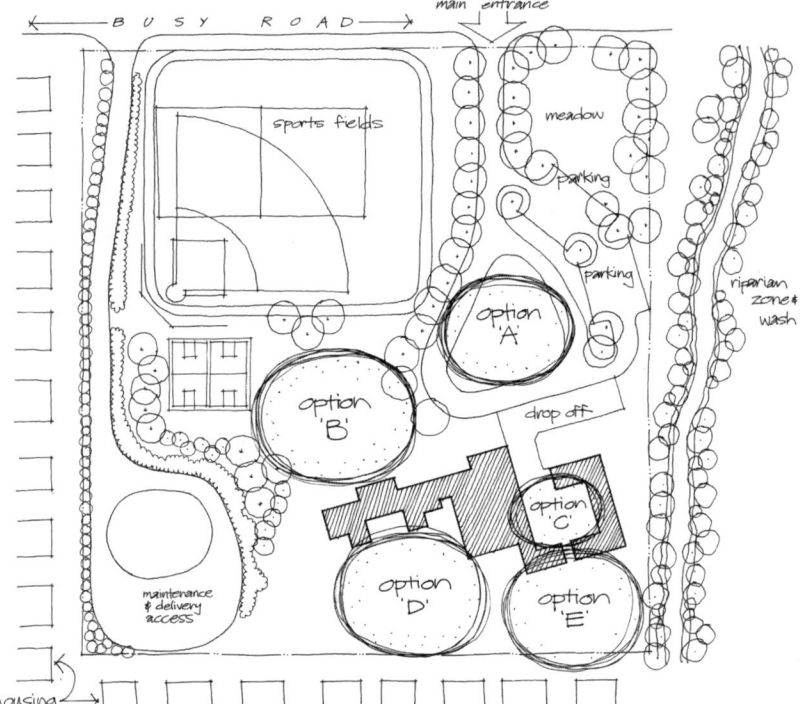

If there are several choices for the location of the wildlife habitat, select the spot that offers wildlife the best conditions—existing shade, vegetation, location near adjacent natural areas, and perhaps even a riparian area like the one shown in this diagram. Notice that option "E" has the most advantages for wildlife and is away from active play areas.

desert sun and hot, desiccating, or cold winter winds. If possible, select a site that is at least a half acre in size. Larger areas create greater opportunities for a diversity of plants and wildlife. Smaller spaces, however, can certainly be utilized for habitat design, and schools should not be discouraged if the outdoor classroom or habitat site is limited in this way. Linear sites, or sites that weave throughout the campus, offer possibilities for trail design as well as spatial sequencing and can be utilized for natural areas that might be conducive to habitat creation. Additionally, these linear sites, particularly when adjacent to native vegetation areas, could demonstrate the importance of connected wildlife corridors.

The wildlife habitat site should be protected from areas where noisy, frequent school activities occur that would interfere with wildlife needs, such as bus loading and unloading areas, cafeteria rooms, and garbage pickup locations. If possible, try to obtain a site within the school grounds that is near undeveloped public land or other large natural spaces such as drainage washes or even parks.

Site Inventory

The concepts of site inventory, site analysis, and site design may be most clearly defined by an analogy from the medical profession: the routine medical checkup is like a site inventory, in which the conditions of the patient (or site) are measured and understood. The subsequent diagnosis of the patient (or site) requires the professional evaluation of these conditions (site analysis). Medical treatment, like site design, is the prescribed plan of action.

The process begins with a site inventory (or site survey) to create a record of human-made and natural conditions. This information must be carefully researched, understood, and recorded onto a site map before a site plan is created. This inventory of information is measured and recorded as a base map, which provides the means of measuring and recording inventory information.

It establishes technical aspects of mapping, such as scale, units of measurement, legal description of the area and land divisions, political boundaries, and geographic (map) projection. The site inventory should record all existing conditions that are relevant to a given project, including the historical, cultural, scenic, and ecological resources, onto the map base. In detail, the inventory might record things like site boundaries, legal restrictions (including setbacks and easements), orientation relative to true north, topography, vegetation, utilities (above and below ground), and existing site features such as adjacent buildings and sidewalks. Good sources of publicly available information, such as air photos, satellite images, maps, and climate data, include:

- Google Earth, free software that allows you to explore the earth's surface through satellite images and aerial photos: earth.google.com
- World Wind, NASA's Google-Earth-like free program that allows users to view Earth images from a variety of directions and scales: http://worldwind.arc.nasa.gov/
- NASA, extensive catalog of free images of the earth: http://visibleearth.nasa.gov/
- U.S. Geological Survey Data Server, which allows free download of elevation data; imagery; and geographic, political, and land-cover data: seamless.usgs.gov
- National Resources Conservation Service Geospatial Data Gateway for publicly available GIS data, including NRCS Soil Surveys, elevation, topographic, hydrologic data, and more: http://datagateway.nrcs.usda.gov/
- USGS/NBII (National Biological Information Infrastructure) GAP Analysis Program, providing biological/species geospatial data, maps, and reports to the public: http://gapanalysis.nbii.gov/portal/server.pt
- NOAA/National Weather Service meteorological data and information: http://www.nws.noaa.gov/gis/

The site inventory is a record of existing conditions.

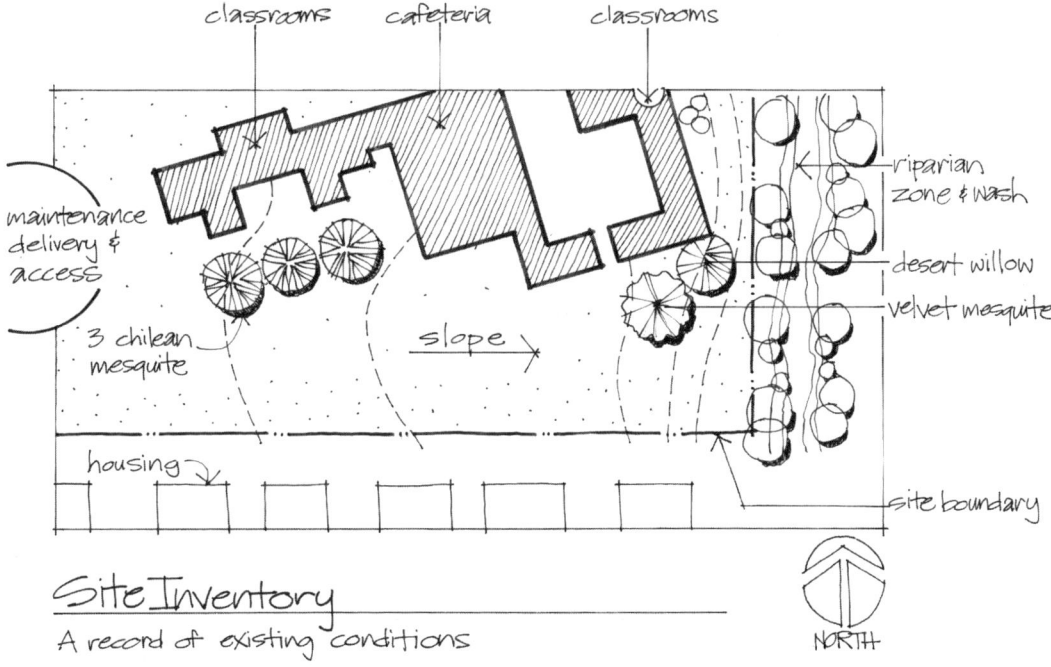

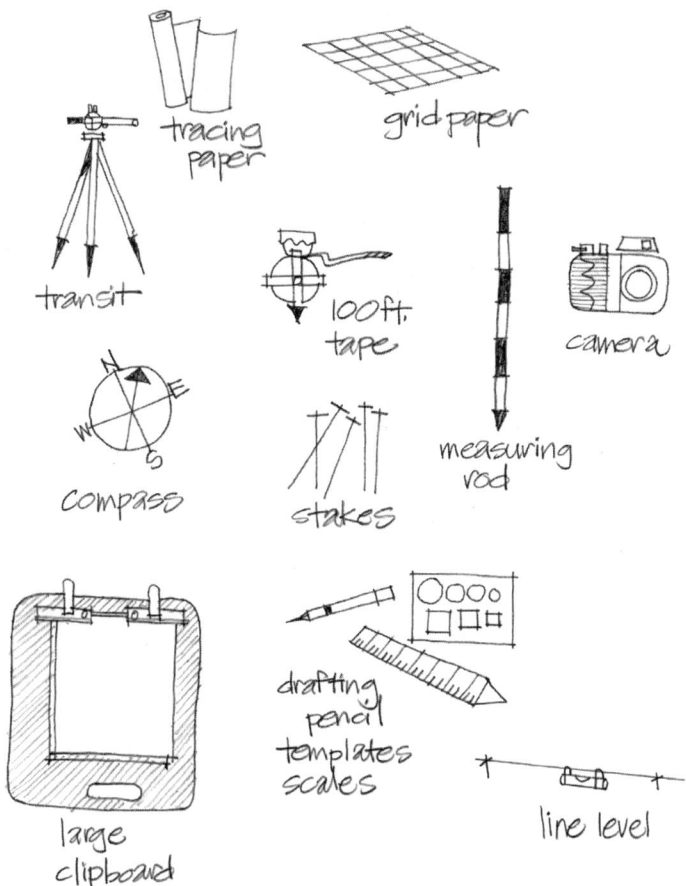

Tools and materials used in making a site inventory.

- NOAA/National Climatic Data Center, free and for-pay data downloads: http://www.ncdc.noaa.gov/oa/ncdc.html

The site inventory maps should be as accurate as possible. Individuals from the community who have surveying skills are the best choices to oversee the production of these maps. Survey maps for the site may already exist; the architect or landscape architect responsible for the original school plans could help obtain these.

If a site survey is not attainable, less accurate methods can be used. Designers can measure sites by pacing them off or with tape measures. The pace method is the least accurate but fastest means of estimating sizes and locations of existing features (an adult or young person can determine their average pace by walking a known one-hundred-foot length, then dividing the number of paces by one hundred to determine the length of that person's average pace). A measuring tape (a 100-foot metal or plastic tape works best) is more accurate when stretched the length of the site, with site elements measured from positions along this baseline. Measurements can be recorded on grid paper in the field and later transferred to an appropriate scale on tracing paper. Alternatively, an architect's or engineer's scale can be used to locate site features on a map (the following scales will probably work best: 1 inch = 8 feet, 1 inch = 10 feet, or 1 inch = 20 feet). Photographic documentation can be helpful in supplementing the mapped record of site conditions. Design professionals often photograph or sketch sites as a way to better see and understand the physical components and visual qualities of places.

Site Inventory Materials
transit (use a trained surveyor to oversee the process)
100-foot tape measure
compass
stakes
line level and string to determine slope and height of objects
measuring rod (ruled post to use with line level)
large clipboard
grid paper
tracing paper
drafting pencils, tape, circle templates for drawing trees and shrubs
camera and film

Site Analysis

Every site has a unique set of features and conditions that create the identity and character of the place. Natural factors such as wind, sun, and topography and cultural factors such as structures on adjacent lands exist in complex and dynamic interrelationships with one another. All of these conditions together create the *genius loci,* or *spirit of place.* As René Dubos wrote in *A God Within* (1972, 22): "Like individual human beings, landscapes and civilizations display distinctive characteristics. While they change in the course of time, they retain a uniqueness derived in large part from the set of conditions under which they emerged and also from the factors which influenced their subsequent evolution. The phrases *genius loci* and *spirit of place* symbolize the forces or structures generally hidden beneath the surface of things which determine the uniqueness of each place."

Just as people have personalities with good traits and bad ones, sites, too, have good conditions, or *opportunities,* and potential problems, or *constraints.* The intended site function also affects how these conditions are perceived in site analysis. For example, a steep hill creates an opportunity for activities such as rock climbing, while that same piece of land has serious constraints as an ath-

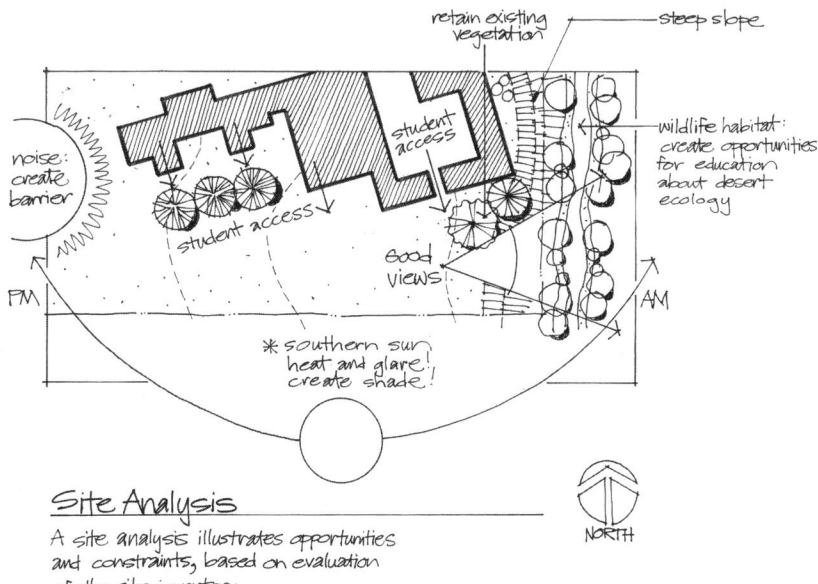

Site Analysis
A site analysis illustrates opportunities and constraints, based on evaluation of the site inventory

The site characteristics—both good and bad—should be fully understood before a design is developed.

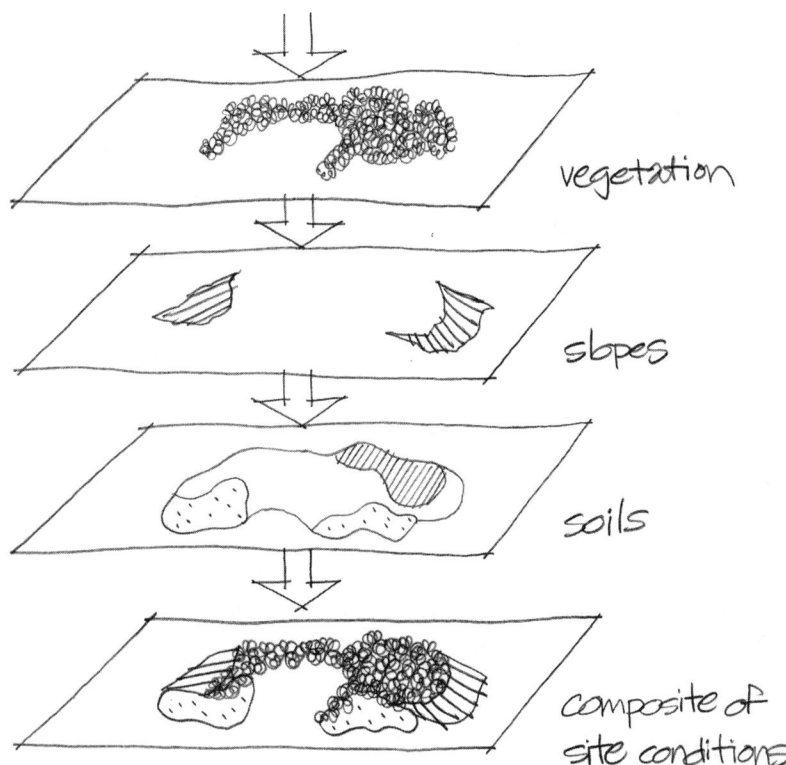

Ian McHarg's method of analysis, often called an overlay system, locates each site characteristic—slope, vegetation, existing structures, wildlife, and so on—on a separate map; these maps are eventually sandwiched together into a final composite map or summary of site conditions that, through interpretation or analysis, will indicate opportunities and constraints.

letic field. For the open-minded outdoor classroom designer, constraints often spur creative adaptations and, thus, become opportunities.

Good design maximizes opportunities and minimizes constraints in a series of *design tradeoffs,* a process of synthesizing site knowledge that is based on a comprehensive understanding and interpretation of site conditions. Each physical aspect of the site (vegetation, wildlife, topography) can be recorded separately in maps on transparent paper. When layered upon each other, these topical maps can be assembled into one composite map of all the site and cultural features. This *overlay analysis system,* as it has come to be called, was developed by Ian McHarg (1969) as a tool for design decision making. Important site qualities, such as ideal building locations and sensitive natural areas, are more readily seen through this cataloging of information. The overlay analysis process is currently generated through a computer application known as Geographic Information Systems (GIS).

While analysis of schoolyard projects may not employ this overlay system, it is important for designers to find a similar, comprehensive way to evaluate all existing site features before site plans are prepared. Detailed analysis notes can be made on copies of the inventory map. These notes will lay the foundation for design decisions.

The decision-making process used in site analysis may follow a course like this: imagine that there is a native mesquite tree (*Prosopis* spp.) found within the proposed outdoor classroom site. The inventory would locate the tree and identify its species and size, while the analysis would describe the condition of the tree. Suppose the tree is mature, healthy, and a good potential habitat *opportunity* for birds. Pretend also that the thorny tree is poorly located near an existing pathway, a condition that is a *constraint* for safety. Designers might sug-

In the site analysis, it was decided that this thorny mesquite tree located very close to a pathway would be a safety hazard; at the same time, it was also determined that the tree provided good shade and habitat for birds. In this regard, the tree possesses both positive and negative qualities—it is both an opportunity and a constraint. Designers will have to decide to remove the tree, relocate the path, or address the safety concerns through tree pruning.

gest tree pruning, relocation, or removal. However, as the design progresses into greater refinement, designers may decide that the tree is more important than the path and should remain. Budget permitting, the path might be rerouted to allow the tree to flourish, and the area where the tree stands could be enhanced with additional plantings.

This example, in which a single site feature is both an opportunity and a constraint, illustrates the potential complexity of site analysis as both an informed and a subjective process of interpretation. The resulting design recommendations are generated through tradeoffs based on the site analysis. The information that follows shows a checklist of site inventory and analysis topics for both natural and cultural conditions. Selected site-analysis examples have been included to add clarity.

CHECKLIST FOR SITE INVENTORY AND ANALYSIS
Climate
Identify average annual temperatures and precipitation for different times of the year, as well as depth of frost and the accepted plant hardiness zone(s) for the area. Describe and document the limitations and benefits that these conditions create. For example, if the project is in plant hardiness zone nine, for instance, be sure to choose plants that can survive in these conditions.

Microclimate
The specific climatic conditions of the schoolyard site, including the vertical and horizontal movement of the sun (rise, set, and high noon), should be measured during each season of the year. Identify year-round sunny and shady areas, winter wind exposure, and cooling summer breezes. Locate the places that need protection from the sun and wind, and determine those areas that are naturally protected. For example, if the site has strong winter winds from the northwest, wind screens may need to be provided. This constraint (wind) also

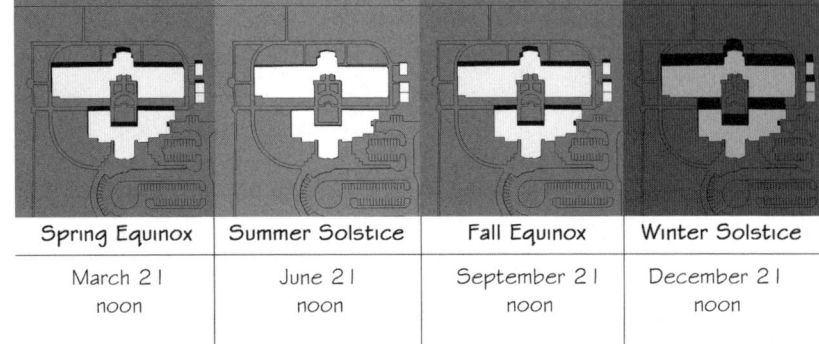

Microclimate—Shade, drawn by Hampton Uzzelle

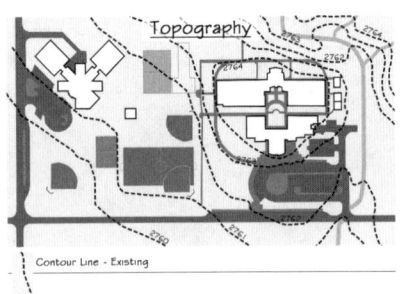

(above) Topography, drawn by Hampton Uzzelle

(right) Building foam-core topographic models provides a good way to understand the site contour.

provides opportunities for creative dramatic effects and artworks (wind harps, chimes, sculptural sails).

Geology

Identify and describe the regional geological structure of the area, including land formations such as mountains, basins, streams, and underlying geology (rock and mineral deposits). Identify potential hazards within the area (landslides, groundwater pollution, and flooding), regional sources of inspiration (natural sites of beauty or cultural features of significance), and viewsheds (from the site) toward points of geological or cultural interest. Also identify and describe the geology within the school site, including specific deposits, rock outcroppings, and soil layers. For example, the analysis might indicate sand deposits within the school site; this information could eventually lead designers to develop these sandy locations into play areas.

Topography

Identify topographic contour lines at specific intervals (every two feet, for example), noting the degree of steepness in slope percentages. Locate high and low spots and sinkholes, and establish spot grades for existing conditions, such as building elevations, walkways, and other ground surfaces. Identify potential

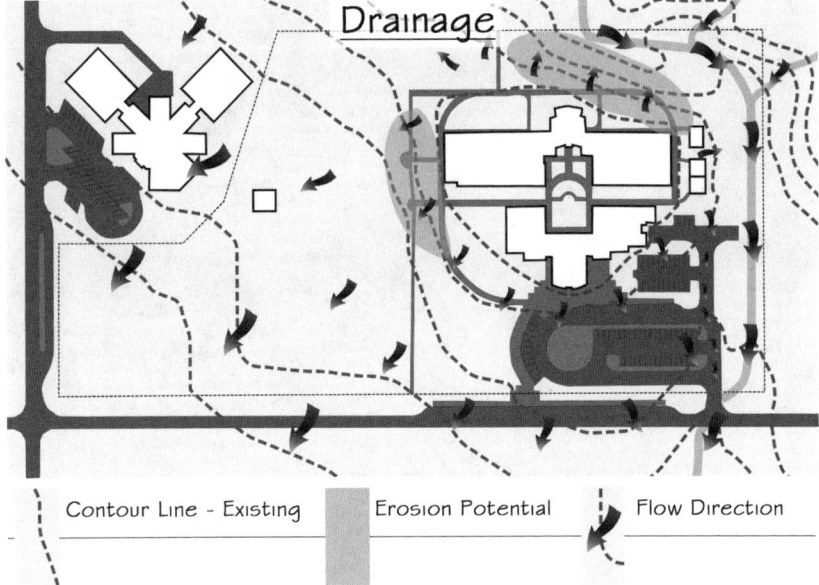

Drainage, drawn by Hampton Uzzelle

problems, such as soil erosion; poor drainage; or slopes too steep for sheds, ramadas, walks, and other features. Identify potential accessibility problems and determine topographic points of interest, such as hills and valleys. For example, a portion of the site may have slopes of 20 percent or greater. This area should be avoided for the placement of site structures. Another example would be the discovery of a low, depressed area within the site that could make a good location for a pond.

Drainage

Locate and note the direction of water flow for drainageways and surface water runoff (water running away from the site and toward the site). Note subsurface water, downspouts, standing water, and wet spots. Evaluate drainageways and low spots for potential habitat areas, including planted areas and ponds (water is naturally directed to low spots, which can become locations for ponds and planted areas). Identify all drainage problems resulting in soil erosion, wet spots, and muddy areas. For instance, a drainage problem might be identified; perhaps water from a building downspout is not being drained away from the building, creating a muddy area. This water could be channeled or directed toward planted areas or a seasonal stream.

Soil

The physical and chemical properties of soil provide important baseline information that may be used as a determinant in site design. For the purposes of the schoolyard garden, soil texture (i.e., sand, silt, clay, or loam) and the pH (level of acidity or alkalinity) are important determinants for the selection of plant materials and their nutrient needs. In addition, soil porosity, the volume of water that can be held in the soil, and the permeability of the soil, the ability of water to move through the soil, as well as the soil horizon and depth to parent rock, should be determined. Describe these conditions as opportunities or constraints; this might include potential problems with caliche hardpan, poorly drained soil, and soil fertility advantages or disadvantages. For example, a site

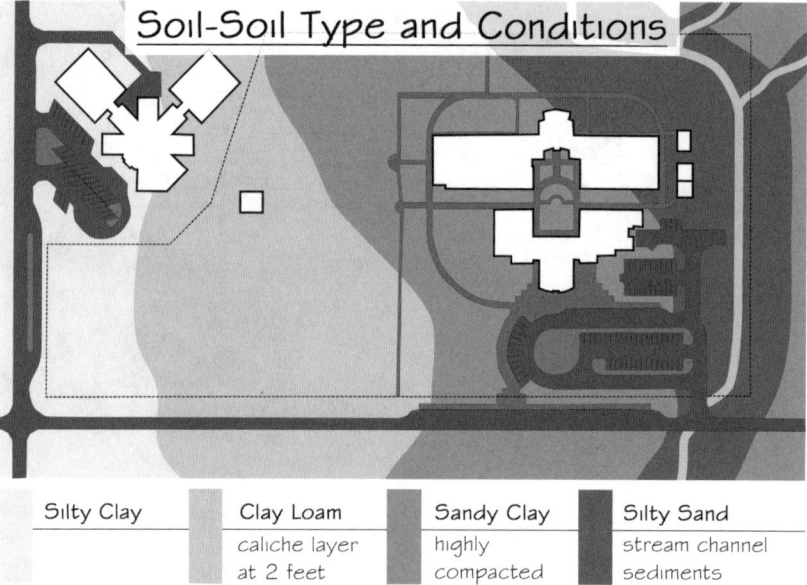

| Silty Clay | Clay Loam caliche layer at 2 feet | Sandy Clay highly compacted | Silty Sand stream channel sediments |

Soil, drawn by Hampton Uzzelle

Vegetation

with a two-foot layer of caliche would have limitations for new tree plantings, since digging holes might require a jackhammer.

Vegetation

Locate all existing vegetation (trees, shrubs, grasses, and wildflowers), and designate plant species, size, form, color, texture, and other features. Determine plant conditions and potential uses for wildlife and people, such as shade, views, and scenic beauty. Identify problems with plant health, location, and safety concerns, such as thorns or poisonous fruits. For example, perhaps an old London plane tree (*Platanus acerifolia*) exists within the schoolyard; it is not native to the area but provides potential as bird habitat. Furthermore, assume that the tree is appreciated by children and teachers, as its mature size offers much-needed shade and its wind-twisted form provides character. Under these conditions, the site analysis would find the tree to be important, recommending that it remain despite the fact that it is a nonnative tree.

Wildlife

Identify existing wildlife habitats within the region and the corresponding wildlife that use these areas. In the schoolyard, identify existing habitats for enhancement as well as other areas that present opportunities or constraints for habitat development. For example, if there is a drainage wash with mature vegetation along one edge of the schoolyard, this area could be preserved and expanded as a wildlife habitat zone. Another example might present a severe limitation for wildlife, such as a busy street that runs nearby; this street should be avoided and screened to offer protection for wildlife and children.

Ecology

Write a description of the natural history of the region, including general ecology and plant and wildlife communities. Include dominant plant and wildlife species, their location, and the health of their populations. These unique characteristics should be taken into consideration as they may provide inspiration for design ideas. For example, the nearby Sonoran Desert Riparian Scrubland could be represented as a display area in the schoolyard design.

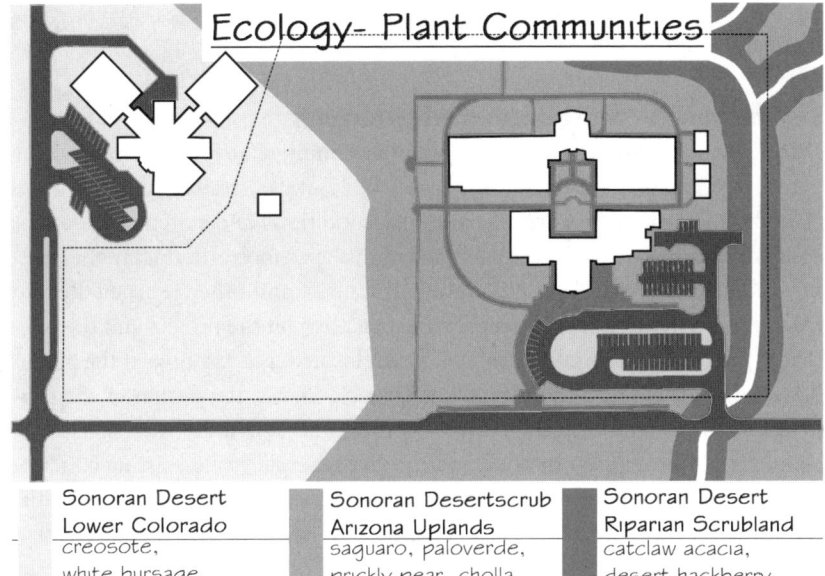

Ecology—Plant communities, drawn by Hampton Uzzelle

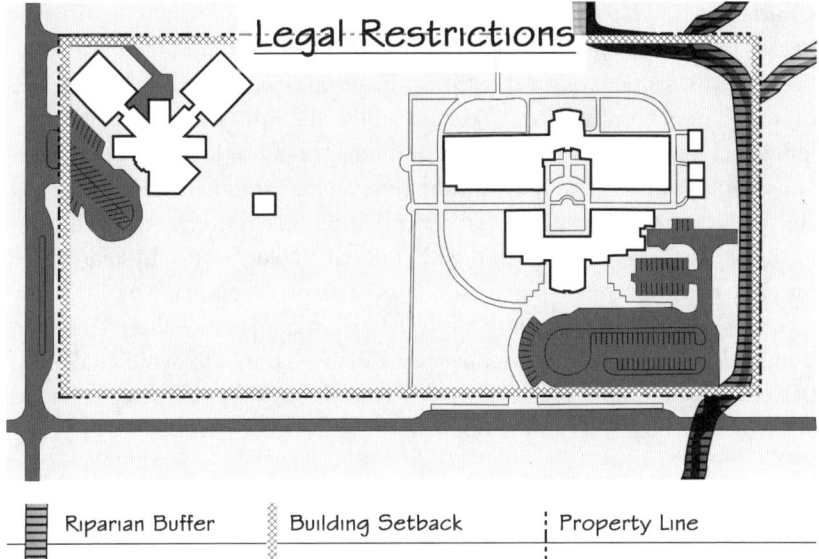

Legal restrictions, drawn by Hampton Uzzelle

Site Context

Use a regional map to investigate the location of the site with respect to important natural and human-made features, including nearby mountains, forests, towns, and roads. This regional information will provide the contextual framework for the site. For example, it might be learned that a nearby road-widening project will greatly impact the site and will need to be considered in the design. Another scenario could include the discovery of an old discarded copper mine within the region; this topic could provide an interesting avenue for student research projects, perhaps resulting in a display within the schoolyard.

Legal Restrictions

Determine site boundaries within the schoolyard site and note city and/or county building and landscape restrictions, such as building setbacks. Describe the impact these restrictions will have for outdoor classrooms. If the regulations call for periodic design review by a county or city review board, designers should make early contact with this board and encourage ongoing dialogue.

Existing Land Use and Human-Made Structures

Document surrounding land use (residential, commercial, recreational), noting existing buildings, circulation patterns (roads, walks, trails), neighborhood character, and other features. Record the conditions and potential assets or conflicts. Suggest areas for screening. Within the schoolyard, document existing human-made items such as walks, structures, and other features. Record these conditions and describe the features that benefit the project and the ones that restrict use and should be removed or relocated. For example, if the neighborhood is on the National Record of Historic Places, the design of the proposed outdoor classroom should not disturb or be in conflict with the special character of the neighborhood. Or, as another example, if the existing concrete walks within the schoolyard are laid out in a manner that restricts the potential for development of a habitat garden, perhaps these walks or portions of them should be removed.

Utilities

Locate and map all electric, gas, sewer, telephone, cable, and water lines; irrigation systems; septic tanks and leach fields; storm sewers; electrical boxes; and cooling system pumps. Often, states have Blue Stake programs through which individual homeowners, companies, and other organizations can obtain, free of cost and prior to excavation, information on the location of utilities such as electric, gas, telephone, cable, and water. Various utility companies will come to the site and mark the ground with a specific color—typically red is used for electric power, yellow for gas lines, orange for telephone, blue for water, green for sewer lines, and purple for reclaimed or nonpotable water. Designers should also determine site boundary easements, hazards to avoid, and views to screen. For example, if an electric line runs through the site, designers must avoid planting near this limitation.

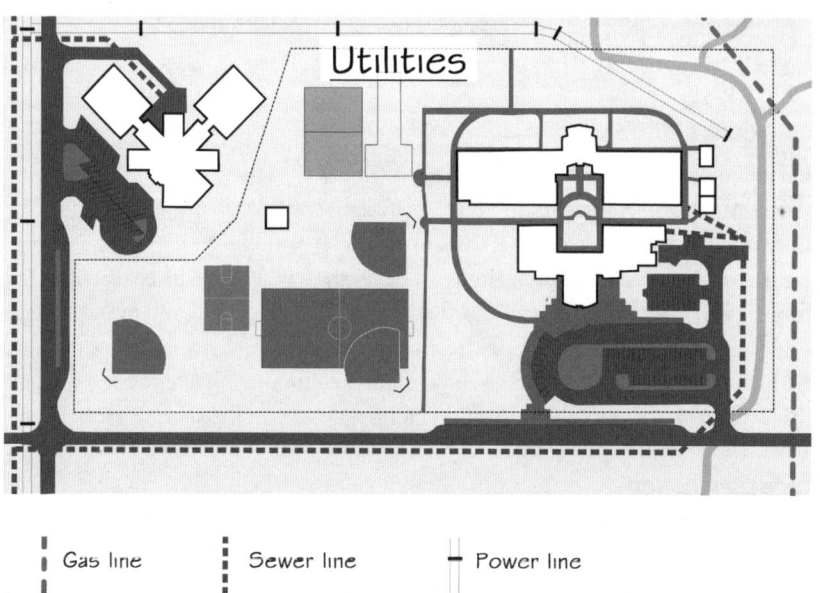

Utilities, drawn by Hampton Uzzelle

Views

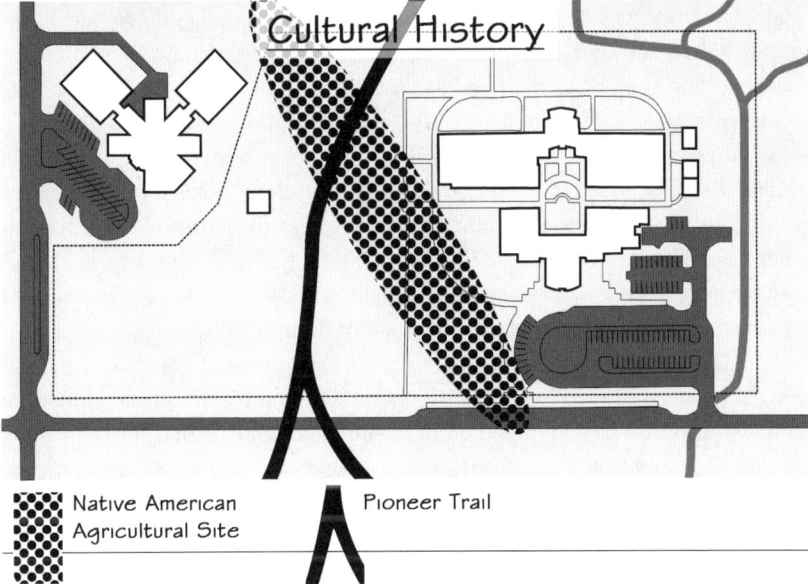

Cultural history, drawn by Hampton Uzzelle

Views

Photograph views from all sides of the site, looking out from the site and into the site. Label views—for example, "looking north from site." Observe daily and seasonal changes. Note good and bad views, short and long views. Identify bad views that should be screened, good views that need to be preserved and/or enhanced. For example, perhaps an unsightly view of the adjacent property parking lot and busy street become an obvious negative impact determined in the site analysis; these bad views can be remedied through screening.

Cultural History

Use a regional map to locate significant cultural features within the area, such as museums, historic sites, and sacred places identified by local Native Americans. Describe the cultural history of the region from Native American influences through early pioneer and ranch life. Outline the potential impact or benefit these have as a source of inspiration for design ideas, and identify related potential guest speakers and field trip locations. Indicate culturally significant or sensitive areas within the specific site, such as archaeological areas and historic structures, and document their potential impact. A new site might have to be selected if the impact is too high. Determine educational opportunities that might be incorporated in the design solution. For example, if the nearby town was supposedly named for silver deposits once found there, this story could inspire design ideas such as artwork or story murals. Or if evidence of primitive dwellings was found within the site, this would warrant protection and preservation. These provide great learning opportunities in the school setting.

Design Synthesis

With the site research completed, designers are ready to make informed decisions as they develop a design for the various schoolyard gardens. In this next phase, it is important to note that the information gathered and generated previously will be reviewed and evaluated, and it is completely natural for some of this material to be changed and adjusted as the design progresses.

Developing a design will involve the creative synthesis of information and ideas into drawings depicting physical forms for the layout of the schoolyard project, a challenging endeavor that requires an understanding of *design theory* within the context of the specific region in the arid Southwest. Theoretical guidelines (Chapter 2, "Design Theory") and the basics of ecology in the arid Southwest (Chapter 6, "Ecological Principles and Wildlife") are presented for reference and used throughout this process of design.

Site design involves the placement and configuration of zones, spaces, and design features (light fixtures, plants, walls) within an interlocking landscape composition. Design is approached in a sequential manner that starts with the general placement of areas (zones and spaces) and design features and progresses toward greater and greater refinement. Design stages within this process are often referred to as *conceptual, preliminary,* and *final* levels. *Conceptual design* is an experimental stage in which the sizes of zones and spaces, as well as their proximity and relationship to one another, are sketched in loose diagrams to test alternative layouts. It is important to determine whether zones, and spaces within zones, will be physically adjacent and connected to one another, or if they will be separated. Three-dimensional study models made with clay or molded sand also prove helpful.

In *preliminary design,* a schematic and more refined stage of plan layout, the ideas begin to solidify. The shapes and sizes of zones and spaces will be determined, and their connections or separations to and from one another will be defined through the massing of plants, walls, level changes, or other devices. Pathways will be shown with broadly accurate dimensions and other features (seats, drinking fountains, shade structures) and will become realistic in depiction. This level, although more developed, continues to allow for changes and refinements. *Final design* is a well-articulated and more precise layout in which dimensions are accurate and construction materials (including plant names) are specified.

Design is an experimental process that involves testing ideas. Many alternative layouts must be developed and evaluated according to the parameters set in the design program. This will help designers achieve their ultimate goals.

Conceptual Design

The conceptual design of the schoolyard site will consist of several alternative loose arrangements of zones and spaces. Pathways might be included but will remain diagrammatic and can be drawn on site-plan maps as dashed or dotted lines. Designers use conceptual diagrams called "bubble" diagrams at this stage to determine the size and relationship of these components before a more specific layout is attempted. To achieve a good design solution, a discussion of zones, spaces, design features, spatial sequencing, and circulation patterns follows.

Zones, Spaces, Design Features, and Spatial Sequencing

Site planning involves a hierarchical division of outdoor areas that is organized according to the conditions of the site and the intended use of each area. *Zones,* the larger areas within the landscape, are characterized by a theme and designed for a specific function or experience, such as a butterfly garden or a place for a set of related activities, like a free play area. Zones are made up of smaller units, or *spaces,* which could include a shaded sitting space, a work station, an open space for small gatherings, a quiet space, and planted areas. *Design features,* the smaller objects or groups of objects in built landscapes, may be functional amenities (such as drinking fountains, water features, and signs) or objects used to define the boundaries of a zone or space. An overhead trellis feature, for example, will certainly provide needed shade, but it will also help to define the work-station space situated under the trellis.

Keep in mind that it is possible to develop only one zone. In this case, the hierarchical model still holds true, as the zone, perhaps a wildlife habitat zone, will include several smaller spaces and will be distinct from other schoolyard zones such as the athletic and playground zones.

Circulation Patterns

The sizes of and relationships between zones, spaces, and connecting circulation pathways are organized as a progression or *spatial sequencing* of visual and physical experiences for users. As people move through the environment, the garden unfolds its scenes to them, evoking a medley of sensations. This succession of unfolding scenes is similar to the art of filmmaking, since a filmmaker also leads the viewer through a series of scenes in order to tell a story and produce, along the way, a set of controlled visual effects and emotions. Similarly, garden designers provide visual interest and excitement by creating a variety of settings that reveal themselves as one travels through the series of outdoor spaces. The arrangement of spatial sequences within the landscape is an art form of the highest level.

Since circulation is such an important aspect of site design, it is included here to offer ideas that could help in the preparation of design alternatives. Pathways and trails offer people access from one place to another. This should happen in coordination with a variety of sights, sounds, and smells. Sometimes mysterious, delightful, or even funny, a path within the outdoor classroom should take people on a journey of experience through the sequence of zones and spaces. For example, the pathway might twist sharply around a boulder and

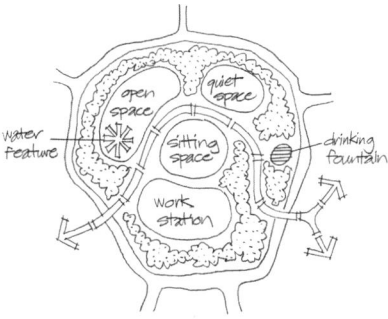

This diagram shows a butterfly garden zone made up of several spaces: a sitting space, a work station, an open space, and a quiet space. Design features include a drinking fountain and water feature.

This garden scene, like a still photograph, is only one piece in the total experience users might have in the landscape. There will be many other views, as well as other sensory characteristics to perceive, as people sit, walk, and enjoy the garden. Schoolyard designers must try to orchestrate this collection of sensations: visual scenes, olfactory delights, tactical surroundings, and kinesthetic experiences that are felt as users move through the spaces.

A pathway is not just a way to get from point A to point B; it should be a delightful experience.

become a narrow passageway through a tight thicket of bird of paradise (*Caesalpinia*) plants. Suddenly, the same path widens and opens into a meadowlike clearing dotted with wildflowers. Experiences like these will make the schoolyard project meaningful and engaging for people while also satisfying wildlife needs.

Testing Design Concepts

Many alternative conceptual designs should be generated before one (often a synthesis of two or more conceptual designs) is taken to a more refined stage. Designers should start by developing an ideal diagram for their outdoor classroom, wildlife habitat, or garden. At this point, they should disregard the specifics of the site and think only of the ideal functions and their relationships to one another. To begin, designers should describe each requirement, activity,

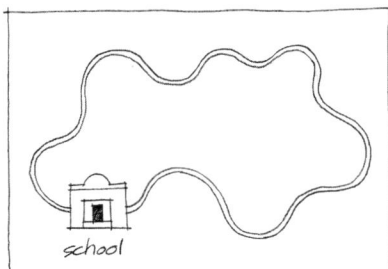
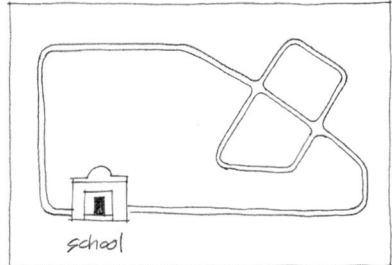

The layout of the pathways within the schoolyard project could be derived from adaptations of several basic patterns.

S curves mimic the way people naturally walk, which is in slight S shapes. This pattern lends itself to a natural layout.

Straight systems, or grid systems, provide clear-cut methods for defining and enclosing specific habitat zones and spaces within a checkerboard pattern. Straight and grid patterns tend to be geometric and formal, but could be softened with asymmetrical planting arrangements or through the use of a soft paving material such as decomposed granite.

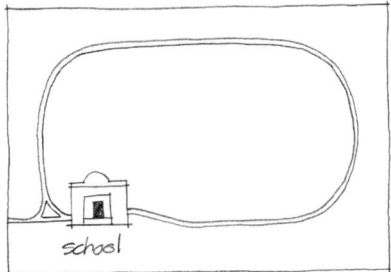
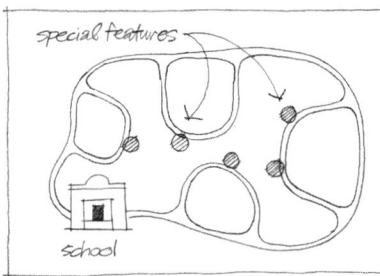
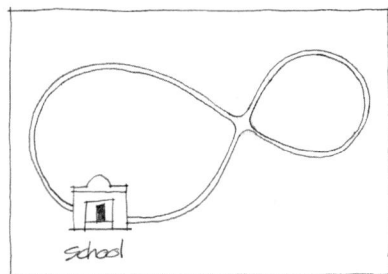

Circular loop paths run along the perimeter of the site. This creates a long pathway for various activities while also providing access to the entire site. This could be a useful circulation pattern for small sites as a way to maximize site experiences.

Multiple loop paths are similar to circular loop paths. The primary path encircles a large area. This main path has several secondary pathway loops that take individuals to special features within the landscape, yet in all cases return users to the main path. This pattern is used in Japanese stroll gardens as well as at many botanical gardens throughout the United States. It is an excellent system that helps prevent people from getting lost.

Figure-eight patterns consist of two loops that meet in the middle. This option creates several directions of movement, which may be attractive within the schoolyard site. It also provides a spot in the middle where the paths come together. This spot could be developed into a classroom, an observation area, or other gathering place that could provide seating and shade structures.

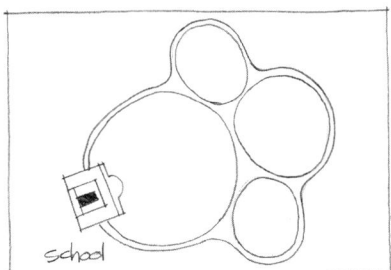
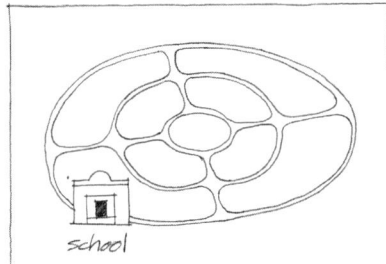

Clover-leaf patterns resemble figure-eight patterns except that there are three or four loops rather than two. These loops could serve to enclose specific zones within the schoolyard project.

Spider-web patterns are mazelike systems that are particularly interesting for children, as they offer a variety of directions for travel and potential activity settings that could be planned along the path. However, in some situations, their complex patterns could be confusing and should be avoided. Their symmetrical nature might be softened with asymmetrical plantings.

The labyrinth pattern, based on historic maze gardens primarily developed in the Middle Ages, offers a fun way to structure the schoolyard site. Labyrinth patterns are intricate networks of pathways and blind alleys often enclosed with plants. Sometimes used to facilitate spiritual enlightenment, the hide-and-seek nature of the maze offers a playful experience for children, who would probably enjoy designing their own versions of this garden form.

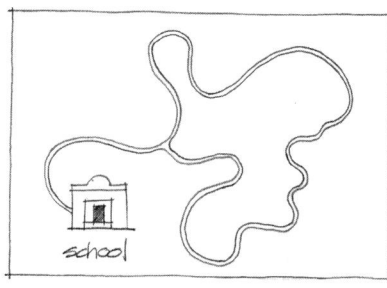
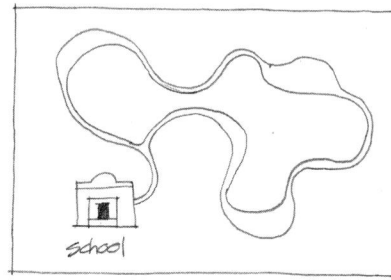

The *"let it happen"* approach allows people to define pathways, as needed, on the site. The circulation patterns are not defined in the design plan. They are determined after the project has been constructed and people begin to wear paths on the ground as they move freely through the various spaces in the site.

Student-designed paths often meander and have undulating forms. Their winding pathways have varying widths, which can be narrow and pinched in spots or take wide, bubblelike forms at others. As often envisioned by the students, the wide spots are places for activities such as meeting, sitting, and watching. This pathway concept would be wonderful within the schoolyard setting and could be applied in combination with other patterns.

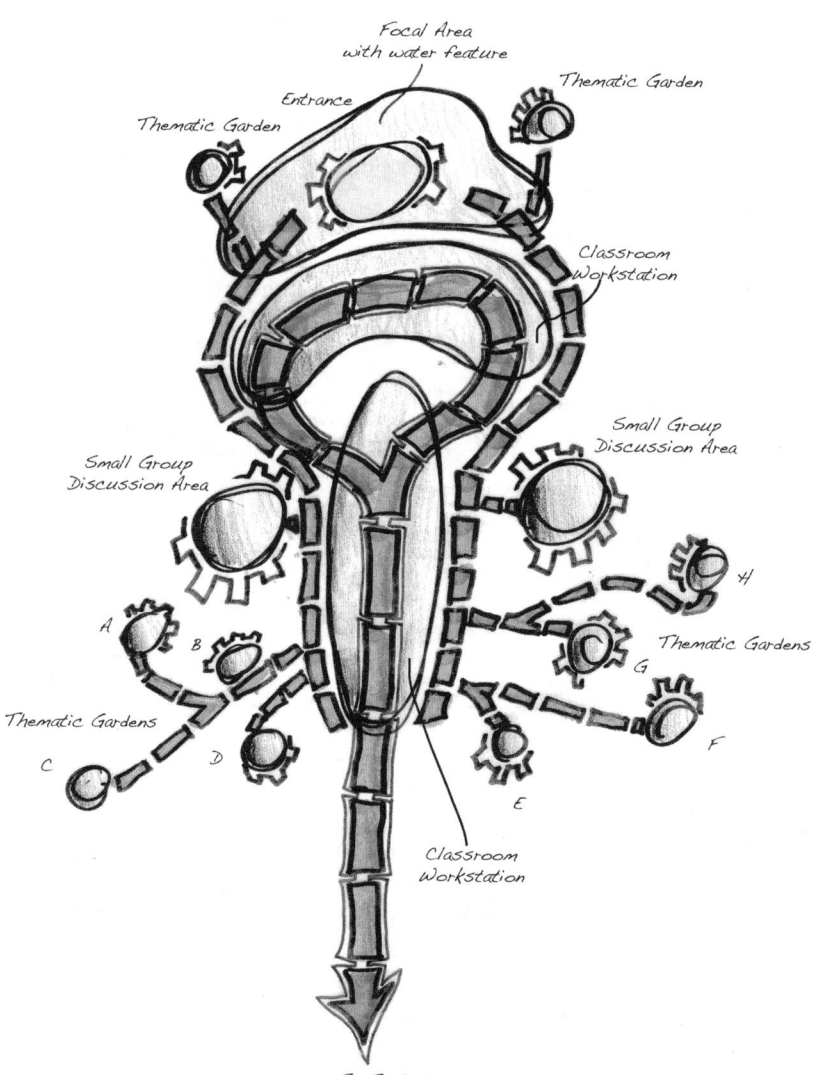

Conceptual diagrams, or "bubble diagrams," should be developed first, without concern for the constraints of the site. Shown here, drawn by Mélisa Kennedy, are three diagrams that explore the relationship between zones and spaces. The thematic gardens shown as letters A–J represent a range of possibilities: vegetable or flower gardens, various habitat gardens, history gardens, art gardens, or any combination of these.

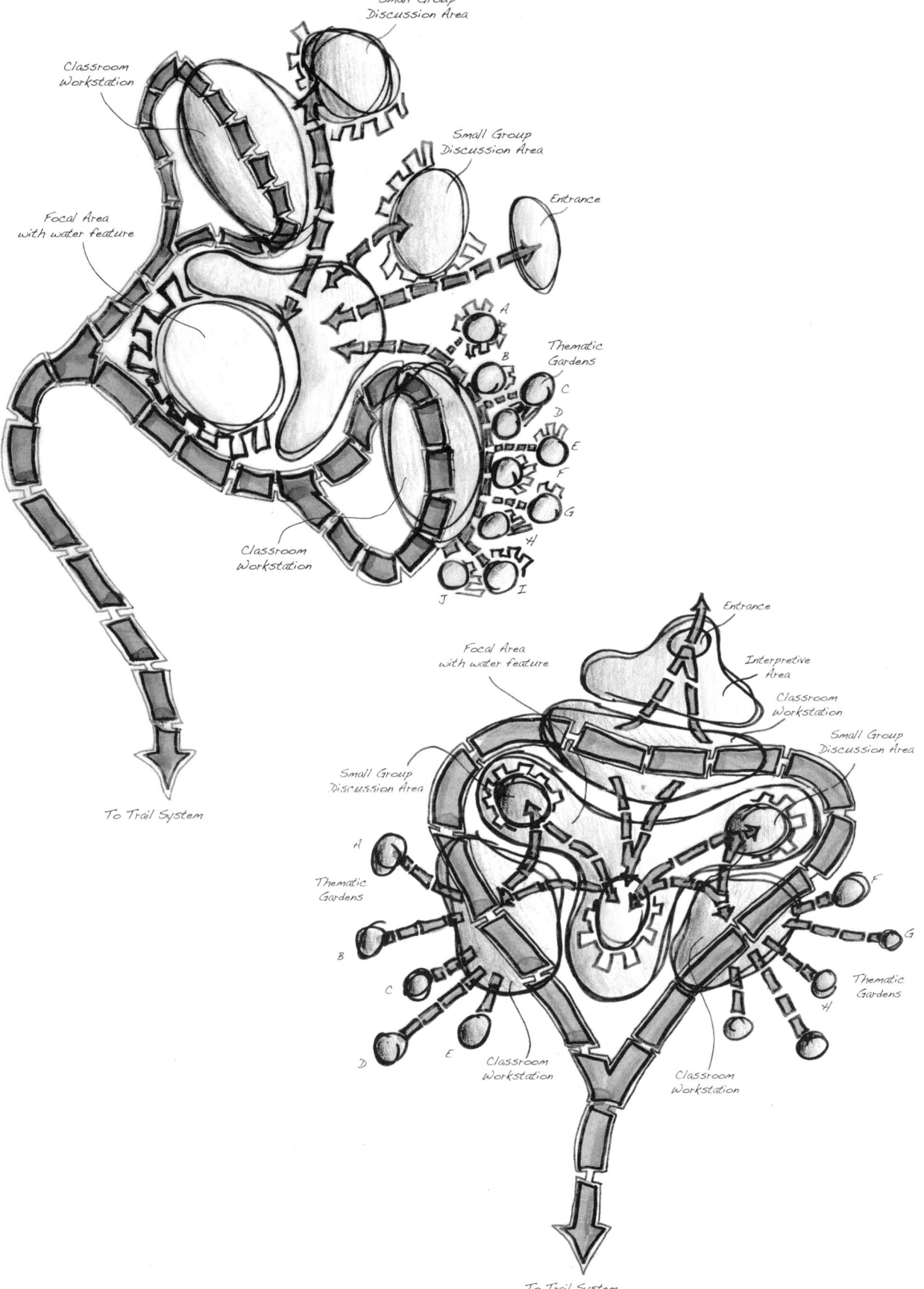

activity setting, design feature, and curriculum idea on a single piece of paper. There will undoubtedly be overlap and repetition among these ideas, so they should be grouped in topical piles on a large table. For example, all of the items that relate to water or pond features would go in one pile. These may have to be organized several times and in several ways before an appropriate pattern emerges. It is also possible that items from one pile will have to be duplicated for use in several of the other piles. For example, the requirement *shade,* or the design features *tables and benches,* might be included in several of the piles. Designers should begin to think of these piles as zones within the ideal schoolyard classroom.

The organization of design ideas using this method will become the basis for testing conceptual diagrams of the ideal site. One option for conceiving these physical areas is to make large circular cardboard shapes for each zone, and smaller cardboard ones for related spaces and features. Arrange these on the table so that related or similar zones and spaces appear together and dissimilar ones are separated. Try this several times until a few exceptional conceptual diagrams emerge.

Designers will now be prepared to move on to the same kind of exercise as above, but now within the physical parameters of their site. This can be achieved easily through the use of a *sandbox study model.* First, build a simple box proportioned to the dimensions of the site (the box length should be at least three feet, with a depth of six inches). Add clean sand to the box. With cardboard, construct the existing human-made and natural features, including the buildings, walls, walks, trees, and other natural features. These items should be created to scale and should be proportionally correct in relation to the dimensions of the site as represented by the box. Add cardboard trees and shrubs to the sandbox and test alternative locations for zones and spaces within the realistic parameters of the site. Pay attention to the information gathered in the site analysis, which might include problematic slopes, ideal potential habitat areas, existing shade from buildings and trees, good and bad views, and conflicts such as nearby roadways. Existing and proposed landforms can easily be represented by adding water to the box and molding the sand. Circulation patterns can be made out of pieces of paper or fabric. By manipulating the card-

This sandbox model makes it easy to manipulate zones, spaces, and circulation pathways. Features like trees and benches can be moved around to create several design alternatives.

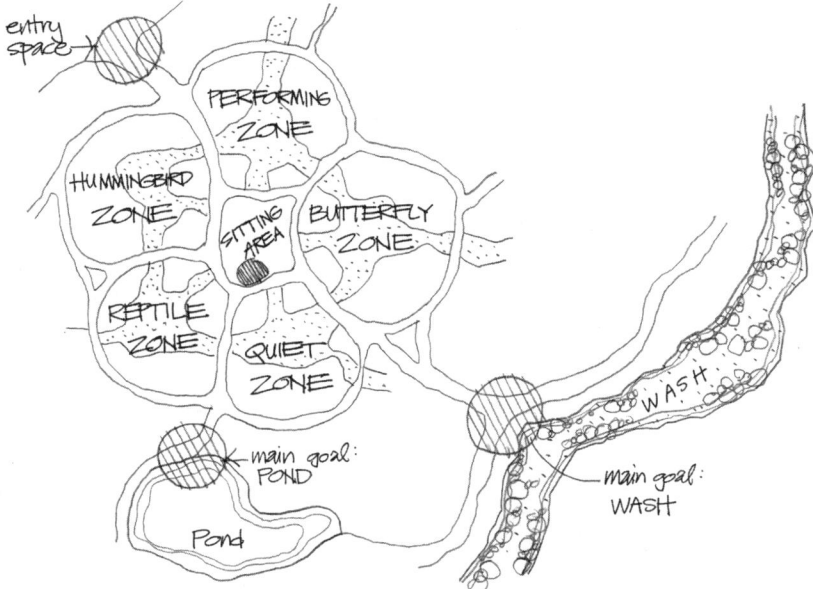

Conceptual bubble diagrams, as they relate to the specific conditions of the site, are used to help designers make decisions. The process of design at this stage involves locating zones and spaces in spots with optimal site conditions. For example, the pond zone would be best if located near an existing riparian area under mature shade trees, while the hummingbird garden zone might find its optimal spot closer to the school building so that students and teachers can see the flowering desert shrubs and small birds from classroom windows. Design decisions such as these might not be obvious—"pros" and "cons" will have to be assigned to each decision, and tradeoffs will have to be made.

board pieces, many conceptual design arrangements can be generated. Record the alternatives with a digital camera for future discussion and evaluation. This design tool works well in community meetings and classroom workshops with students.

While manipulating the cardboard pieces, designers may discover that there are too many zones, spaces, and features, and that these various functions will not all fit within the boundaries of the site. Should this happen, either expand the boundaries of the site to accommodate all zones, spaces, and features, or eliminate some of the ideas.

The size and location of a project's zones and spaces will eventually be determined as designers continue to manipulate the sandbox model. The cardboard pieces will need to be adjusted as designers progress to better fit the various functions within the site. Some zones will begin to take on elongated shapes, while others may twist to follow an existing riparian area. In fact, zones might even be doughnut shapes that enclose smaller zones. Some of the pieces will be interlocking and related; others will be separated with buffers.

Preliminary Design

The loose ideas and diagrams developed in the conceptual design stage will become more specific through the preparation of preliminary designs. This level of design shows the general geometry of the site layout, including zones, spaces, features, and circulation paths. Spatial composition and general forms are determined, but specific materials, including plants, remain unnamed. Preliminary site plans indicate broad plant types such as shade trees, shrubs, and ground covers; they show hard or soft ground surfaces. In this stage, the ideas and drawings are open for revision and modification from the school community. Views, buffers, and focal points can be represented with symbols, while other features (trees and shrubs) are drawn more realistically. Ideas are illustrated through plan view drawings, sketches, and models. Usually, a number of preliminary design alternatives are generated for review by the project users.

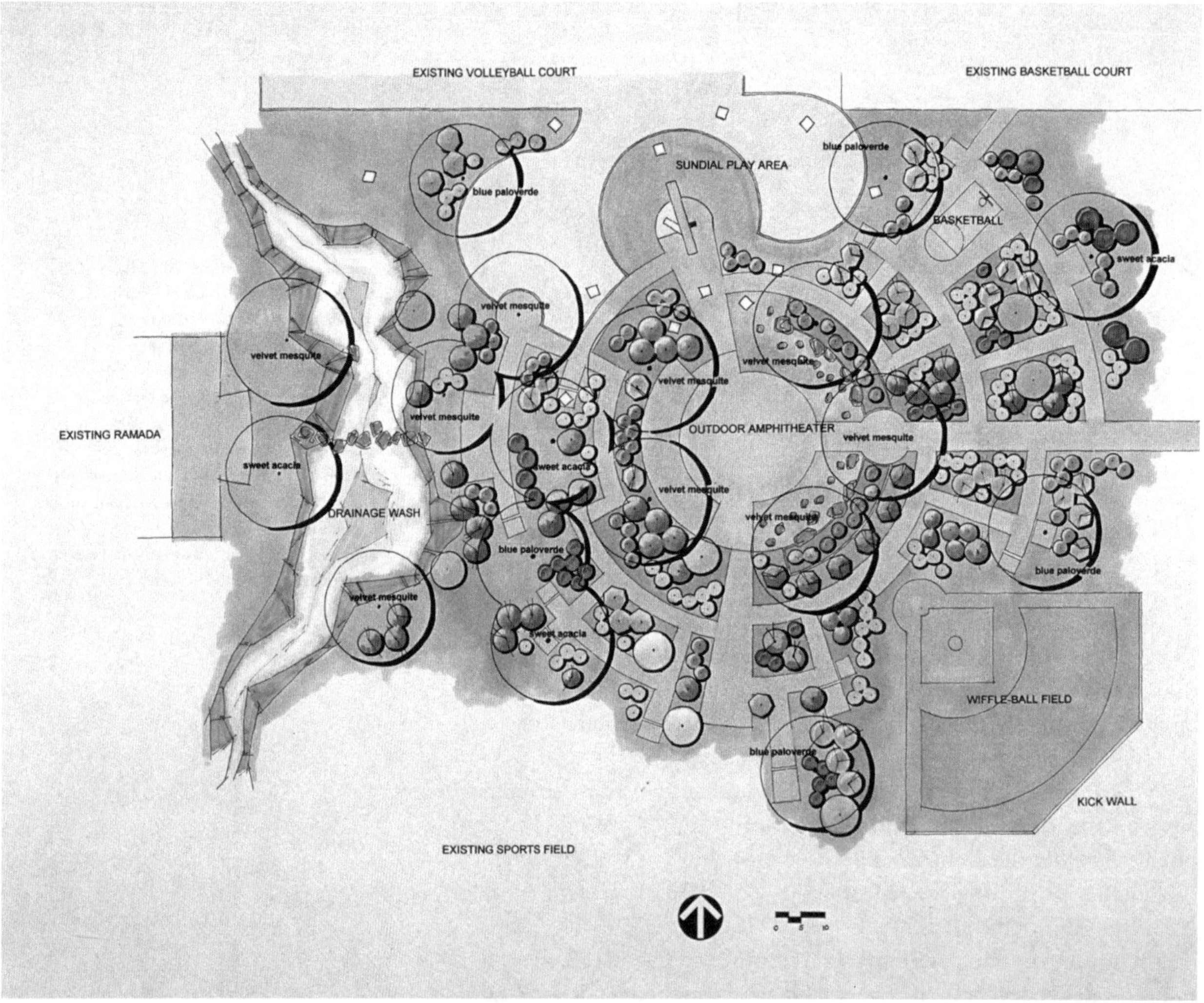

A preliminary design will show, in a fairly articulated manner, the site's pathways, general plantings, level changes, and landscape forms. These plans and models present a good overview of how the landscape will be composed, but they are still works in progress and will need modification and refinement toward the creation of a final design.

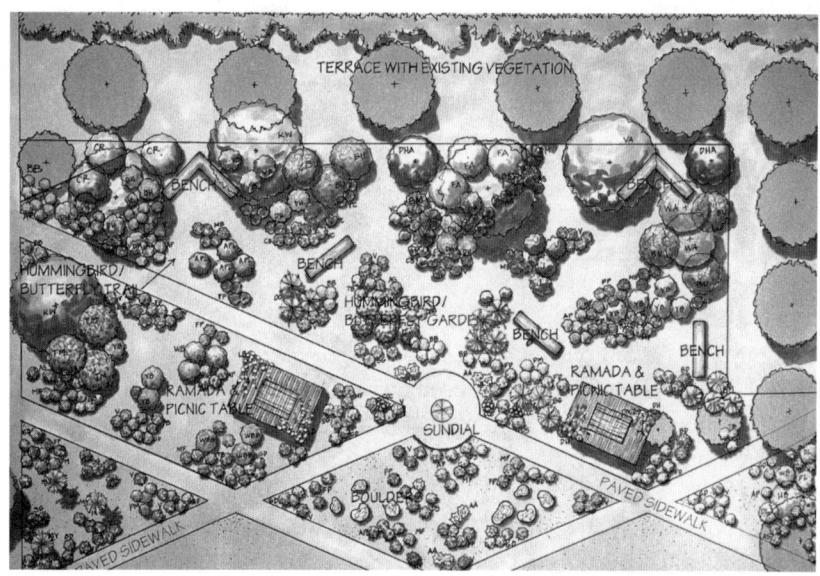

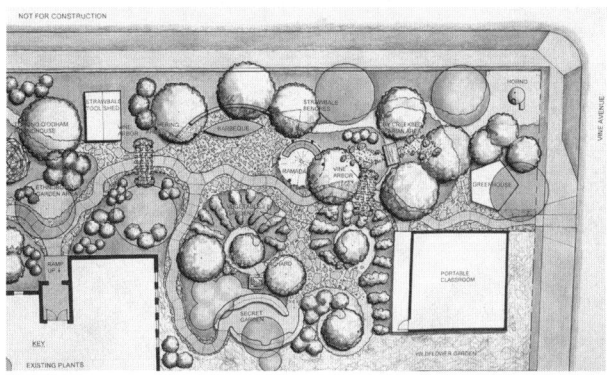

Final Design

One or several of the preliminary design alternatives will be adopted for revision into the final site plan. The final site plan is a refined scheme, which should be presented in a clear and accurately measured set of drawings (plans and sketches) that will make site construction with the assistance of contractors and volunteers a relatively easy endeavor. Keep in mind that design adjustments during construction often occur. The drawings should be colorfully rendered and labeled. Final plan drawings, sketches, and site models will guide the construction process and help with fund-raising efforts.

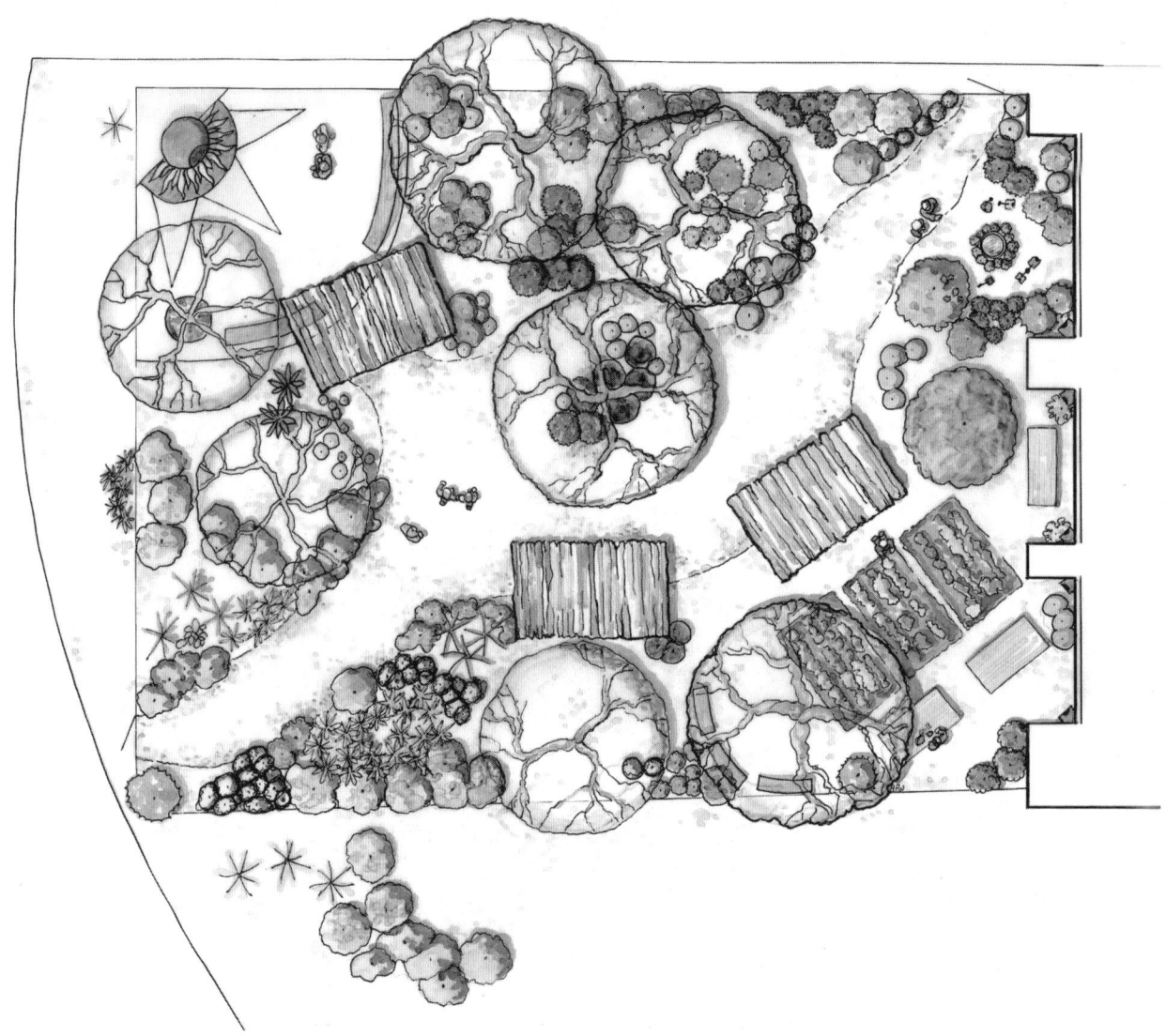

This final design for a schoolyard project clearly shows the forms of the landscape. It is not a legal construction drawing, but it could be used for construction, with adjustments made on-site as needed. These plans make good fund-raising tools, since potential donors can clearly see the proposed amenities. The first drawing was made by Helen Walthier for Margaret Livingston's Planting Design class; the second was designed by Robin Pinto and redrawn by Ariel Fisher.

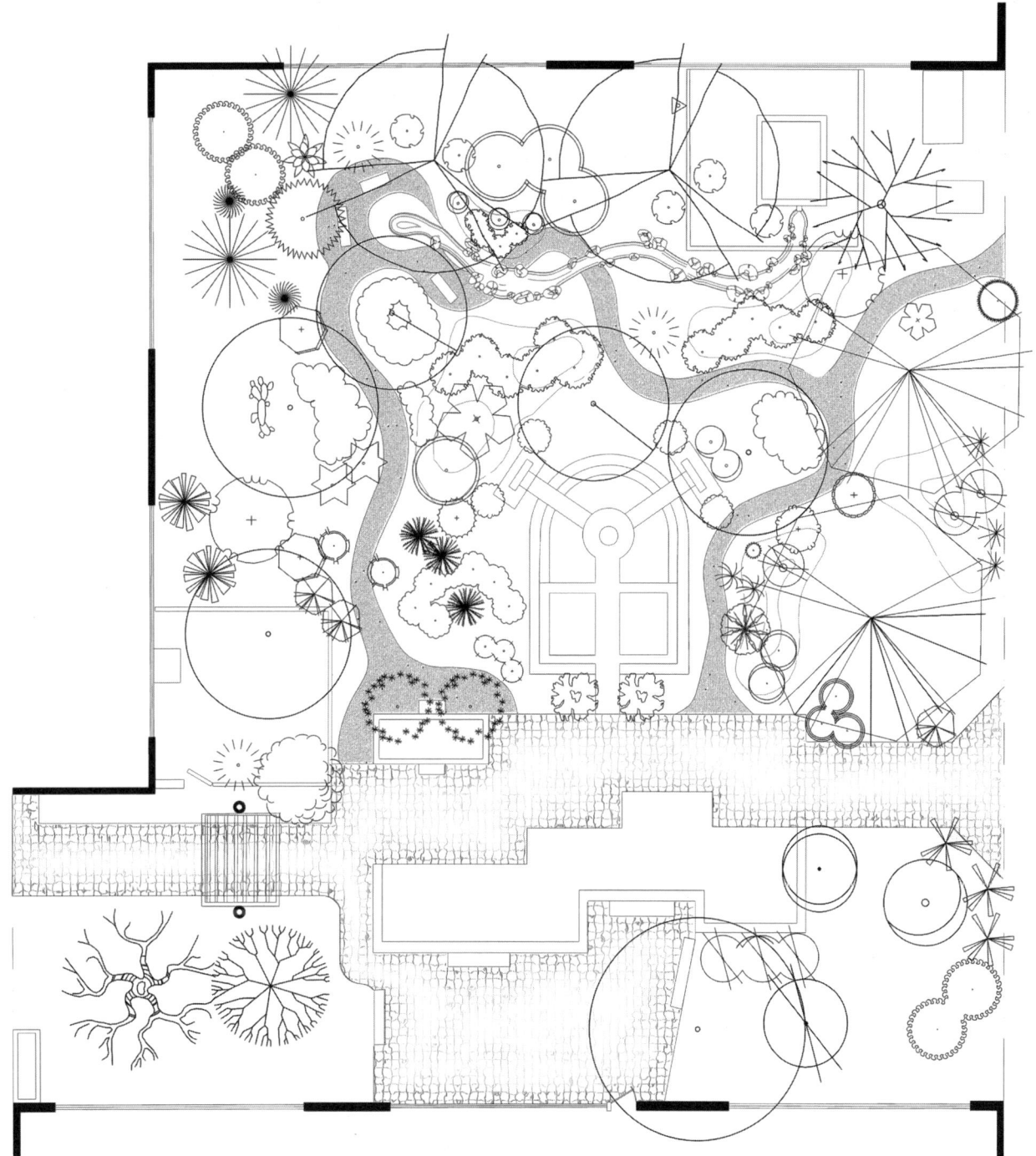

CHAPTER 5 Design Essentials

Introduction

Although this book offers special attention to wildlife habitats, with information on additional selected garden themes, school community groups will identify their own specific outdoor needs. With final designs completed, schools will be ready to begin fund-raising and eventually installing the design. Fund-raising and construction activities can be handled by outside professionals or through community volunteers.

Grant preparation is a time-consuming and sometimes overwhelming endeavor. Consider hiring a professional for the job; it could be well worth it. If licensed contractors build the project, legal construction drawings may be required, as discussed previously in Chapter 3, "Beginning the Design Process." Many contractors, however, will be able to use the final site plan as the guide for construction, with the knowledge that field adjustments might have to be made if the drawings are not completely accurate.

Often, school communities will elect to handle both fund-raising and construction of the outdoor classroom through volunteerism. As administrators, teachers, maintenance staff, students, parents, community members, and outside professionals continue to be involved in these aspects of the project, many individuals will develop a sense of stewardship and will help keep the garden alive and evolving well into the future. Acknowledging the work of these valuable participants, both publicly and with personal letters of appreciation, is essential.

Project Funding

The funding aspect of the outdoor classroom is most successful when it is viewed as an ongoing and organized process. Two approaches will be helpful in obtaining funding for the project: searching for actual dollar contributions, and obtaining in-kind donations. Designers will have to be creative in their search for resources and should look for grants from public and private agencies while accepting different forms of cash donations, contributions of materials (paper, plants, lumber, irrigation supplies), and volunteer services.

Grants and Cash Donations

There are several potential funding sources among individuals and agencies that could provide grants for schoolyard outdoor classrooms and gardens. School communities should begin by identifying both local businesses and corporate agencies that might be interested in offering support. Businesses realize that supporting local schools enhances their public image, so project funding may be as simple as asking. The local Chamber of Commerce can provide a list of businesses in the area. Some funding may also be available within the school district itself. The school administration will know if there are education funds that can be used toward the design and development of the project.

In most cases, designers will need to complete grant applications or formal requests for funding. Often, grant requirements specify the necessity to obtain a matching cash donation, a situation that requires designers to find multiple funding sources. Requests for funding should include a project description, a statement of goals and objectives, a discussion of project benefits, and site-plan drawings. Photographs of models, as well as photographs of the planning process—especially workshops with students and student drawings and letters—will add compelling support materials. Demonstrate the level of participation by administrators, teachers, maintenance staff, students, parents, and outside experts whose time, in some cases, may be used as in-kind contributions. A well-prepared proposal can and should be used for multiple grant applications.

Individuals and organizations, including local businesses and clubs (the Rotary Club, the Lions Club, and garden clubs) might be able and willing to offer cash donations. In all these cases, one of the most persuasive fund-raising tools will be the completed site plan, as this document is a summary of the community's vision. Care should be taken to create a site plan that represents the ideal outdoor classroom for the school and region—it is important to not squelch goals for fear of funding limitations. Most donors will be interested in funding compelling concepts with great ideas, and the site plan can also include construction phases that allow construction and fund-raising to occur over the span of several years. This approach is useful when resources are limited.

This plaque shows recognition for donations that supported the purchase of a specific tree planted in a science garden project.

Another strategy for fund-raising is to earmark specific zones, spaces, design features, and even circulation pathways for specific donations. For example, an agency or person might want to fund one aspect of the site plan, such as signage for the hummingbird garden. Another person might offer funds for a pond or a stone pathway, and so on. Student presentations targeted to these organizations or individuals would be an effective fund-raising device.

In-kind Donations

Many schoolyard habitat gardens and other types of outdoor classrooms are created through a combination of grants, corporate and civic donations, and in-kind donations of goods and services. In-kind donations of goods, which could be landscape materials such as rock, gravel, topsoil, mulch, or lumber for planting beds, or other items like shade structures and benches, could be secured from local suppliers, lumberyards, plant nurseries, retailers, developers, and landscape contractors who may have scrap materials from various jobs.

In-kind donations can also take the form of services; schools have happily received donations of technical assistance services from contractors, plumbers, irrigation specialists, wildlife biologists, horticulturists, architects, landscape architects, artists, professional fund-raisers, and local civic groups. Outside participants can submit *Not-for-Pay* invoices of their time, listing all the services they have provided, with the fees and other expenses they would normally charge. The Not-for-Pay invoice should include a statement explaining that the school does not have to submit payment and that the dollar amount has been donated to the project. This clear documentation of in-kind services will help strengthen the grant proposal.

Organization of the Fund-raising Process

The fund-raising process will probably be most successful if one person is designated to coordinate and oversee all the funding activities. This person should work with a group of individuals who are each responsible for one category of fund-raising: grants, cash donations, or in-kind donations, for example. Each of these respective individuals (or groups) should set goals, establish timelines, and develop a method for reaching their goals. Grant-writing and fund-raising experts within the community might be able to offer advice.

To make the fund-raising process more effective, set target dates for the receipt of funds and commitments for goods and services. On a large poster or bulletin board, track the funding and commitments as they come in and display evidence of all donations received. Participants will find this encouraging, and it can lend energy to the project.

Students can add their efforts and excitement to the fund-raising process. Activities like talent shows, car washes, plant sales, and even a modest penny drive can help raise cash and enthusiasm. The simplest activities can augment grant and in-kind donations and add to the students' feeling of ownership of the project.

Design Features

Design features were discussed in Chapter 3, "Beginning the Design Process," as they related to the development of a written program that identifies community goals and objectives, lists specific requirements, possible activities and their settings, and curriculum ideas.

This section presents some ideas and technical assistance that relate to a few of the most essential design features: earthworks, ponds, plants, shade structures, storage areas, pathways, seating, walls, and signs. As was discussed in Chapter 4, "Site Research and Design Synthesis," *design features* are often the smaller objects or groups of objects in built landscapes that serve as functional amenities or ways to define the boundaries of a zone or space. As this section is only a general guide, designers will have to conduct additional research regarding local building codes and landscape standards established within their state, county, and city. Contact a landscape architect, contractor, and public planning representative early in the process for advice and review.

Earthworks define spaces and create interest.

Earthworks

Earthworks are landforms like hills and depressions that add interest and define or separate zones and spaces. These topographic changes, made in the creation of ponds or barriers such as berms, can be used to make a flat site more interesting or to direct pedestrian circulation (users will naturally walk around a pond or incline). Perhaps most important for the outdoor classroom, manipulation of the earth can redirect surface rainwater to areas in need of water. Many schools create swales or seasonal drainage washes to help irrigate planted areas.

Creating landforms through topographic manipulation is an art form much like sculpture, and the effects can be just as dramatic. It takes skill to understand the schoolyard's existing topography and be able to work with these conditions to create new landforms that look natural. When designing topographic features such as berms, hills, and valleys, refer to any U.S. Geological Survey (USGS) topographic map for general landform shapes. The contour lines shown on these maps indicate changes in grade resulting in landform patterns such as hills and depressions that could serve as a guide for planning earthworks in the schoolyard. Additionally, clay models are useful tools for designing earthworks. Take care not to create slopes that are too steep, as these will be hard to maintain with plants, and soil erosion problems could occur. In arid environments, gentler slopes will be easier to sustain.

Usually, earthmoving and topographic projects strive to balance the areas of cut and fill. In other words, soil is moved around on the site without additional soil being brought in from another location. For example, the earth removed to create a pond might be used to make a hill or a berm nearby.

Ponds

Water is one of the ingredients needed to create a successful wildlife habitat. The most dramatic way to incorporate water into the schoolyard setting is through the creation of a pond, used not only to attract and sustain wildlife but also as a dynamic teaching tool. Wendy Titman (1994, 43) wrote that ponds are "essentially symbolic of 'the living world' for children, and where they existed, ponds were the subject of much comment and conjecture. Children were fascinated with the creatures associated with ponds." Ponds can be used for many learning opportunities as students observe the life cycles of plants and wildlife in ways that cannot be achieved through any other feature in the wildlife habitat.

EARTHWORKS
- Define zones and spaces.
- Create landscape interest.
- Shape pedestrian circulation.
- Direct water flow to help irrigate planted areas.
- Strive to balance areas of cut and fill.
- Strive to appear natural.
- Avoid steep slopes that may cause erosion problems.

CHOOSING A POND SITE

When choosing a location for a pond, study the topography of the site to find low spots where water collects naturally. The pond location will also be determined by proximity to water and electric utility lines (contact local utility companies to determine the location of these lines). Pond location is best if it can occur in existing natural areas, as wildlife may already be present. Existing trees and shrubs will provide shade during the hottest part of the day while also offering wildlife the necessary cover. If shade is not available, designers should create it; the site plan will have to make provisions for this important condition. Ponds should be away from high-litter trees, as debris will fill the pond, and away from fertilized areas that may contaminate the water. Ponds should also be located away from areas of high activity, such as sports facilities, parking lots, or roads, since they might inhibit wildlife. If the pond site is in a windy location, provide windbreaks (walls, trees, or shrubs) for wildlife protection. Wildlife observation is another important element to consider in pond design.

Ponds are one of the most successful features in attracting wildlife to the schoolyard; however, they often pose serious concerns related to liability and safety. Each school must evaluate the pros and cons and decide if pond creation is a valid option. Schoolyard designers may want to contact other schools that have created ponds to learn from their experiences and discover ways to mitigate concerns and maximize benefits. Supervision is one of the key factors needed to ensure safety.

CONSTRUCTION OF THE POND

Essential elements for any type of pond include a water source, a filtration system, and electrical service (to operate the filtration system). Some form of filtration, whether external or submersible, is needed to keep the water in the pond clear and to remove the carbon dioxide that supports the growth of algae.

The pond lining is what actually holds the water. The pond can be lined with a clay liner, PVC sheeting, a rubberized liner, concrete, or fiberglass. Many of these types of liners are prefabricated by pool or pond manufacturers. Pond manufacturers sell materials and pond kits for the construction of ponds in a variety of sizes and shapes. Check local regulations before selecting pond materials, and seek advice from local experts before installing the pond.

POND REQUIREMENTS AND CONSIDERATIONS
- Fit with the natural topography.
- Construct at low spots where water collects naturally.
- Have shade.
- Protect from wind.
- Balance ecology through pond organisms.
- Locate away from fertilized areas.
- Locate away from high-activity, noisy areas.
- Include places for wildlife observation.
- Supervise for safety.
- Determine a maintenance schedule.

Ponds can be used to attract wildlife and create interest.

Ponds will attract and sustain wildlife while providing many opportunities for outdoor learning.

Pond maintenance involves both frequent and long-term responsibility. Water-quality testing should be performed regularly to monitor the overall health of the pond, and dead or diseased plants and fish will need to be removed on an ongoing basis as needed. The pond should be completely drained, and accumulated debris cleaned out, every two years.

FISH AND POND ORGANISMS

Fish help maintain the overall ecological balance of the pond. Insects, tadpoles, and snails, for instance, will clean the bottom surfaces. Note that public, treated water is chlorinated and therefore toxic to many pond plants and fish, so a dechlorinating agent must be put in the water prior to adding living organisms to the pond. When first introducing soil and plants, the pond will go through stages of murkiness as algae levels build and change. In prefabricated or concrete ponds, balance will eventually be achieved and the water will become clear. Ponds with earthen bottoms, however, will retain a murky appearance.

Plants

Plants are critical living materials used to define spaces, enhance views, and attract wildlife. Plants within wildlife habitats will have a variety of uses, particularly as food, cover, and nesting materials for wildlife. Plants can also block unsightly views and noise, frame good views, stabilize slopes, and prevent soil erosion. They help retain soil moisture and clean the air. Plants direct human circulation within the garden and offer protection from the desert sun and wind.

> The Southwestern deserts contain some of the most unique natural landscapes in the world. Rugged mountain ranges, gentle plains, and sandy arroyos support a great diversity of plants, from the gnarled Ironwood tree to the delicate Mexican Gold-poppy. The vegetation may be complex, with an intermingling of trees, shrubs, cacti, other succulents, and groundcovers, or a more simple composition of two to three dominant plant species. Sometimes the plainest landscape becomes breathtakingly beautiful, such as when abundant rainfall coupled with mild temperatures coax forth a tapestry of wildflowers.
> —JUDY MIELKE, *Native Plants for Southwestern Landscapes* (1993, 13)

Various species of plants can be used to attract and sustain different types of wildlife. Wildlife habitats typically focus on small wildlife such as insects, birds, and small mammals. Wildlife viewing blinds constructed with plants provide the opportunity to view wildlife within the schoolyard setting. Viewing experiences will be more successful when viewers conceal themselves. This could be as simple as standing behind a tree or shrub or more elaborate through level changes where viewers are at higher elevations with lookout points that direct views toward protected natural areas.

The selection of plants within the schoolyard should be based on both visual and functional concerns. Designers will need to select plants according to design requirements and environmental factors, choosing the most appropriate plant species for wildlife and human needs. Considerations include plant habit (shape), mature size, branch and foliage patterns, leaf texture, fruit and flowering benefits, and seasonal interest.

Planting designs will have to be prepared in conjunction with the final site plan. Planting design should be thought of as an artistic composition that makes use of both the fundamentals of design, outlined in Chapter 2, "Design Theory," and issues of ecological appropriateness, discussed in Chapter 6, "Ecological Principles and Wildlife." Design principles (unity, variety, scale) and elements (color, form, and texture), as well as site conditions (soil, sun exposure, wind, elevation, rainfall), will guide the selection and configuration of plants. The arrangement of plants usually includes general plant massings to define zones and spaces, with the addition of specialty plants for visual interest. Planting plans should be in keeping with the overall conceptual framework for design or theme, which will include ecological principles, cultural aspects, and art.

"Growing plants in a hot, dry, sunny environment is pioneering in a real sense. Interior valleys and desert areas present special challenges: extremes of heat, aridity and problem soil make gardening different, even difficult, at times," wrote Mary Rose Duffield and Warren Jones (2001, 4) in *Plants for Dry Climates*. To ensure the survival and success of the chosen plants, designers should be sure to practice proper planting techniques. When planting in poor, rocky, or caliche hardpan, it is best to dig a hole at least twice as large as the size of the root ball. Many gardeners in the arid Southwest also recommend improving the soil removed from planting holes by mixing in organic matter, such as animal manure or composted materials, with the native soil before returning it to the hole ("backfilling"). This will improve drainage and help retain soil moisture, giving the plant a better chance to become established. Some individuals believe in using only the native soil for planting backfill and prefer to add organic matter to the ground surface instead. It is not advisable for schoolyard designers to use all imported or improved soil in plant pits, as the plant roots may become "root bound" and not grow beyond the edges of the planting hole.

SOILS

Soil *pH level, characteristics,* and *classification* are important determinants for the selection of plant materials. The various requirements of the plants will have to be matched with the conditions of the soil, especially soil drainage, fertility, and nutrient levels (nitrogen, phosphorus, and potassium). Problem soils in the arid Southwest such as hardpan and calcareous (caliche) soils may warrant extensive measures such as using a jackhammer when making plant holes. Saline soils are also potentially problematic, as they often require the leaching out of soil salts before planting. Extremely rocky soils can warrant time-consuming preparation requirements related to rock removal and building up the topsoil.

Soil conditions in the arid Southwest are highly variable from one region to the next. Specific soil information for a particular area may be available through the local branch of the U.S. Department of Agriculture Natural Resources Conservation Service (NRCS). Information on soil testing is available through nurseries, local cooperative extension offices, or environmental engineering firms. The data generated from soil testing provides an interesting learning opportunity for students involved in the planning of the project, because with this analysis of the soil, they will be able to determine what plants will grow well in which location.

XERISCAPE DESIGN

Xeriscape design promotes the use of native plants and low-water-use strategies that will not require excess supplemental irrigation. The word comes from the

PLANT BENEFITS
- Provide wildlife food, cover, and nesting materials.
- Screen bad views.
- Frame good views.
- Stabilize slopes.
- Prevent soil erosion.
- Help soil retain moisture.
- Direct circulation.
- Offer needed shade.
- Clean the air.
- Provide wildlife viewing blinds.
- Define zones and spaces.
- Provide beauty and interest.

Screen bad views and noise

Frame good views

Stabilize slopes and prevent erosion

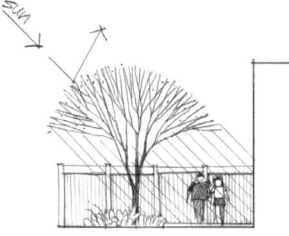

provide shade

wildlife viewing blind

Hydrozoning, or grouping plants with similar water requirements, helps conserve water.
Low-Water Zone: Plants can survive on rainfall once established.
Moderate-Water Zone: Plants require some irrigation but are not "water greedy." This is often called the *transition* group.
High-Water Zone: Plants requiring the most water are limited and grouped together. This group is often called the *mini-oasis*.

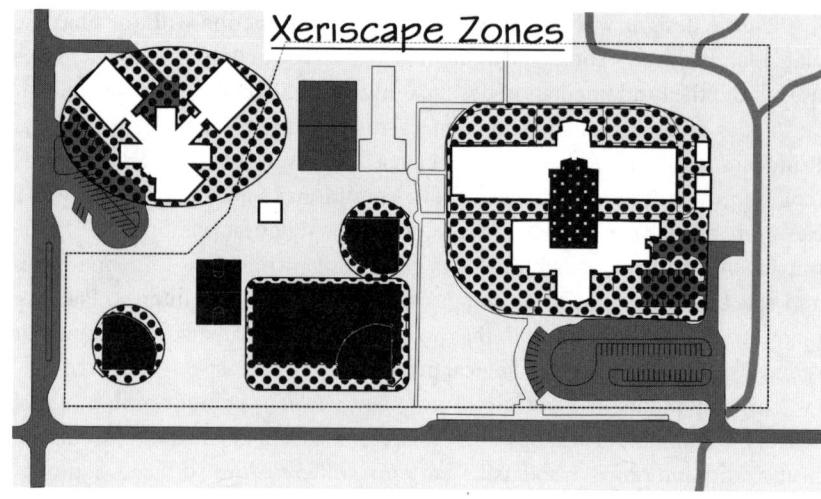

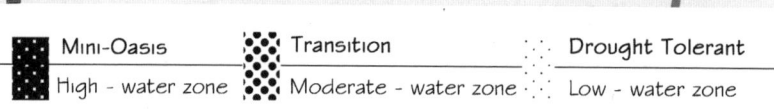

Xeriscape zones, drawn by Hampton Uzzelle

Greek word *xeros,* which means "dry." In her essay "Xeriscape" in the *Encyclopedia of Gardens,* Margaret Livingston (2001, 1455) observed: "Although the practice of xeriscape is a recent effort . . . it was realized long ago in the Mediterranean countries that even in a hot, dry climate, gardens could offer shade and refreshment yet use a minimum amount of water." The design of the southwestern wildlife habitat and outdoor classroom should consider the principles listed below to help save water and money.

Principles of Xeriscape Design

Minimize turf areas that rely on large quantities of water.
Use plants with low water requirements.
Use hydrozoning—group plants according to water needs.
Manage water efficiently.
Water at sundown or early morning.
Use water-harvesting techniques.
Shape the topography to capture as much rainfall as possible near plant roots.
Catch water from building downspouts and paved areas and direct it toward plantings.
Use irrigation (drip systems and soaker hoses often use less water than hand-watering or sprinklers).
Add organic material to improve soil conditions.
Use mulches and organic materials that retain soil moisture.

IRRIGATION SYSTEMS

An integral factor in the success of a schoolyard garden is the irrigation system that supports its vegetation. Within the arid Southwest, newly installed plants require supplemental water, and this is best achieved with an irrigation system. Be sure to install the irrigation system in conjunction with planting, as newly installed plants will need immediate watering for the best chances of survival. Some desert plants may only need supplemental water for the first two to three years after planting, but other plants require lifelong irrigation. A drip irrigation system can be a water-efficient and effective means of watering plants in the arid Southwest if the system is properly maintained and checked regularly for missing emitters and leakage. Sometimes in small gardens where plant spacing is narrow, soaker hoses work well and can have fewer maintenance concerns.

The irrigation system must water plants deeply to encourage roots to seek maximum depth levels. Shallow watering will encourage shallow roots and cause plants to become water-stressed and vulnerable to high winds. Irrigate in the early mornings or evenings when evaporation rates are low, and check soil moisture periodically to better gauge and determine an appropriate watering schedule. Garden designers may consider using the planning, implementation, and maintenance of the irrigation system as a valuable part of teaching water conservation.

Simple irrigation layouts can be prepared by most irrigation equipment suppliers, while more complicated designs may require the expertise of a landscape architect or irrigation designer. These professionals produce irrigation drawings, which are important tools for installation as well as good records of what lies underground; these plans could prove useful should future repairs to the system be needed. The specific irrigation requirements vary greatly from region to region within the arid Southwest. Schoolyard designers may want to check with local landscape contractors to find out the standard irrigation specifications for their area. National supply companies often offer great assistance and may even help install the schoolyard irrigation system. Rain Bird Sales and Technical Service, a nationally recognized irrigation company, is one particular company that can offer advice. For additional help or information, contact the local water company, the university cooperative extension service, botanical gardens, nurseries, and irrigation system suppliers.

Zoning the Irrigation System

Zoning the irrigation system for water flow allows designers to customize the amounts of water provided to the different types of vegetation in the garden project. As some plants have higher water needs than others, the designation of water zones will be helpful. For example, when designing the irrigation system, trees—which typically have different watering needs than shrubs, grasses, and ground covers—might be within a separate zone and perhaps on a separate irrigation line from other plant materials. High-water-use shrubs, grasses, and ground covers might also require a separate line to ensure that their water needs are met.

Maintaining the Irrigation System

Regular maintenance of the irrigation system extends its longevity and promotes efficient water use. Check for leaks, damage from rodents, and malfunctioning emitters or sprayers as part of a regular maintenance program. Adjust times and duration of watering according to the seasons of the year; during the hotter seasons, evening and morning watering are the more efficient times of the day to water, since less water is lost through evaporation.

WATER HARVESTING

Water harvesting is a conservation technique that provides an ethical approach to water use in arid environments. The term is used to describe the capture of rainwater runoff for use in the landscape. Water harvesting is a valuable technique for environments within the arid Southwest, where it has been used by Native American groups for centuries. The simple water-collection ditches and

WATERING AND THE IRRIGATION SYSTEM
- Water deeply to encourage deep, strong roots.
- Consider locating plants in water zones (hydrozoning) so that the irrigation system can be designed to conserve the maximum amount of water.
- Drip systems (properly maintained and checked for water leaks) may use less water than hand-watering, which loses water through evaporation.
- Irrigate when evaporation rates are low.
- Check soil moisture periodically and develop a watering schedule.
- Use the irrigation system as a water-conservation teaching tool.
- Get assistance, when needed, from an irrigation specialist.

SIMPLE WATER-HARVESTING TECHNIQUES
- Create irrigation channels that release water to planted areas.
- Use historical techniques such as *ak-chin* farming—planting in natural drainage areas.
- Use gray water or sink water to irrigate plants.
- Capture water from pavement and roof runoff and direct to planted areas.
- Collect rainwater in barrels or cisterns.

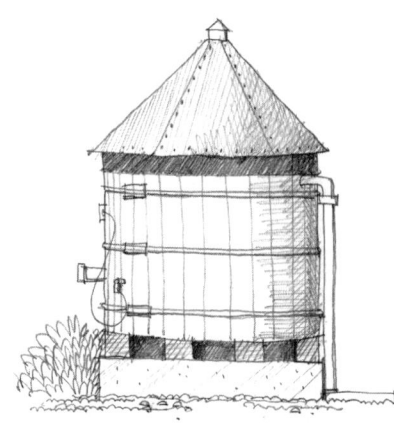

Shade structures help extend the use of the outdoor classroom into the hot season, when the conditions of the sun make outdoor activities prohibitive. They help protect children in arid environments from harmful solar radiation.

irrigation channels of the Hohokam, for example, could be re-created for use and demonstration within the school environment. *Ak-chin* farming is another historic water-conservation technique that uses natural erosion patterns. *Ak-chin* is an O'odham word that means "place where the wash loses itself in the sand or ground" (azcentral.com, accessed June 25, 2004). This refers to the type of farming they used, which depended on the floodplains created by winter snows/rains and summer rains for water. *Ak-chin* farmers sited crop fields on the moisture- and nutrient-rich soils of alluvial deposits. Early Hispanic cultures used gravel as a mulch to reduce water evaporation and moderate soil temperature. These historic techniques, updated with new technologies, offer great potential for teaching water conservation.

Water-harvesting techniques provide a natural and cost-effective means to help sustain the natural outdoor classroom and wildlife habitat garden. Water-harvesting systems can be as simple as capturing roof runoff through downspouts and channeling it to planted areas within the habitat. There are also more complex systems that involve catchment basins, high filtration, ultraviolet treatment, and water recycling for human use.

When designing a water-harvesting system, simplicity can often be rewarding. Runoff from patios, roofs, and drinking fountains can supply a portion of the water needs of the landscape area. School maintenance staff are excellent resources for assessing the possibilities of harvesting water from these areas. Designers may also want to consider cisterns and rain barrels as collection devices. Some schools have gray-water lines that enable sink water to be used in the habitat, but be sure to investigate the sanitary and safety requirements of the county and school district before proceeding with such an installation.

Shade Structures

Within the landscape, designers should consider adding structures that will protect people from the hot sun, strong winds, and rain. These structures will provide activity settings, frame views, and serve as transitional places (from one pathway to another or one ground elevation to another). Shade structures will have visual dominance within the site and therefore serve as important focal points that add to the unique identity and character of the site. They can be used as visual references to the history and culture of the site by incorporating the architectural forms and construction techniques of historic cultural groups.

The effects of the southwestern sun warrant serious concern and make shade a very important asset for the design of all outdoor spaces. It is a critical feature in the outdoor classroom, wildlife habitat, and garden for the comfort of people

and the survival of wildlife and certain plants. Shade can be provided through tree canopy, shrub plantings, or built structures such as ramadas or overhead trellises. Trees and plants are particularly good choices for shade because they add water to the air through transpiration, providing an extra cooling effect. Often, human-made shade structures are used in conjunction with natural materials: vines are used effectively on trellises or ramadas to shade and absorb solar radiation. Self-climbing vines can be used on textured surfaces or trained to climb cables strung from overhangs, which can provide shade to east and west walls.

Shade can also be provided through site orientation with respect to shadows cast by landforms, vegetation, walls, or buildings. North-facing slopes and buildings or walls with northern exposures will receive the most shade, while eastern exposures offer secondary shade benefits in the late afternoon when the sun can be harsh. In the arid Southwest, western exposures receive the most extreme conditions of sun and summer heat. Designers can offset this by locating deciduous trees on the west sides of buildings to shade the roof and outdoor spaces. This will not block beneficial winter sun, since the trees will lose their leaves in the cold season, allowing sunlight to penetrate.

When selecting trees for shade, consider their size and form. Trees with broad, round forms will cast wide shadows, maximizing the benefits. The following list, modified from Gregory McPherson and Charles Sacamano's book on southwestern landscape architecture (1989), provides considerations for the use of vegetation in controlling sun and wind within the arid Southwest.

- Locate trees to shade east- and west-facing windows, walls, and outdoor spaces.
- Shade the south roof only if solar access is not a concern.
- Select deciduous trees with dense canopies in summer and open canopies in winter for placement south and west of buildings.
- Locate large shrubs to shade east-, west-, and south-facing walls.

(below left) Trees can be planted to shade east- and west-facing windows.

(below right) Use vines for shade and wind protection.

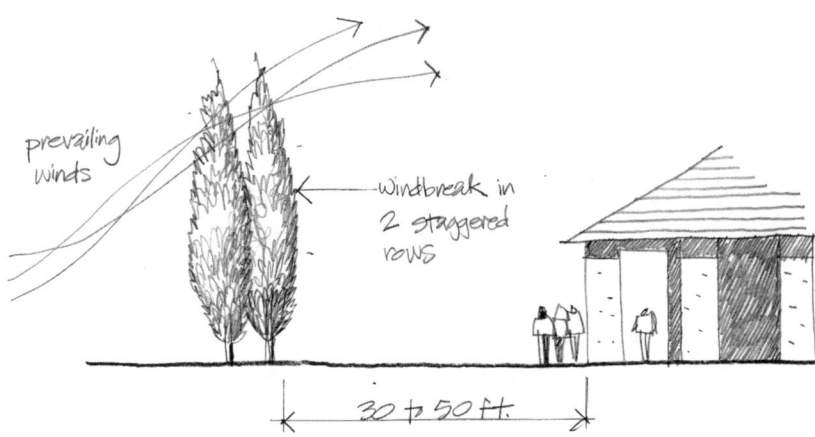

Windbreak.

Use deciduous vines to shade east and south walls, and evergreen vines to shade west walls and protect north walls from winter winds.

Use ground covers to shade reflective surfaces and reduce building heat gain.

Place windbreaks thirty to fifty feet upwind from the building and place those trees close together in a staggered arrangement.

Use dense-branching conifers, if appropriate to the region, for maximum wind protection.

Extremes of heat and full exposure to the harsh sun will have a negative impact on many plants. Reflected light, or sunlight that bounces off nearby bare walls and uncovered soil, may also affect sensitive plants. Plants must be carefully selected for their ability to tolerate these conditions. Planning the orientation of the habitat or other gardens with proposed or existing areas of shade and varied sunlight patterns will provide greater opportunities for plant and wildlife diversity and human enjoyment.

Storage Areas

An often-overlooked feature in the design of outdoor classrooms is storage facilities. There are many tools, educational materials, and general supplies that will need to be stored at the school as the garden is created, used, and maintained. Items such as shovels, rakes, wheelbarrows, buckets, water-testing kits, collection jars, butterfly nets, wildlife food, and irrigation-system parts all require storage, and these materials should be conveniently located in or near the wildlife habitat. Storage structures can be constructed on-site or purchased as prefabricated ready-made units, preferably with shelving and other organizing systems to minimize clutter and make access to materials easier. Storage areas should also be placed over pavement and located near water areas for easy cleanup. They should be screened, if possible, or decorated with art to provide visual interest.

Pathways

A pathway is a means of getting from one place to another, but in the context of the school habitat garden, it is, perhaps more importantly, a vehicle for student exploration. As students travel along the pathway, there will be many plant

CONSIDERATIONS FOR STORAGE AREAS
- Locate the storage structure for easy access to materials as needed.
- Make sure the door or entrance to the storage structure is safe.
- Ensure good ventilation.
- Provide good drainage and visual screening.
- Protect the storage structure from the sun.
- Provide adequate room for the materials.
- Use shelving and other organizing systems.
- Protect wildlife supplies stored inside.
- Use lighting (a window or skylight may be sufficient).
- Locate the storage structure near water for ease in cleanup.
- Decorate with artworks for visual interest.
- Place the storage structure on paved areas for wheeled access and ease in cleanup.

Storage systems within the schoolyard outdoor classroom are essential.

textures to discover and small wildlife to encounter. Pathway layout is a critical component of the overall site design, as paths will connect a series of activity settings and separate or define zones and spaces. Pathways can be designed with wide spots, or nodes, which make good places for seating, small group gatherings, and outdoor classrooms.

A wide range of possible materials can be used in the development of pathways: *soft materials* include bare soil, soil treated with a resin stabilizer, sand, decomposed granite, gravel, rubber, manufactured safety surface, mulch, wood chips, pine needles, and straw; *hard materials* include flagstone, cobblestone, brick, concrete, and wood decking. In the Southwest, dryness makes wood decking problematic, and designers should avoid it unless they are willing to provide considerable maintenance to keep it sealed and protected. Drainage and water runoff is another important aspect of pathway design. Dry-laid

PATHWAYS
- Connect activity settings.
- Define and separate zones and spaces.
- Can have wide spots or nodes for gathering places or outdoor classrooms.

Pathway with wide spots for gatherings

SEATING: OPTIONS ARE KEY
- Accommodate small, medium, and large groups.
- Consider fixed seats and movable ones.
- Design the shape of seating arrangements for the type of activity.
    - Circles for group discussions.
    - Semicircles for performances and lectures.
    - Clustered seating for several small-group discussions.
    - Right angles for conversation.
    - Seats with tables for working with materials and tools.
    - Single seats placed under trees or in small spaces for contemplation.
- Variety in heights—people like to sit on walls, benches, curbs, and steps.
- Variety in materials—logs, stones, bales of straw, and others.
- Seating designed for the winter sun and the summer shade.
- Seating connected to circulation pathways.
- Seating to take advantage of good views.

methods of construction, in which paving blocks are set over a layer of sand to allow water percolation, offer benefits, as water goes back into the ground and not into city drainage systems.

Seating

Seating is desirable for students, teachers, and all visitors in the outdoor classroom, so the site plan should include several seating options distributed throughout the site. Some seating plans should be designed for small groups, and others for large gatherings such as school performances. Seating should also accommodate quiet contemplation and solitude. In *Natural Learning,* Robin C. Moore and Herb H. Wong (1997, 72) describe their creation of a schoolyard that incorporated wonderful seating options: "As spaces were formed and shaped, we kept in mind the small-scale character of the child's world. We constantly looked for opportunities to create little corners, alcoves, shelves, ledges, hooks, nooks, cubbies, and crannies. We wanted to provide places where children could perch themselves, play with small objects, or stash personal belongings. Many elevated, comfortable spots were provided by logs, tree trunks, elevated cable spool tops, rocks, railings, raised spots in the sand area, and tables and benches throughout the Yard."

Seating options should include choices between fixed seats or movable ones. Movable chairs provide the most flexibility, and, according to William H. Whyte (1980, 34), they give people a sense of control over their environment, as they can move the chair anywhere they desire: "Now, a wonderful invention—the movable chair. Having a back, it is comfortable; more so, if it has an armrest as well. But the big asset is movability. Chairs enlarge choice: to move into the sun, out of it, to make room for groups, move away from them. The possibility of choice is as important as the exercise of it. If you know you can move if you want to, you feel more comfortable staying put."

Seating arrangements should be designed to accommodate proposed activities. For example, if the activities include group discussions and presentations, then group seating is needed. If the activity includes writing, measuring, or microscope use, then the seating area must also include tables. Sometimes a concrete amphitheater is the most appropriate seating plan; other times movable bales of straw serve the desired need. Seats can be benches, chairs, seat walls, curbs, stairs, stools, logs, stones, or other materials. The shape of a seating arrangement might vary throughout the project to allow for different functions. Seats can be arranged in a circular or curved fashion, a rectangular pattern with right angles, a linear pattern, or random clusters.

Climatic considerations are another aspect of seating design. Seating locations must not be vulnerable to strong prevailing winds. Within the arid Southwest, much of the seating should occur under shade structures or tree canopies. However, as many schools use the outdoor classrooms year-round, winter sun might also be appreciated. Choices regarding seat materials must also consider climate, as metals often become too hot in desert environments, and wood splinters and ages poorly. In general, seat selection should consider the body dimensions of the user, comfort, maintenance, and durability. Seating layouts should provide shelter from the wind and sun, take advantage of views, be connected to circulation pathways, and facilitate structured curricular activities as well as unstructured activities.

Walls

Walls have numerous uses in school gardens. These include seat walls, which serve both as seats and walls, and retaining walls, used to hold earth for the creation of terraces or raised planting beds. Walls can be used to display information, create outdoor spaces, frame beautiful views, and screen unsightly ones. As mentioned in Chapter 2, "Design Theory," Japanese moon-gate walls, which have circular view ports or openings that frame objects on the other side, would be particularly useful in wildlife habitat gardens, as wildlife areas could remain relatively undisturbed, yet students would be able to watch wildlife through the moon gate.

Walls can be constructed using many construction methods and materials, including reinforced concrete, concrete block, masonry brick, dry-laid stone, railroad ties, tires filled with soil or concrete, frame and stucco, wood board, gabion, adobe, rammed earth, and straw bale. Adobe, rammed earth, and straw bale, in particular, have benefits related to climate control and the cultural traditions of the Southwest. Opinions regarding material selection vary. For ex-

Stone seat at Meridian Arch entryway, Seattle.

This example of straw-bale construction shows the innovative use of this technique in the outdoor classroom.

The design and construction of adobe walls in outdoor classrooms make good cultural heritage projects.

ample, the authors of *The Straw Bale House* naturally believe that "building walls from straw is much less labor intensive than using other materials such as concrete block, brick, adobe, or stone, and requires considerably less skill. Bale building is forgiving, encourages individual creativity, and leads to final structures that are climatically adapted and energy efficient" (Steen, Steen, and Bainbridge 1994, 22).

Adobe is a traditional building material used in the Southwest by many cultural groups. It is a sun-dried brick (adobe bricks can also be kiln dried) made out of a blend of water, straw, sand, and clay, the latter usually excavated from the site. Adobe bricks are relatively low-strength and have problems associated with their propensity to absorb moisture, but proper maintenance and stabilization of walls will help mitigate most problems identified with adobe. Within the schoolyard project, low-cost adobe construction projects could serve as useful demonstrations of historic building techniques.

In general, wall construction should be a cultural component of the site. Local cultural heritage can be showcased through building materials, building forms, and methods of construction. Donated materials and labor for these potential schoolyard projects will offset the otherwise high construction costs of most walls. Designers will benefit from involving local experts in design and construction.

Walls can retain the earth.

Walls are used to:
- define zones and spaces;
- retain the earth;
- make terraces;
- make raised planting beds;
- frame good views and screen bad ones.

Signs

Signs provide useful information for the garden. They can be *directional,* helping people find their way to and around the site. Way-finding through signage alone, however, will create difficulty. Rachel and Stephen Kaplan (1998, 50) observe, "Way-finding is made easier by having distinctive, differentiable elements. Such elements can be specific objects or places that serve as landmarks. They can also be regions, making it clear that one is in one zone or area as opposed to another. The distinctiveness of such elements, where they are placed, and the number of them are all key aspects of designing for way-finding."

Walls can create terraces.

Signs can be used for *identification* of the zones, spaces, and features within the schoolyard project. They can label a sensitive wildlife area or describe and illustrate the life cycle of one of the bird species living in the habitat garden. Elaborate educational signs are often referred to as *display* signs that provide in-depth information. Display signs make excellent research, design, and construction projects for students.

Sign information can be presented in an artistic and graphic manner, and coordinated with photographs and artwork. The size, shape, and location of the sign is another consideration.

Signage plans can strive to reinforce the hierarchical arrangement of zones and spaces and related experiences. For example, the schoolyard outdoor classroom itself could have a large entry sign that sets it apart from other functions on campus. Within the outdoor classroom, various zones could be identified

Walls can frame views.

with informational signs that reflect their unique character and use. Smaller spaces within the zones could be indicated with smaller signs that continue to define this hierarchical scale. With this approach, the signage plan would help reinforce the spatial order of the site design while adding to the overall understanding of the environment.

Maintenance

Deciding to have an outdoor classroom, wildlife habitat, or any type of natural learning area is an excellent method of connecting students with the outdoors, but outdoor classrooms and gardens of any type require constant maintenance. Gardens can be compared to kitchens in this regard. We would never think of a kitchen as maintenance-free; we know that meal preparation ends with washing dishes, putting leftovers away, and sometimes even mopping the floor. It is much the same with outdoor classrooms and gardens—we have to clean up planted areas, put tools away, and sweep pathways.

Habitat designers will have to write a maintenance plan to address the specific maintenance requirements of the habitat garden. Because the natural environment is dynamic and ever-changing, maintenance of the garden must reflect concerns for natural systems and ecology. Plant forms should be allowed to retain their natural shapes. Manicured lawns and pruned hedges and shrubs are static and not in keeping with the natural environment of the arid Southwest. They should be avoided in the schoolyard classroom, along with poorly adapted or non-native plants. These types of plants will be difficult to sustain and will not promote important values related to arid land ecology.

The following list of maintenance tasks and tips will help ensure a natural and safe outdoor classroom for students, teachers, and wildlife. Students should be involved in maintenance activities, possibly as a part of curriculum components.

Weeding

Weeds are plants that do not meet the needs of wildlife or are harmful to wildlife, other plants, or people. They can threaten beneficial habitat plants and become a fire hazard. Most of the native beneficial plants used in the schoolyard are vulnerable to herbicides, so the safest method of controlling weeds is hand-pulling. Although more time-consuming, this method also allows for a more selective approach to weed removal.

Fertilization

In the school garden, it is important to use slow-release, organic methods of fertilization. Heavy, fast-release fertilizers can kill many of the microorganisms and insects that are beneficial to the health of the soil. An alternative method of fertilization involves enriching the soil with mulch or organic compost. Additionally, beneficial plant materials such as native grasses or trees will improve soil quality over the years. "Mesquite trees have long been known to be nitrogen pumpers," writes Gary Paul Nabhan in *Gathering the Desert*. "That is, their extensive root systems pull in whatever available nitrogen exists in the soil and rock strata below, and it is pumped into the canopy. Leaves and pods falling are

TYPES OF SIGNS
- Directional (top): for way-finding, helping people get where they are going.
- Identification (middle): telling the name of something: the building, the park, or a specific plant within a botanical garden.
- Display of educational information (bottom): such as a list of the wildlife that live in the schoolyard garden, with a description of their particular behaviors and habitat needs.

essentially dumping nitrogen as litter below the canopy, enriching the topsoil" (Nabhan 1985, 72).

Pruning

Heavy pruning removes wildlife food and shelter, and thus it is not appropriate in the wildlife garden. When plants are in bloom or producing fruit, heavy pruning will limit flower and fruit production. Pruning is appropriate for the removal of dead or diseased portions of a plant, as it may rejuvenate these shrubs or trees, or for select branches that create safety hazards. In general, pruning involves the selective removal of whole branches at the base of larger branches (it is not recommended to cut branches in the middle). The natural shape of the tree or shrub should be maintained, and the branches of shrubs should be allowed to make contact with the ground in order to provide wildlife cover.

Moderation is the key in seasonal pruning and cleanup. Many of the materials typically removed from residential gardens are beneficial to the diversity and succession of plant materials and wildlife in the habitat garden. Leave a portion of the organic debris in the habitat area. Clippings of leaves and branches provide good nesting and shelter materials, as do dead trees and rotting logs. Flowers should be allowed to reseed, as this will enrich the next year's crop and provide wildlife with food sources. To add to the dynamic nature of the habitat, retain seedlings and volunteer plants. Although much of the seasonal maintenance deals with retention of beneficial plants and debris, diseased plant material should be removed.

Bird Feeders and Birdbaths

Feeders and nest boxes should be thoroughly cleaned once a year to remove parasites that may build up in old nesting materials. Birdbaths also require regular cleaning, especially in the summer, to remove the buildup of bacteria and parasites.

Accessibility

The natural outdoor classroom provides rich opportunities for study, and it is up to the designers to ensure that all students can use and enjoy it. Thus the design of such a place must include universal accessibility, based on the requirements of the Americans with Disabilities Act, which was established in 1992 by the U.S. Justice Department. The substance of the Act and related design guidelines can be found in the "Americans with Disabilities Act Design Guidelines," available through the Americans with Disabilities Access Board in Washington, D.C. (http://www.access-board.gov). The spirit and intent of the Act is to provide equal access and experience for all individuals, without discrimination or segregation due to variations in ability. These guidelines apply to pathways, ramps, seating, and other functions such as drinking fountains and restrooms.

Requirements

The minimum width for any circulation pathways is thirty-two inches, but forty-eight inches is preferable. If the path is only thirty-two inches wide, a

Schoolyard outdoor classroom designers should develop a maintenance plan—a written document that describes all the specific maintenance needs. Tasks from this maintenance plan should be incorporated in the curriculum so that students will learn the importance of caring for the garden.

Tree and shrub pruning should be minimal, and wherever possible, plants should be allowed to retain their natural shapes to better provide wildlife cover.

The outdoor classroom and other learning gardens must be accessible for everyone.

wheelchair turning and passing zone is required at every two-hundred-foot interval. Pathways should be free of hazards, such as slick surfaces and wet spots created as a result of poor drainage, and pathway surfaces should be hard enough for wheelchair access. They may be constructed from stabilized earth, asphalt, or concrete. The optimal slope of the pathway is 2 percent, and a 5 percent slope is maximum. If the topographic change is greater than 5 percent, a ramp is required. Overhead obstacles are particularly hazardous to individuals with impaired vision.

The site plan must also make accommodations for the parking of wheelchairs within group seating areas. Outdoor wheelchair parking areas typically include a three-by-four-foot concrete pad, accompanied by adjacent seating for peers and a special education teacher.

With respect to water features in the garden, the safety of disabled users must be considered. Wheel stops and railings mitigate the danger of a wheelchair or walker accidentally rolling into the water. Platforms may be needed to allow wheelchair access to water features.

Safety

In the design of places for children, safety issues must be addressed. Administrators, teachers, and parents are very good at identifying these concerns. The *National Action Plan for the Prevention of Playground Injuries* (Thompson and Hudson 2000), developed by the National Program for Playground Safety (NPPS), has created a Playground Maintenance Checklist that outlines many considerations, including general upkeep, ground surface, hazards, equipment deterioration, and hardware security.

General safety concerns for schoolyard projects include inappropriate behavior; accidents during use (perhaps during construction or maintenance projects); outside threats; and shortcomings with the physical environment, such as objects at children's eye levels, slick pavement, misplaced steps, or poor construction techniques. The most critical behavioral concern lies in the lure of ponds for swimming. Safety problems can also arise when children are involved in the construction process, as misplaced tools might become hazards and children might accidentally injure themselves. Unwelcome harmful visitors are another source of danger. These concerns and many others must be addressed in the planning and construction process and on an ongoing basis in conjunction with daily activities. Good maintenance practices, combined with careful supervision, will keep outdoor classrooms and other gardens safe.

Sometimes the designers of playgrounds for children are overly concerned about safety. Afraid to create an unsafe environment, they limit equipment selections and minimize equipment complexity. This actually makes safety issues even more of a problem, as children sometimes invent ways to enhance the dull playground by using it inappropriately.

SAFETY CONCERNS
- Misuse of facilities
- Poor maintenance
- Poor construction
- Objects placed at children's eye levels
- Misplaced tools
- Lack of supervision

Project Evaluation and Revision

Schoolyard natural outdoor classrooms are dynamic living systems for wildlife, students, teachers, and community members. They should not be thought of as fixed, rigid, and manicured landscapes, but as evolving and growing places

Evaluation and revision of the outdoor classroom is essential. These drawings were prepared by students in a workshop in response to questions like: What do you like about your outdoor classroom? What do you not like about your outdoor classroom? How should the garden be changed to make it better?

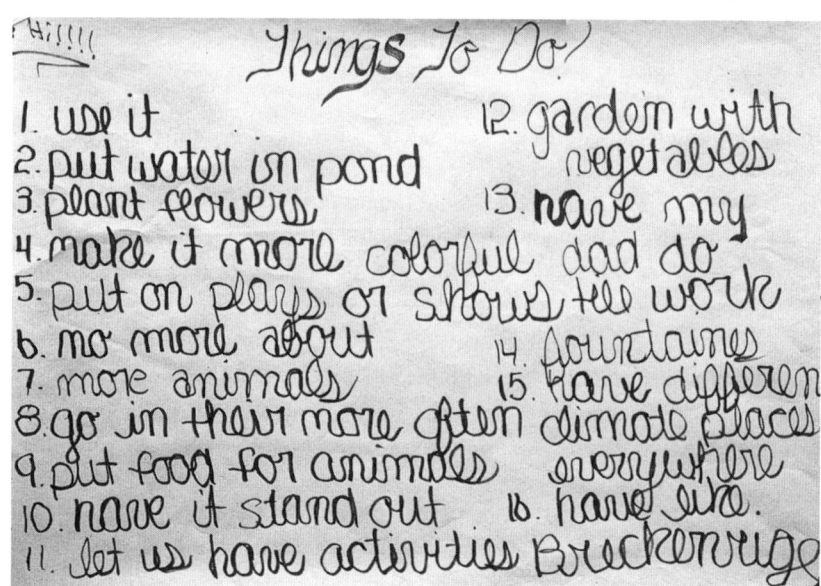

that will need modifications and improvements to better reflect the needs of the changing school population. Ongoing review of the area will help maintain the overall function and quality of the environment for both people and wildlife.

The natural classroom should be evaluated on an annual basis to assess the ecological and environmental conditions, learning and curriculum effectiveness, participant or user appropriateness, and functional and visual qualities of the place. The following "Outdoor Classroom and Schoolyard Habitat Assessment Criteria" have been developed as a basis for the evaluation of existing school learning gardens. Each school should modify this list for specific application to their own project. Portions of this list were modified from Renee Schaefer's (2003) schoolyard assessment criteria.

The annual evaluation will probably reveal strengths and weaknesses in the project. Revisions will be necessary, and perhaps a new site plan will need to be developed. Site boundaries might be expanded, zones or spaces added or

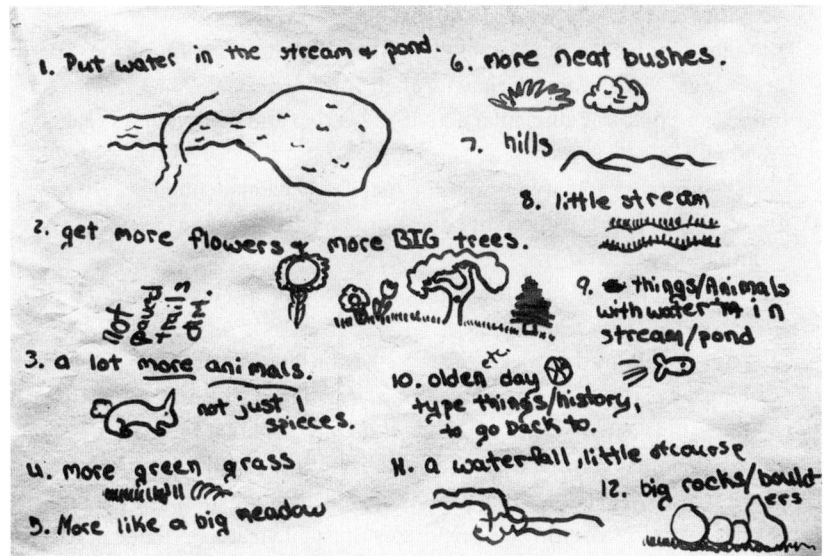

removed. New artworks might be placed in the schoolyard, plants moved, and pathways adjusted so as to constantly improve the learning environment. New teachers, parents, and students should be involved in making design revisions and implementing new ideas. Participating in additions or revisions to the outdoor classroom will make the project meaningful for new users, and will also help hold the interest of returning students as they progress through the grade levels.

Outdoor Classroom and Schoolyard Habitat Assessment Criteria

Ecological/Environmental
The site is well suited to and in harmony with its specific regional context.
The site mitigates hazards and site constraints and maximizes the environmental opportunities of the site.
The site includes examples of ecological aspects of its region within the arid Southwest, such as native plants or rain-harvesting procedures.
The site includes adequate food, shelter, and water for wildlife.
The site uses renewable energy and natural resources (sun, water, wind) efficiently.
Plants within the site are healthy and diverse; many or all are native to the area.
Climate-mitigating features (shade structures, wind screens, rain shelters) occur within the site.
The site emphasizes quiet and buffers noise.
The site enhances views.

Learning/Curriculum
Teachers are using the site as a theme for integrated learning.
The site is being used to teach students about the place where they live through place-based learning activities.

Activities and activity settings support classroom curricula.

The site includes a variety of activity settings (including multipurpose settings) that are appropriate for their intended use.

Indoor and outdoor curricular activities overlap and complement each other.

The site provides activity settings for specific, teacher-defined objectives.

The site addresses the different educational needs of various age groups and both genders.

Students enjoy learning in the outdoor classroom, and teachers find it to be a resource and a teaching asset.

Students are allowed to make creative revisions to the outdoor classroom.

Students have the opportunity to choose learning activities some of the time; some activity settings are *child-defined,* or unstructured.

The site includes some activity settings that allow for wildlife observation.

There are activity settings that encourage socialization among students.

Numerous activity settings incorporate adjustable features (that can be manipulated by users).

The site includes areas that are both accessible and inaccessible to students; that is, portions are secure for wildlife.

Maintenance responsibilities are incorporated into curriculum activities.

Participants/Users

The site design responds to the cultural context of its area or region.

The site offers exhibits and/or demonstrations of historic cultural technologies or practices.

Administrators, teachers, maintenance staff, students, parents, and community members feel a sense of ownership and find the place meaningful.

Everyone feels welcome to use the site.

The site includes activity settings for all users and ages, and increases and promotes interaction among them.

The site has allowances for ongoing revision (design adjustments) and change over time. Administrators, teachers, maintenance staff, students, parents, and community users have opportunities to say what they like and do not like about the outdoor classroom.

The site is appropriate for children.

The site responds to the needs of the neighborhood and is being used by community members.

The site includes private areas for children to find solitude.

The site has a natural area for free exploration.

Conflicts in use are minimal.

Functional

The site is separate from other schoolyard activities that might create conflicts that interfere with teaching and wildlife needs.

The site is well maintained and has a maintenance program.

The site is comfortable: it provides varied and adequate seating and shade.

The site has drinking fountains.

The site accommodates pedestrian access and circulation.

The site has signage for navigating and way-finding.

The site is barrier-free and accessible for wheelchairs.

The site minimizes vandalism through lighting, frequent use, adult supervision, and (possibly) fencing.

The site is a safe place.

Visual Qualities

The site has a unique character and identity.

The overall design layout includes an interconnecting (interlocking) network of zones, spaces, design features, and circulation pathways.

The zones, spaces, design features, and circulation pathways are delineated in a clear and pleasing manner. They are separated or connected appropriately.

The schoolyard demonstrates an overall cohesive design style.

The overall design of the site includes multiple sensory experiences.

The site has a strong visual composition of *design principles:* balance, contrast, diminishing detail, direction, emphasis, figure-ground relationships, movement, overlapping, proportion, repetition, rhythm, scale, transparency, unity, and variety.

The site has a strong visual composition of *design elements:* color, form, light, lines, masses, planes, points, shapes, textures, and volumes.

KIM DUFFEK **CHAPTER 6** # Ecological Principles and Wildlife

Introduction to Wildlife Ecology

Ecology is the pattern of relationships between organisms and their environment. An environment is everything that acts upon an individual or species to shape it, and it contains the elements that ultimately determine survival. Physical factors (such as geologic features and climate), chemical factors (such as soil makeup), and biotic factors (such as plants, animals, and microorganisms) can shape entire biotic communities. All organisms in a biotic community are interrelated in some way, in what many refer to as the web of life.

Local environments are shaped by climate and topography. One need only compare the cool north side of a mountain to the warm south side to understand these forces. In doing so, contrasts in the makeup of plant and animal communities will be observed. Deserts occur primarily in the rain shadow of larger mountain ranges. In these areas, moisture-laden air rises up and over the high slopes, cools, condenses into rain, and falls at the higher elevations. Once the air reaches the far side, or rain shadow, of the mountains, it has lost most of its moisture.

Within these broad environments are small local environments and even microenvironments where species that could not otherwise survive on the hot, dry desert find a place to live. Washes, or arroyos, present conditions that serve the requirements of species adapted to loose soil and higher, intermittent, sometimes violent, water availability. On rocky north-facing slopes, crevices provide shade and shelter for plants and animals not adapted to the harsh open desert. Garden designers can take advantage of shady spots to plant species with different needs than those that thrive in the hot sun. A spot near a roofline or a gutter will support plants with higher water needs. Grouping plants by their needs makes them more likely to thrive.

The survival of any species depends upon the provision of food, water, shelter, and space in its habitat. Habitat is the type of place where a particular plant or animal lives. Some organisms live in a wide variety of places, while others have very limited habitat due to their narrow requirements for existence. At first, it does not seem advantageous for a species to occupy a narrow niche because it will be less likely to survive changes in its environment. But in a stable environment, monopolizing a certain commodity is more advantageous than being a generalist, expending energy in competition with many other species. For any organism to survive in a particular environment it must be able to utilize the resources available. Limited nutrients, moisture, and cover must be adapted to in a harsh desert environment, through either physiological or behavioral traits. For example, the body of a Kangaroo rat (*Dipodomys* sp.) metabolizes the moisture it needs from dry seeds. The Kangaroo rat lives underground in a cool burrow, where it stores its seeds, coming out only at night. The seeds take up a small amount of moisture from being underground. These behavioral traits conserve and trap water. The rodent then metabolizes its food efficiently and excretes urine so concentrated it can crystallize as soon as it contacts the soil. This animal is the epitome of desert survival.

Interdependence occurs when two or more species rely strongly on each other for survival. Bat-pollinated flowers open only at night, excluding daytime pollinators, and also produce the copious quantities of pollen and nectar that long-lived and far-flying nectivorous bats need for survival. Some plants have forged so tight a relationship with a particular animal species that neither could continue to survive without the other. Sometimes it is not so clear. In the northern part of their range, saguaros, which are adapted to bat pollination, keep their flowers open longer into the morning than their southern counterparts, thus attracting a second major pollinator, the white-winged dove. This is advantageous to the plant because the bat's range is limited to the extreme southern Southwest, while the dove's range extends throughout the range of the saguaro. The saguaro is limited in the north by frost.

Studying wildlife ecology is like trying to put together a huge and complex puzzle. Often what seems obvious becomes less so when looked at more closely. An ugly caterpillar that eats garden plants, for example, will metamorphose into a beautiful butterfly that pollinates those same plants.

Some scientific discoveries related to wildlife ecology can be used to benefit humans. The microorganisms that live in bat guano and break down the chitin in old insect parts can help humans convert piles of old shrimp, crab, and lobster exoskeletons into fertilizer. The chemicals produced by a delicate flower can save a person's life. Jojoba fruits produce a compound that can replace whale oil in cosmetics and for machinery lubrication. The possibilities are seemingly endless, as long as we protect what remains of the natural environment. As we lose species, our options become slimmer.

The need to preserve intact habitat is important. A migratory pollinator, such as a rufous hummingbird, a monarch butterfly, or a long-nosed bat, must have migratory corridors with all the necessary provisions for survival available. If a long stretch of natural habitat is destroyed, the animal will run out of energy before it can reach the next available stopover place. In some instances, we are losing critical islands of habitat before their benefits to wildlife are discovered. The piece of habitat may only be used for a few days by a bird, bat, or butterfly species, but it is nonetheless an indispensable stopover site for refueling and rest. We have little understanding of the full consequences of losing one species, as it is difficult to anticipate the ripple effect upon all organisms that indirectly depend upon its actions. Every thread we remove from the web weakens the whole system until it is no longer the healthy, diverse ecosystem it once was. It

White-winged doves pollinate saguaros and disperse seed when feeding chicks. Drawing and photograph by Kim Duffek.

was thought that passenger pigeons, which once filled the sky by the millions, would never go extinct, yet man reduced their numbers below a critical threshold and they perished. There is still so much about the natural world that we need to know.

There are stories to be discovered and lessons to be learned by working in a garden. These lessons are more than ecological: they can be applied to the other sciences, as well as to math, fine art, and writing activities that increase one's perception and problem-solving abilities. There is no better teacher than the natural world because it taps into an inborn curiosity that textbooks cannot always reach. Keeping that wonder alive enriches a life in countless ways and gives one the ability to step back and see the big picture in every facet of life. To bring nature into our world, one simply needs to provide the basic requirements of the species desired.

Elements for Survival

To attract wildlife to a habitat garden, four basic needs must be met: food, water, shelter, and space. If the site is lacking any of these four requirements, animals may visit the garden, but they will probably not linger for long. When houses are constructed, and exotic plants and animals introduced, humans destroy living space for wildlife. A garden can provide refuge in an otherwise harsh urban area. By providing a comfortable refuge in a habitat garden, we make life more possible for at least some wildlife in humankind's world.

Food Resources

Food is necessary for all living things to survive. The way a mountain lion obtains the nutrients essential for its survival is, of course, different from the way a fungus meets its needs. Plants may rely on both the mountain lion and the fungus to provide nutrients in the soil necessary for growth and reproduction.

The soil is actually more alive than most people think. It is made of weathered rock and many microorganisms that break down both organic and inorganic substances into the building blocks that plants use to make roots, stems, leaves, flowers, nectar, pollen, fruit, and seeds. Even fragrance and other chemicals the plant may use for attraction or defense are manufactured from molecules made available from waste products by microorganisms in the ground. In turn, the plants provide food for animals, and the cycle continues.

Wildlife need food, water, shelter, and space to be provided in a habitat garden. Photograph of bamboo fountain by Kim Duffek.

The balance of nutrients in the soil is important for plant health. Plants that grow in a specific soil are adapted to the availability of certain nutrients and the lack of others. In desert environments, the breakdown of sparse dead material contributes a small amount of nitrogen and other chemicals to the soil. Yet, plants that are adapted to growing in these substrates not only survive but thrive.

When these plants are placed in a garden setting, their food resources are usually plentiful, yet imbalances occur. With the use of commercial fertilizers, a plant can actually suffer more from imbalances because the application of these manufactured chemicals kills the microorganisms that fix nitrogen and other nutrients to the plant's root hairs. Nutrients become unavailable to the plants because their beneficial partners are gone.

A better way to keep plants healthy is to feed the microorganisms that feed the plants. This can be accomplished by using compost and organic mulches before problems start. Mulch is slightly decomposed plant trimmings, leaves, and shredded branches. Compost is mulch that has been decomposed by microorganisms into substances that are more immediately available to plants. Worm castings are plant materials that have been broken down by worms. The resulting material is very rich and should be used sparingly. The art of keeping worms for this purpose is called vermiculture. Worm castings and compost should be mixed directly into the soil. Mulch is usually placed on the surface of the soil, around the plants, to hold moisture in the soil. The mulch gradually breaks down through the action of weather and microorganisms, and the nutrients are carried by water into the soil, where they become available to plants. The plants build stronger roots when the soil is healthy, and they will then utilize water more efficiently when it is made available to them.

In an arid environment, a plant that can live with little water on a dry, rocky slope has more opportunity for survival than the water-loving plants competing for space at a small desert seep. Many animals are smaller in the arid Southwest than their northern and eastern cousins, as a smaller animal needs less food and water to stay healthy. Tolerance to drought and dehydration is often necessary in dry climates. Some animals have become specialists in their desert environment. A Kangaroo rat has kidneys that are so efficient that it obtains all the water it needs from metabolizing dry seeds, so it never needs to drink. These rodents are found primarily in the desert and not in urban areas.

Not all animals can tolerate living in close proximity to humans. And not all plants can adapt to horticulture. With loss of natural habitat, we lose organisms with requirements incompatible with the human way of doing things. We can enhance the lives of those wild things that adapt to human encroachment by planting plants that provide essential elements of survival, most importantly, food and shelter. For the others, we need to preserve native natural areas without the intrusion of exotic species.

In your garden, strive to use native plants that provide a diversity of resources over a long season. Dense shrubs that produce edible fruits provide both food and shelter for many animals. The sections that follow on pollinator gardens and wildlife gardens give some guidelines as to what specific animals, such as hummingbirds, seek in your garden. The appendix lists some suitable plants for the various arid bioregions of the Southwest. These lists are by no means complete, and further exploration is encouraged. Finding and studying the makeup of local native biotic communities in various seasons may provide inspiration for the garden design and plant palette. Sometimes, observations from an undisturbed natural drainage can give vital clues to what neighborhood wildlife needs. A field trip to a wild area can provide information on which plants are important to animals. Local ecologists can offer a wealth of information for students planning a habitat garden.

Water Availability

Water is an important element to survival. With it, plants can grow and animals can thrive. The richest concentration of plants and animals in the desert occurs around riparian, or streamside, habitat. This is not an arid environment itself, but is an oasis that provides a critical provisioning place for local and migratory wildlife. When the Santa Cruz River flowed past Tucson over a hundred years ago, cottonwood forests and mesquite woods proliferated around the river and

Water is a critical resource in the arid Southwest. Photograph of river scene by Kim Duffek.

adjacent marshes. Beaver and fish lived year-round in the river as migratory birds flocked there on their annual journeys. Desert-adapted animals found temporary respite in the lush vegetation and cool shade. In the eighteenth century, European people arrived and began cutting many trees for lumber and firewood. They also brought so many cattle that the grasses filling the Tucson Valley would eventually disappear. When a drought hit in the 1880s, starving cattle were moved to the river to eat what they could. The cattle trampled what vegetation still existed, and when heavy rains finally came, the river soil was washed away, for not enough vegetation was left to hold it. What was once a wide, marshy perennial stream is now a channelized dry ditch most of the time. There are people who wish to bring the river back by using treated effluent water. But the water table below Tucson is so low from pumping fossil water from the aquifer for the last one hundred years that most feel that the Santa Cruz near Tucson will never be a river again. This story and others like it have played out all over the West. With the rivers gone, along with the plants and animals they supported year-round, so also went many migratory birds that depended on these green hotels as stopover places to refuel and to rest. The impact extends beyond the American Southwest to the Arctic and down to the Tropics, as birds who were unable to survive their long migratory journeys never returned to their nesting grounds to breed.

Riparian areas are not the only ecosystems diminished by human encroachment. Habitat destruction occurs in our delicate desert areas as well. With every acre of land that is cleared to build houses, the homes of countless organisms are lost. These losses can be mitigated by providing oases for wildlife in habitat gardens. If whole neighborhoods could plant just a corner of each of their yards with wildlife-friendly gardens to create a patchwork of minihavens for wildlife, both the animals' and the humans' lives would be enriched. In addition, the vegetation would create a sound barrier and afford a more peaceful privacy to everyone's backyard.

With ever-increasing population growth, water conservation is becoming very necessary to ensure water for future generations. In fact, the future is now, as communities in the West face critical water restrictions for landscape use in order to provide sufficient water for basic household needs. To mitigate the pressure on western water, we must plant water-thrifty gardens. Animals adapted to the desert do not need a landscape straight out of the tropics. A garden can be fairly lush looking and conserve water at the same time through the planting of appropriate species and proper watering techniques. Lawns are not very useful to wildlife. Ubiquitous American lawns are not only water guzzlers but big polluters as well. The more a lawn is watered and fertilized, the faster it grows and the sooner it needs to be mowed. Gasoline burned in inefficient lawnmower engines contributes to air pollution. Fertilizers and pesticides are applied to the grass to keep it green and weed free. Runoff from treated lawns contributes alarmingly high levels of pollutants to our washes and waterways. If a lawn is considered necessary, there are western drought-adapted lawn grass alternatives (such as buffalo grass and some grama grass species) that need less water and grow more slowly. Organic fertilizers and occasional deep watering will keep the lawn healthy and green.

Wild animals rely heavily on free water to drink, and they will travel great distances daily to obtain it. Swimming pools are attractive to all forms of wildlife, but not all those who come to drink survive when they accidentally fall in. Installing a water feature, which can be as diminutive as a small, steady drip of water onto a concave rock, provides a safer alternative. Although animals can find water outside the habitat garden, having a water feature will attract a great many more of them for greater periods of time. Hummingbirds love to bathe in the splashing droplets when water falls.

Providing Shelter

Shelter is important for every species of terrestrial animal and many plants as well. In nature, the canopy of a tree will provide the protection from cold and heat and predation that a young, tender plant needs to survive. It forms a microclimate where species that could not survive in the open can find refuge. A garden can provide refuge to wild species in an otherwise harsh urban area.

Thick, thorny branches form favored nest sites for cardinals, pyrruloxias, verdins, hummingbirds, thrashers, and cactus wrens. In the desert, many birds, including roadrunners, build their nests in cholla cacti to protect their young from predators. Shrubs such as the desert hackberry provide seasonal food and shelter for birds, mammals, insects, and reptiles.

Observe the vegetative makeup of a local undeveloped area. Are there large trees or shrubs, with another layer of medium-sized shrubs, and then smaller ones below that? Are plants overlapping and growing close to one another, or do they tend to be separately spaced? What differences are there between the top of a hill and the bottom of a drainage? Do different insects and birds, for example, use different types of plants? Are any of the birds eating the insects off a particular plant? Does the plant also provide shelter for resting or nesting? If so, maybe it is a good one to consider for the limited space in your garden.

The key to attracting as many species as possible to your garden is to learn the needs of the local fauna and optimize plantings to suit those needs. Designers will feel more confident in planning a garden if they have firsthand knowledge to draw from. Providing a little shade as well as sun, and high shrubs as well as low ones, will give animals more choices for meeting their needs. The appendix provides information on the characteristics of some commonly available plants.

Building houses for bats and birds is another way to enhance garden habitats. There is little information on the use of bat houses in the Southwest, but prebuilt models and plans are available from many sources. Joining Bat Conservation International's Bat House Project (http://www.batcon.org) would allow students to be involved in a bat-related scientific study on what kinds of artificial roosts bats prefer in different parts of the country. Students should be encouraged to be creative, for they may hit upon the perfect design for a bat house in the Southwest. The "Birding/Wild Birds" section of About.com has information on birdhouses (http://www.birding.about.com). Parameters necessary for birdhouses to attract particular species are well known. Many plans are available to suit the needs of birds seen in the habitat garden. Butterfly houses generally do not work. Most butterflies overwinter as pupae in leaf litter and use other places for temporary shelter.

The best way to provide shelter for wildlife is to plant a diversity of dense trees and shrubs that will attain various mature sizes. Giving animals choices for meeting their needs is essential, because their needs may change from day to day and season to season. Shelter provides a refuge from the elements, predation, and human disturbance.

Desert cottontails can feel at home in a habitat garden. Illustration by Kim Duffek.

Space to Survive

Wild animals also need space. Some animals tolerate the stress of being near humans, and it is easy to provide for these creatures in a garden. Most animals, however, need wild places where the entire web of life is intact, and where plants and animals can interact and provide for each other in a healthy and balanced system.

Unfortunately, many ecosystems are not as they were before humans arrived. Those species that can survive under the pressures of a rapidly changing environment will be the best at adapting. Those that decline under the pressure of change will need human understanding and protection, or they will perish. The easiest, cheapest, and best way of ensuring the survival of wild species is to preserve sufficient healthy habitat before it is destroyed. Trying to put together what is left of the pieces of a broken vessel is much more difficult, if not impossible, than being careful with an intact one.

Careful planning of communities can help protect open space while providing room for urban growth. Cities cannot continue to sprawl into wild areas without compromising the natural attributes that make those cities unique. People must remember the childhood wonder they experienced as they discovered the natural world. Staying connected with that experience provides for open, multilevel thinking in solving problems. Open space is important for relaxation and rejuvenation of the human spirit. In this time when families often live far apart and people move around so frequently, it is important to have the natural world to come home to.

Migratory species of wildlife are particularly hard-hit by habitat destruction. Because these species travel between various countries and through diverse biotic communities, a missing piece in the great puzzle can mean the difference between living and dying for a bird or a bat, or between hunger or feeding, exposure or shelter, exhaustion or being rested. Even a small garden can be an attractive stopover spot for migratory animals. Plan with the big picture in mind, even if your garden is just a small plot of ground. Over the years, people will be amazed at the wealth of wildlife being nurtured from the plants living in a schoolyard, or a backyard, habitat.

Providing food, water, shelter, and space for creatures in the habitat garden is not effortless, but what effort it requires is amply rewarded by the rich experiences to be had there. Contributing to the health of the wild creatures present in the urban environment contributes to the health of the planet. One person's actions may seem a small contribution, but, collectively, a great many small deeds add up to something of significance.

To attract particular species of animals, one must understand their special needs. The next section addresses the requirements of some specific animal groups, which will enable the designer to create gardens for pollinators and other wildlife.

Pollinator Gardens and Wild Visitors

Introduction

Pollinators come in many shapes and sizes, and they vary in their habits and abilities. Flowers also come in many forms, often shaped by the preferences of a specific pollinator. These partnerships provide for efficient transfer of pollen from one plant to another, which ensures diversity in the plant population. In return, the pollinators are rewarded, usually in the form of nectar. We often create gardens with hummingbirds or butterflies in mind, but moths, bees, and, in some areas, bats, perform important pollination services for food plants critical not only to wild animals but to humans as well. Many common food crops rely on pollination by insects, particularly bees. Throughout the world, important fruit and lumber plants worth billions of dollars annually rely on bats for pollination.

The shape of a flower correlates with the type of pollination strategy it employs. A wind-pollinated plant lacks showy petals and nectar rewards, and the pollen is abundant but small so that it can drift easily on the wind. At some point during the Mesozoic era, which was the age of dinosaurs, insects such as beetles started eating the pollen and inadvertently transferring some of it to other flowers. Plants developed strategies not only to cope with the theft but to exploit this situation. Over time, speciation occurred in flowering plants when

Pollinator gardens provide excellent learning opportunities in the outdoor classroom.

genetic variation created a flower that was more attractive to a particular pollinator species. The success of that flower in producing seeds led its offspring to be attractive to the same pollinator, a trend that continued until many flowers took on special shapes, and produced less pollen and more nectar to attract the animal species they had seduced through the generations.

Plants that attract particular pollinators tend to bloom during times of the year when the animal is present. Many hummingbird flowers in the Southwest bloom in spring and fall when the largest number of these birds are migrating through the area. Bat plants flower in sequence from south to north in spring, and from north to south in the fall, as the bats follow their migratory route. Insect-pollinated plants bloom when their pollinators will be present in greatest abundance, mostly in the warmth of summer.

Gardens created to attract specific pollinators should be rich with other organisms that contribute to natural processes. A healthy garden requires seed dispersers, predators, and decomposers to complete the web of life. Depending upon the location of a site and its surrounding conditions, the diversity could be high or low. Some sites may yield surprising visitors. Remember that gardens are not static, but are constantly changing. Plants grow and die and reseed themselves. Wild visitors come and go. What follows is an overview of some common pollinators and what is necessary to attract them, as well as descriptions of some other guests that may be discovered in the vicinity of the habitat garden.

Hummingbird Gardens

Hummingbirds are agile creatures with the ability to hover, and even to fly backward. Most North American species nest in the United States and Canada during the summer, then migrate south to escape the cold and shortage of food during the winter. Therefore, if a southwestern flower depends upon hummingbirds as pollinators, the best times for the plant to bloom are spring and fall and, to a lesser extent, summer.

The forms of flowers attractive to hummingbirds adhere to a general pattern that was molded by the characteristics of these tiny birds. The eyes of these

Costa's hummingbirds visit red tubular flowers. Illustration by Kim Duffek.

Hummingbird gardens make great additions to the schoolyard. Flower photograph by Kim Duffek.

avian wonders are adept at seeing red; therefore, a plant that tends to run to red in color would better catch the attention of passing hummingbirds. To exclude other potential visitors, hummingbird flowers are deeply tubular in shape. Only a hummingbird's long, narrow bill can reach the nectar reward at the bottom. Anthers in these flowers are strategically located above the floral tube to transfer pollen to the head of visiting hummingbirds. As the bird travels from blossom to blossom, the pollen is rubbed off its head onto the pistils of other flowers. The partnership ensures that the pollen is more often transferred to the same species of plant.

A garden for hummingbirds needs plants with nectar-filled red tubular flowers to meet the needs of these high-energy birds (the appendix provides a list of plants in specific regions that attract hummingbirds). Nectar high in sugar is important, but protein is also critical to their survival. They obtain protein by eating small arthropods such as gnats and very small spiders. The birds are also very sensitive to pesticides and other chemicals, so none should be used on or near the plants in the hummingbird garden. A small, shallow pool with a gentle trickle of clean, splashing water will be used regularly by the birds for bathing. Hummingbirds also like some shade and a place to retreat, so trees in and around your garden will provide the birds with additional benefit. Females usually seek out dense shrubs to build their nests of spider webs and other materials.

Hummingbirds are territorial around food sources. In the wild, males will defend a good patch of flowers from other hummingbirds (watching the social dynamics around a feeder is entertaining and educational). Try placing several feeders in various locations with visual barriers between them to determine which placement best reduces competition for the most feeders by one bird. Keep in mind that because hummingbirds are visual animals, a large shrub or corner of a building can serve as a divider for territories of competing hummingbirds.

To make nectar for your feeder, boil four cups of water, then add one cup of cane sugar, and stir until dissolved (red food coloring is not needed and may harm the birds). You can store the mixture in the refrigerator for up to a week.

Hummingbird Feeders: Supplemental nectar will not hurt hummingbirds as long as the feeder is kept clean and filled with fresh nectar. Deadly bacteria can grow in old sugar water and on the inside of a dirty feeder, so proper maintenance is essential. Rinse the feeder and change the nectar daily. On a weekly basis, or sooner if mold is observed, clean the feeder with bleach solution, rinse it, and let it dry completely before refilling with fresh nectar.

Hummingbird Basics
Plant reddish, tubular-shaped flowers as high-energy nectar sources.
Plan the garden to have various species of plants that will provide a long season of blooms.
Do not use pesticides and other chemicals.
Preserve leaf litter as a place for small insects that the birds can eat.
Plant dense, shady trees and shrubs for nesting and resting.
Provide a trickle of clean water for bathing.

Butterfly Gardens

Butterflies are both fun and relaxing to watch. Most members of the butterfly family in the arid Southwest are rather sedentary, although occasionally they may wander. As summer progresses and insect numbers increase, many butterfly populations slowly expand northward. Some, such as the monarch, are truly migratory. If a garden is agreeable to butterflies, several species will probably make it their home.

Butterflies have four stages of development: egg, caterpillar, chrysalis, and adult, in that order. The needs of the animals during two of these stages must be met to ensure that butterflies are present on a regular basis in the garden. First, of course, nectar must be provided for the adults. Flowers that attract butterflies will have a landing pad with short tubes leading to the nectar. Most insects do not see the color red, but the color-range vision of butterflies is considered to be greater than that of any other animal, and ultraviolet (vc) color, which is invisible to humans, is found on both butterfly plants and butterflies. Flowers that are both yellow and open in structure seem to attract butterflies most often, but mass plantings of color located in the sun will draw many butterflies. Butterflies also need cool, shady, preferably moist spots in which to rest. Protection from the wind will keep them more active in your garden.

The larvae, or caterpillars, of each species feed on specific host plants. Many butterflies have only one host plant species on which their offspring depend for survival. The adult female will deposit a few eggs on a plant appropriate for

Southern dogface butterflies lay their eggs on *Dalea* species. Illustration by Kim Duffek.

Monarch butterflies migrate over long distances. Illustration by Kim Duffek.

Migratory Monarchs: Monarchs are the only butterflies in the world known to migrate to specific overwintering sites each year. In the spring and fall, these amazing insects travel great distances to reach favored territory. In the northern reaches of North America, and during migration, monarchs mate and the females lay eggs on milkweed plants. Monarch caterpillars feed only on this family of plants. Adult monarchs migrate south in the fall, to overwinter in California, Florida, and central Mexico. During the journey, the butterflies rely on nectar-rich flowers to provide the energy needed to make the long trek. However, habitat destruction is putting the monarch species in peril: Deforestation and land development are destroying the plants that these incredible insects depend on for survival. There is much about monarch migration that is still unknown, especially in the arid Southwest. Schoolchildren can become young scientists by observing and reporting monarch sightings. For more information, visit the Desert Museum's Web site at http://desertmuseum.org/pollination/index.html (accessed August 7, 2007).

its hatchlings. In the appendix, some known larval host plants are identified for each region. Many people view caterpillars as destructive pests that eat the leaves from their lovely plants, but they fail to notice that the so-called pests transform into the lovely butterflies they enjoy. Furthermore, plants in a healthy garden usually recover from even heavy nibbling by caterpillars.

Butterfly Basics

Plant your garden in a sunny location, with some shade available.
Protect your garden from wind.
Provide a puddle.
Plant food sources for caterpillars and nectar sources for adults.
Pack flowers into masses of individual colors.
Do not use pesticides.

Bee Gardens

Bees exhibit amazing diversity and provide billions of dollars in free services to our world economy. About 80 percent of the plants in the desert Southwest and at least 30 percent of our agricultural crops are dependant upon bees for pollination. Unlike non-native European and African honey bees, which form large colonies, native bees in the United States tend to live in small groups or, more often, are solitary in their nesting habits.

There are over one thousand species of bees in the arid Southwest, a diversity greater than in tropical forests. Bees are mostly herbivorous, collecting pollen and nectar from flowers to feed themselves and to provision their young. The eyes of bees can detect ultraviolet, blue, and yellow. Many bee-pollinated plants are yellow and have UV nectar guides leading to the nectar source in the flower. The predominance of bees is reflected in the number of desert plants that have yellow flowers. Some of the plants that attract bees are noted in the appendix.

In addition to yellow or blue flowers as a food source, bees need sites to raise their young. Many bees, including orchard mason bees (which are important crop pollinators), nest in old beetle burrows in the dead or dying wood of old trees. Artificial nests for bees can be made by drilling soda-straw-sized holes

Bee pollination is necessary for food production.

in blocks of wood. The bee blocks are then hung around the garden, providing places for females to lay their eggs.

Africanized bees, which have established themselves in the southwestern United States, are not aggressive near flowers. Although they will sting in self-defense, they will only attack when defending their nests, which are made in spaces such as those found in hollow trees. They will not use bee houses made for native bees.

Pesticides are deadly to bees and other living things even if they are not the targets. Spraying for mosquitoes actually increases mosquito populations by killing off the predators that would normally keep the blood-sucking insects at reasonable levels. It also kills pollinators (Williams 2001, 38–47).

Bee nest blocks can be constructed out of four-by-six-inch untreated lumber. Drill holes that are five-sixteenths of an inch wide, about four inches deep, and set on three-quarter-inch centers. Do not drill the holes completely through the lumber. Try to hang the blocks firmly where they will receive morning sun. The bees also need mud available to them to build the partitions, so provide a small mud puddle as well.

Bee Basics
Plant yellow and blue flowers.
Provide nesting places.
Do not use pesticides.
Provide a mud puddle.

Moth Gardens

Moths are more often viewed as ugly pests than as beautiful and beneficial insects, but moths and their caterpillars feed many a hungry wasp, spider, bird, and bat. Many moths are actually quite beautifully patterned, not just with browns and grays but with pink and yellow and black and white.

There are over three thousand species of moths in the Southwest, and many beautiful flowers attract these mostly nocturnal insects (some are noted in the appendix). A few flowers, such as datura, have such deep flower tubes that only those species of sphinx moths with a very long, four-inch proboscis can reach the nectar and pollinate the plant. Sphinx moths can often be seen feeding on flowers at dusk and dawn and on cloudy days. Other moths and plants are totally dependent on one another. This is true with yucca moths and senita moths. These animals live their entire lives on or near their host plants, and the plants must have these moths present in order to produce fruit and seed.

Moths smell with their antennae, and many have ears on their abdomens. In general, a moth will pick up the sweet, strong scent of a night-blooming flower and follow the trail until it can see the target. As a moth's vision is finely tuned to seeing in darkness, its host flowers are white or pale in coloration, attracting the animal to the food source. Some species of moths can be lured to a bait station by painting a fermented mixture of rotting fruit, bread, and sugar or molasses onto a log or board.

Like butterflies, moth caterpillars often have a limited number of plant species that they consume. Moth caterpillars are voracious herbivores, and many plants have responded by producing poisonous chemicals to protect themselves. The caterpillars that eat the plants, however, either remove these chemicals from their bodies or utilize them as poisons to ward off hungry predators. This arms

Homes for the Small and Solitary: A small, blue-black bee native to most of our country is the gentle and beneficial Orchard Mason Bee (*Osmia* spp.). It is active in spring and pollinates not only native plants but economically valuable fruits, flowers, and vegetables as well. The females make nests in old insect holes and hollow twigs. They first collect pollen and nectar and form it into a ball. The food ball is packed into the tube, then an egg is laid upon it. The female bee then builds a wall of mud in front of the food ball and egg to seal off the cell. More cells are built until the tube is full.

Orchard mason bees are excellent pollinators of food crops. Illustration by Kim Duffek.

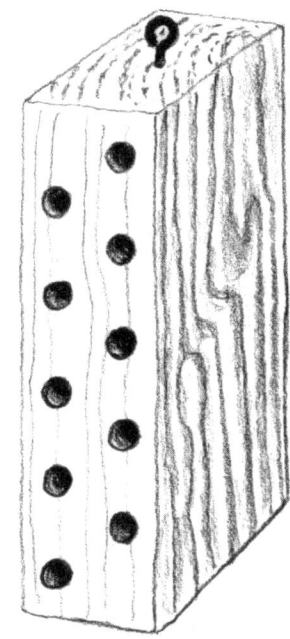

Bee blocks can easily be constructed. Illustration by Kim Duffek.

White-lined sphinx moths pollinate deep, night-blooming flowers. Illustration by Kim Duffek.

Mutualism: One of the closest relationships between plants and moths is the partnership between yucca plants and yucca moths. These species have developed such a close relationship that neither could survive without the other. After mating, the female yucca moth finds an open yucca flower and begins providing for her young by making a ball of pollen with her specialized mouth parts. She then carries this pollen ball to another flower, lays a few eggs in the ovary of the flower, and stuffs the pollen into the stigma. This ensures pollination of the flower and the development of seeds, some of which are eaten by the growing caterpillars. When the moth caterpillars are fully grown, they chew a small hole through the wall of the yucca seed capsule, crawl out, and drop to the ground on silken threads. They burrow under the soil at the base of the yucca plant and spin a cocoon in which they pupate until spring, when the cycle starts all over again.

race takes many forms and is fascinating to study. Many of the chemical defenses used by plants and moths are utilized by humans in medicine and other beneficial products.

Moth Basics

Plant light-colored, sweet-scented night-blooming flowers.
Provide bait stations for attracting more species.
Plant larval food plants for caterpillars.
Do not use pesticides.

Bat Gardens

Bats are amazingly diverse creatures. There are over one thousand species of these mammals in the world, and they eat everything from pollen, nectar, and fruit to fish, frogs, and small mammals. Most bats in North America eat insects. There are three species of nectivorous (nectar-feeding) bats that range into the United States in small areas near the Mexican border: the Mexican long-tongued bat, the lesser long-nosed bat, and the Mexican long-nosed bat. For North American bats, these animals are large, with a wingspan of fourteen to sixteen inches. If your garden is in or near Tucson, Phoenix, Sierra Vista, San Diego, or Big Bend, it may be worth planting a bat garden. For a few suggestions of bat-pollinated plants, see the appendix.

Long-nosed bats pollinate some Agaves and Saguaro cacti. Photographs by Jeff Medkeff; courtesy of Jeff Medkeff. Bat illustration by Kim Duffek.

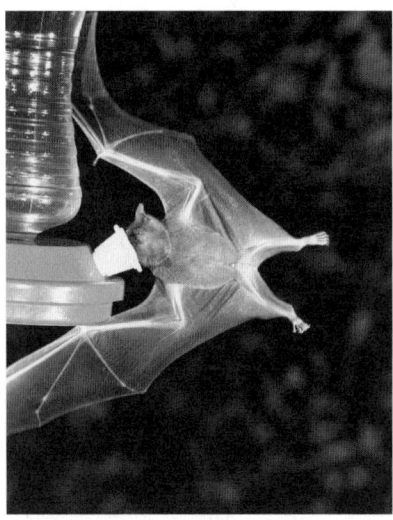

Bat flowers are light pink or white. Blooming at night, they attract bats with their light color and a musky-sweet scent. The flowers are borne high up and in the open on stems or stalks, where the bats can reach them, and are built sturdily enough to withstand the weight of these relatively heavy animals. All three of the species of nectivorous bats ranging into our area have large eyes with good night vision, and a keen sense of smell. To find food, they use both senses. Unlike the insectivorous bats in our region, the pollinators have weakly developed echolocational abilities, using this skill to navigate inside their roosts more often than in foraging for food.

Both listed as endangered, the lesser and Mexican long-nosed bats roost in warm caves and mines, where one roost can be home to thousands of these bats, mostly females and their young. The Mexican long-tongued bat can often be found in small numbers in shallow rock shelters or near the entrance to a cave or mine. Sometimes old buildings are used as roosts, especially during the night, when the bats rest between foraging bouts. All three species migrate to central and southern Mexico for the winter, where tropical plants provide food for them. They migrate north for the summer to escape competition from other bats for limited food sources and to have their young.

The flowers attractive to bats provide copious quantities of nectar and protein-rich pollen to support the health of these long-lived animals. Having only one young a year, bats rely on quality maternal care and the relative safety of the night and of their roost for survival. Unfortunately, with so much misunderstanding regarding bats, humans have become the largest threat to bats throughout the world.

Bats of all species are suffering from habitat loss. As the quality of the ecosystems they inhabit is degraded and their roosts are destroyed, lost are some very important but unknown neighbors. Bats are beneficial in many ways. They pollinate some of the foods that we eat and devour the insects that eat our commercial food crops. To learn more, visit Bat Conservation International's web site at www.batcon.org.

Bats and Hummingbird Feeders: Some lucky people within the range of nectivorous bats report finding their hummingbird feeders drained of nectar during the night. If they stay up and watch, they may witness bats circling their feeders in small flocks, taking turns at slurping up the sweet nectar. There was concern that the bats would suffer if they drank only sugar water and did not eat enough pollen to give them the protein and amino acids they needed for staying healthy, but the bats seem to be visiting the flowers as well.

Bat Basics
Plant plants with night-blooming, heavy-structured, musky-scented flowers.
Provide open space for the bats to fly in.
Preserve overhangs on buildings that may be used as rest stops.
Do not use pesticides.

Fly Gardens

No discussion of pollinators would be complete without the mention of flies as pollinators. Flies are as fascinating and diverse as any other animal group, with habits ranging from providing live flesh for parasitic offspring to sipping nectar from flowers. If a flower smells like sweet, rotting flesh, it is probably trying to attract flies to pollinate it. Many exotic plants, some with bizarre flowers, could be used to demonstrate the role of flies as pollinators. Stinky and gross are always a hit with kids. A local entomologist may be able to help identify fly-pollinated flowers native to the area.

Desert tortoise habitats are good additions to the schoolyard. Desert tortoises distribute saguaro seeds after eating the fruit. Tortoise photograph and illustration by Kim Duffek.

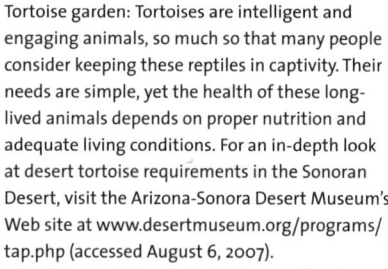

Tortoise garden: Tortoises are intelligent and engaging animals, so much so that many people consider keeping these reptiles in captivity. Their needs are simple, yet the health of these long-lived animals depends on proper nutrition and adequate living conditions. For an in-depth look at desert tortoise requirements in the Sonoran Desert, visit the Arizona-Sonora Desert Museum's Web site at www.desertmuseum.org/programs/tap.php (accessed August 6, 2007).

Wild populations of tortoises are threatened due to habitat degradation and introduced respiratory disease, therefore they must never be taken from the wild nor should captive-born tortoises be released into the wild. Laws and regulations regarding the possession of tortoises vary from state to state. Contact your state's game and fish department for more information.

Wildlife Gardens

Wildlife species vary in their needs. They come in all sizes and forms and utilize different food and shelter in an effort to reduce competition. Imagine if all animals ate nothing but apples: there would not be enough food and most would perish. Instead, herbivores often specialize in eating grass, twigs, fruit, or roots, while carnivores specialize in catching and consuming prey suited to their sizes and abilities. Seasonal food availability can alter an animal's diet. For example, American kestrels feed on insects during the summer, and rodents and sparrow-sized birds in the winter. Quail will eat dry seeds through most of the year, but they consume nutrient-rich spring wildflower seedlings prior to nesting.

An important part of plant survival depends on seeds being dispersed to locations where conditions are favorable for growth and reproduction. Animals such as coyotes, bats, tortoises, and birds eat the fruits offered by many plants and pass the seeds, dropping them with a bit of fertilizer in areas away from the mother plant. Rodents often eat seeds, killing them in the process. But squirrels and mice have a habit of storing seeds in the ground and forgetting them, so that the seeds have an opportunity to grow where they have been buried. White-winged doves often drop saguaro seeds under their nest while feeding jostling chicks, aiding the young saguaro's establishment under a suitable nurse plant. Some ant species also move seeds from place to place, but the vast majority of the seeds they collect are eaten.

Gardens for birds and other wildlife include plants that provide fruits, seeds, and berries. Trees and large shrubs, providing shade and shelter, should be integrated into the garden plan. Locate a source of clean water away from dense shrubs where predators such as house cats may lurk. Plant species of differing sizes and fruiting seasons to meet the varying needs of diverse wildlife species.

Wildlife Basics
Plant a diversity of fruiting plants.
Provide a clean water source.
Plant dense shrubs and trees for cover.
Do not use pesticides.

Completing the Web

Pest Control

A healthy ecosystem has built-in controls to balance nature. For example, without predators such as wolves and mountain lions, deer populations rise unchecked. Too many hungry deer decimate plant populations and, as a consequence, the deer slowly starve to death while destroying the habitat they need to survive. People tend to have a less romantic view of caterpillars starving to death, but the same scenario holds true if predators are not present to keep the insects under control. Possible predators in a southwestern garden include lizards, predacious insects, bats, birds, snakes, foxes, and coyotes. Skunks, armadillos, and raccoons can help by eating pests, or they can do damage with their digging. All of these animals are part of the dynamics of a garden.

Often today, pest control is equated with pesticides. Pesticides are harmful to all living things. When a pest is found in the garden or habitat, it is best to take a wait-and-see approach for a few days before taking any action. And, if action is taken, water spray should be the first weapon. Daily hosing off of the plants infested with pests will often control the problem sufficiently while allowing the predators to escape. Remember that a wildlife habitat garden should reflect the dynamics of the natural world.

Skunks eat pests but also cause damage. Illustration by Kim Duffek.

All over the West, bridges and abandoned mines provide safe harbor for a number of species of bats. A growing number of communities recognize these creatures as allies in the control of mosquitoes and crop pests. Some of the most famous bridge bats—and valued city residents—are the Mexican free-tailed bats that roost under the Congress Avenue Bridge in Austin, Texas. Residents and visitors will reserve restaurant tables early or set up picnics on the lawn along the waterfront during the summer months to watch the bats emerge for their evening of foraging. This enthusiasm for bats would not have existed if one man, Merlin Tuttle, founder of Bat Conservation International, had not worked hard to forge a public understanding of the importance of this resource to the community. In fact, this large colony of bats would have been removed from the bridge permanently if the people of Austin had not been educated about bats. This example holds true in other communities where education concerning bats is an integral part of the planning process.

Preserving bat roosts can be easy. Some bats do not need large structures. The Southwest's species of bats are varied in their eating and roosting habits. Big brown bats are often urban dwellers that specialize in eating beetle pests, and they will roost in anything from a hole in a saguaro cactus to the attic of an old house. The Southwest's smallest bat, the western pipistrelle, roosts singly or in small numbers, often behind loose bark and boards and sometimes in holes in the ground.

The tiny western pipistrelle bat can eat up to six hundred mosquitoes in an hour. Illustration by Kim Duffek.

Bats should be welcome in the garden, as they are an effective means of pest control. Pipistrelle bats can eat hundreds of mosquitoes in an hour. A colony of Mexican free-tailed bats can consume literally tons of corn earworm moths a night, reducing farmers' dependence on pesticides. Bat houses may be used seasonally by bats in some areas.

Other small predators such as lizards, snakes, insects, and birds are easily welcomed into a habitat garden. Providing the necessities for lizards, snakes, and insects is simple, as they can hide in small spaces. Lizards need leaf litter and small crevices such as those under rocks to hide in, and insect pests to eat. They will lick water droplets off rocks and leaves. Lizards in the Southwest can be long, narrow, and smooth, such as the whiptail lizards, or, as with the horned lizards, they can be flat, spiky, and pancakelike. Most of the lizards in the desert Southwest are insectivores. Some, like the horned lizards, which eat ants, can be quite specialized.

Snakes are often maligned, but they are amazingly diverse in their habits. Most snakes, such as kingsnakes and gopher snakes, are generalists, eating mostly rodents but also eggs, birds, lizards, and other snakes. Some snakes are very specialized. Blind snakes spend most of the time underground and are seen occasionally after a rain searching for termite and ant burrows, where they feed. Coral snakes are small predators of other small snakes such as blind snakes. Although their venom is similar to that of a cobra's, the small mouths and tiny fangs of the coral snake greatly reduce their danger to humans. Many snakes in the Southwest mimic the red, yellow, and black warning coloration possessed by the coral snake. Longnose and western shovelnose snakes are often mistaken for coral snakes. Nonvenomous gopher snakes are often mistaken for rattlesnakes, due to their coloration and habit of shaking their tail when threatened. They are valuable predators of rodents and are harmless to humans. Rattlesnakes, of which there are twelve species in the southwestern United States, are highly specialized predators of small mammals. They possess heat-sensing pits on their faces and a sophisticated venom and delivery system for subduing rats and mice. Although a rattlesnake in the schoolyard is unacceptable, it is important to remember that they, as all snakes, are a natural part of maintaining balance in the wild ecosystem.

In sheer numbers, the largest component of an ecosystem is the insects. Predatory insects are diverse. Dragonflies need a small pond in which to lay their eggs. Assassin bugs simply need a place to ambush other arthropods, as both larvae and adults are carnivorous. Praying mantids need vegetation in which to hide and branches on which to make their egg cases, which resemble tiny loaves of sliced bread. Remember that all these creatures are susceptible to pesticides and that such harmful chemicals should be avoided in a habitat garden.

Larger terrestrial predators such as foxes and coyotes may be present in an urban area. They eat rodents, rabbits, birds, snakes, and fruit. It is always a thrill to witness the appearance of one of these canids. In towns and cities, medium-sized predators can coexist with humans if sufficient natural areas are available, but should deliberate feeding occur, these animals will lose their wariness of humans, and trouble, including bites, can happen. This usually results in the animal being relocated or killed, a measure that would not have been necessary had the individual been left to be wild. It is best to enjoy wildlife from a distance.

Although some groups of birds, such as the sparrows, eat seeds, many birds supplement their varied diet with energy-rich insects. A number of southwestern birds are predators of insects and other arthropods. Hummingbirds, known for their consumption of flower nectar, catch many gnats and small spiders for their protein source. Cactus wrens relish large moths and cicadas as a part of their diet. A roadrunner may be seen picking caterpillars off a plant as often as it is glimpsed pursuing a lizard, a snake, or a mouse.

Large avian predators such as hawks and owls may visit the garden to hunt for prey. If sufficient sites are available, some may even nest nearby. Cooper's hawks, Harris's hawks, peregrine falcons, and American kestrels are diurnal raptors that sometimes make their home in an urban setting. Although the

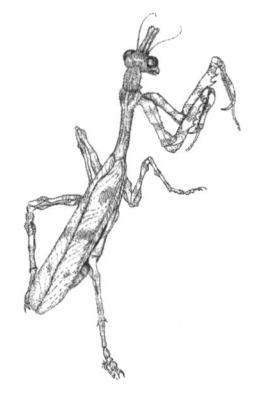

Unicorn mantids prey on other insects. Illustration by Kim Duffek.

peregrine and the kestrel are both falcons, they are very different in size. Peregrines will often feed on the abundant non-native pigeons that are considered pests in many urban areas. Kestrels, being much smaller, will eat insects in the summer and small animals such as mice and sparrows in the winter. Cooper's hawks often hunt birds in dense vegetation, but will also add excitement at the bird feeder. Limited to a small range in the United States, but fairly common south to the tropics, Harris's hawks are unique raptors in that they hunt in groups the way wolves hunt in packs. Only one other raptor species in the world, the Galapagos hawk, shares this amazing social structure. Harris's hawks hunt mostly rabbits and small rodents. Other raptors may visit urban areas as well.

Owl species most often seen in urban areas are the great horned owls and screech owls. These nocturnal raptors will occasionally nest in urban areas. The great horned owl will use the nests that hawks build. The screech owl is a cavity nester that needs holes in trees or nest boxes in which to raise young. Great horned owls will eat anything from scorpions to skunks. The ferocious little screech owl will capture anything up to the size of a quail. The diet of an owl can be studied by examining regurgitated pellets, which consist of indigestible animal parts such as bones, feathers, and fur. Unlike hawks, owls swallow their prey whole or in large pieces. Usually an owl regurgitates a pellet before it goes feeding at night, leaving a clue to its favorite roosting spot for an observant person to find.

Although some may see the habits of birds of prey as horrifying, it must be remembered that these avian hunters contribute to the balance of life. They are teachers of our children as well, since death is inescapably a part of life. All must eat to survive.

Born to Be Wild: Although Nature and its creatures are the best teachers, handling, approaching, or harassing an animal puts stress on it, so these activities should be limited. Even a wild animal in captivity requires this respect. Overvisitation to a bird's nest may cause the parents to abandon the nest. Normally an animal will avoid being approached too closely. If an animal is acting oddly, it may be sick. Never handle a sick animal, as it may bite or scratch, and, in the process, potentially pass on the disease to the handler.

Decomposition

The recycling of nutrients through the food chain is critical to life. These chemicals must return to the soil so that new plants can utilize them for growth. Decomposition can start when a plant is eaten by a herbivore and the unused, indigestible portion is passed through. Beetles and crickets eat and digest decaying plant material. Bacteria and fungi work to further break down the plant matter, but in the arid Southwest a lack of moisture inhibits these actions. Enter the heroes of the desert ecosystem: termites. Termites live in subterranean colonies protected from the dry desert air. Within their gut live bacteria that break down cellulose into mostly sugar, which the termites use as food. Every termite born has to ingest some of the bacteria from its relatives in order to survive. Contrary to popular thought, not every termite species is attracted to the wood in houses. Many termites envelop dead sticks and grasses in mud to protect themselves from drying out and from predation. They then devour the old plant material inside. Very few termite species do damage to human structures. Take the time to learn about native termites in your area. Without termites, the dry land we live in would be littered with dead wood, the soil would be depleted of nutrients, and nothing could survive.

Unwanted Visitors

Our view of a perfect garden sometimes suffers from the desires of the wild creatures that visit it. When we create a lush retreat for ourselves and for the

Rattlesnakes in a schoolyard should be removed to a safe place by trained professionals.

animals we wish to attract, we also make a cool retreat for unwanted and even potentially dangerous animals as well. Rattlesnakes are a concern in areas where your garden is in close proximity to native habitat. These sophisticated snakes are not looking to make a meal of humans. The venom they create is very expensive for them to make (in terms of energy expended) and is necessary for them to be able to subdue their prey. They would prefer not to waste it on someone who was too big to eat. A snake would rather slip away unnoticed and avoid contact with large animals such as ourselves, whom they consider potentially dangerous. Leaving a rattlesnake in a schoolyard habitat is not an option. Trained professionals, such as fire department personnel, should move the snake to a safe place nearby. Rattlesnakes are excellent rodent controllers and have their place in the web of life.

Microscopic visitors in the form of bacteria, viruses, and fungi can pose an invisible threat to the animals attracted to the garden. Not all microorganisms are bad; in fact, most are beneficial and necessary to other life. But there are some that are potentially deadly. Water sources and feeders should be cleaned regularly with bleach to avoid contamination from droppings of sick animals and from bacteria that could spread disease under unsanitary conditions.

As for visible pests, if possible, tolerate unwanted guests. Eventually, a balance may be struck. Many plants can tolerate much damage from insects and still recover when the pests' numbers decline. If you have too many caterpillars, know that there are parasitic wasps that will eventually prey on some of the caterpillars and strike a balance in your garden. In the meantime, you can pick off some of the excess caterpillars from overly damaged plants. Should an outbreak of insect pests occur on a few plants, try spraying the pests off with water on a regular basis to keep their numbers down. In difficult cases, a solution of soap (such as Palmolive or Dawn or natural dish soap) can be sprayed onto the affected plants. Remember, this will also kill any predators and caterpillars that cannot escape the spray. Be sure to spray in the cool part of the day so as not to burn the leaves of the plant. Much information on managing pests is available in natural gardening books and magazines.

Rodents and rabbits, skunks and raccoons, even deer and javelina, can cause damage to a garden. A well-watered garden is like a salad bar to wild animals. To solve problems with unwanted vegetarian guests, either different kinds of plants may need to be planted or fences may need to be installed. Eventually, suitable results will be achieved if the needs of the garden and the pressures put on it by hungry animals are observed and compensated for.

Seeds for Thought

The natural world is infinitely filled with lessons to be learned. For every question answered, nature offers up dozens of new questions. Because the web of life is so intricately balanced, the stories can be complex. A six-year-old and a sixteen-year-old may look for answers to the same question, and their exploration can be as in-depth as the mind can accommodate.

From writing to mathematics, teaching through an outdoor classroom requires a twist on the normal lessons in a given curriculum. Since nature provides any number of ways to look at the world, there are numerous ways to use this environment as an opportunity for learning. What follows are just a very few examples of activity ideas for teaching outdoors.

Pollination Strategies: Explore the reasons why flowers come in so many shapes, sizes, and colors by looking at the shapes, habits, and needs of various pollinators such as hummingbirds, bees, moths, bats, and butterflies. These animals help move pollen from one plant to another and have formed special relationships with certain plant species.

Flower Dissection: Learn the parts of a flower and their function in order to understand pollination and its role in plant reproduction.

Interdependence—The Web of Life: Examine how every species depends on others for survival. Study how plants need the sun and nutrients in the soil to make food. Observe how herbivores eat plants, carnivores eat herbivores, and bacteria break down the waste so that nutrients can return to the soil, where plants can take them in to make food.

Seed Dispersal/Traveling Seeds: Identify methods of seed dispersal and describe characteristics that help the seeds move, such as wind, water, and animals.

What's the Buzz on Native Bees? Learn to identify some common native bees and their habits. There are over a thousand species of native bees in the desert Southwest, yet all the attention goes to the non-native European honeybee and its cousin, the African honeybee.

Bats—Need Nectar Will Travel: Learn about the perils for bats and the benefits they provide to the whole ecosystem. For example, three species of bats in the Southwest depend on the flowers and fruit of tall cacti, such as saguaros, and of century plants for food. Female long-nosed bats winter in Mexico and migrate north to the Sonoran and Chihuahuan Deserts to have their babies.

Growing Places: Study the growth of seeds into plants in order to learn the space requirements (vertical and horizontal) of various species. Develop planting plans for specific garden types.

Soils: Compare types of soil at various sites (home and school) and understand soil physical characteristics such as structure and water-holding capacity.

Seasonal Changes: Explore the changing needs and appearances of plants, and learn how this relates to variations in watering and maintenance through the seasons.

Microhabitat Requirements: Observe the needs of different plants with regard to shade, sun, water, frost, etc. What special requirements do they have? Where does each species manage to survive best?

Phenology and Presence of Pollinators: Keep long-term records on temperature, bloom time, plant growth, seeds, and animals present. How does a plant's condition relate to pollinators' behaviors?

Predator and Prey: Learn to identify these on a small scale.

Work: Compare the work done in the garden by students versus wildlife.

Total Habitat Requirements for an Animal Species: Learn what is needed and ask questions: Are wildlands necessary? Are wildlife habitat gardens necessary? How do humans share this planet with other organisms?

Adaptations: Learn how plants and animals successfully survive in different environments.

Baby Insects: Study the reproduction and survival of caterpillars, lacewings, antlions, spiders, beetles, and other insects.

Diversity of Wild Visitors to Garden: Keep species lists and write down observations.

Plant Identification: Flowers, leaves, fruit seeds; sizes, colors, shapes; numbers of flower parts.

Sustainability: Understand how local wild natives are adapted to the local climate. Could humans adapt to living with limited resources?

The aforementioned are just a few ideas to explore in teaching scenarios. Certainly, teachers would have many other ideas on ways to tie wildlife gardens and outdoor natural areas to learning. This text offers only a few insights into the complex world in which we live. To understand natural systems, one must develop cognitive skills to solve complex puzzles. The study of nature thus can be used to provide students with problem-solving skills that prepare them for success in their personal and professional lives.

Words of Inspiration

Although an outdoor classroom and garden requires some work on a regular basis, it will not be overwhelmingly burdensome if planned properly. A wildlife habitat garden should, by its nature, be wild and unruly, inviting the wild creatures to participate. By choosing locally adapted native plants, the garden will be easy to maintain, leaving more time to enjoy the dynamics and wonder of the plants and animals present. The information in this book gives the reader the tools necessary to plan and implement a garden in a variety of genres. Designers must now let the imagination soar, and when the collective spirits of the children and adults participating in the planning process touch the ground together, wonderful things will happen.

KIM DUFFEK   APPENDIX Regional Plant Tables

Introduction

The following tables contain plants tailored to each of the arid bioregions of the American Southwest. There is some possibility for overlap between tables, meaning that many of the plants listed on one table will be suitable for other regions as well. Feel free to experiment with those on other tables, for some will meet a project's requirements and may naturally occur in your region. But pay close attention to frost tolerance. Also, some plants from cooler regions may suffer in high-heat areas without extra water or shade. Using native plants will ensure a minimum number of problems, since the plants are adapted to the climate, whereas plants from other climates may have special needs.

In every city, bioregional plant and animal communities are shaped by factors such as the amount and distribution of rainfall, high and low temperatures, topography, and soil type. Each table in the appendix has a summary of typical factors for each region. Keep in mind that wild plant and animal communities thrive in their undisturbed native element, so using lots of native plants will provide good sources of food for wild animals. These plants are adapted to their native climate so will require less water and maintenance, which will save time and money and will attract local wildlife to the habitat garden.

Many books on southwestern plant care are available, and many are sold at local botanic gardens and even at big national stores with nurseries. The local university agricultural extension agent is a wealth of information on plants for a particular area, as are many of the resources listed in this book.

Arid Bioregions of the American Southwest

Southern California Coastal Edge (Beachside Metropolitan Los Angeles and San Diego)

Southern California Coastal Edge is located on the hills and valleys between wetter chaparral areas and the sea. It is predominated by low-growing aromatic shrubs such as California sagebrush; white, black, and whiteleaf sages; California buckwheat; and bush

Map of the bioregions of the arid Southwest prepared by Steve Phillips of the Arizona-Sonora Desert Museum.

Southern California Coastal Edge. Illustration by Kim Duffek.

Southern California Inland Valleys. Illustration by Kim Duffek.

Mojave Desert. Illustration by Kim Duffek.

sunflower. Unfortunately, very little of this native community still exists. Average rainfall is ten to fourteen inches, falling mainly in winter. Average temperatures range from highs of 78°F in the summer to lows of 50°F in the winter. Only two to three days of frost below 32°F may occur each year. Severe freezes are rare; temperatures have dipped to the low twenties in some areas; other areas have never recorded freezing temperatures.

Southern California Inland Valleys (Inland Metropolitan Los Angeles and San Diego)

Southern California Inland Valleys consists of California chaparral, which is characterized by vegetation between three and fifteen feet high, such as chamise, which is well adapted to summer drought and fire. Average rainfall is twelve to thirty inches, falling mostly in winter. Most of the region occurs on steep mountainsides, with some spilling onto *bajadas*, or erosional plains. Average temperatures range from highs of 92°F in summer to lows of 40°F in winter, with an average of fourteen days of frost below 32°F. Temperatures have dipped to 21°F in some areas.

Mojave Desert/California High Desert (Las Vegas, NV; Twenty Nine Palms, Lancaster, and Barstow, CA)

The Mojave Desert is the smallest North American desert. The region is dominated by mountains and plains formed by the erosion of uplifted rock. It shares many of its animals, and plants such as creosote bush, brittlebush, and big sage, with the other North American deserts. Joshua tree, a yucca, is the hallmark native of this region, where there are many winter annual plants. Average rainfall is two and a half to seven and a half inches, falling mostly in winter, which makes this an unusual southwestern desert. Average temperatures range from highs of 100°F in summer to lows of 32°F in winter, with much variation from one place to another. Much of the Mojave experiences temperatures below 32°F on most winter nights.

Arizona Uplands Sonoran Desert (Tucson and Northeast Phoenix)

The Arizona Uplands subdivision of the Sonoran Desert is characterized by vegetation consisting of leguminous (pea family) trees, such as palo verde, mesquite, and ironwood, and perennial succulents, including the well-known saguaro cactus. Average rainfall is eight to twelve inches, distributed in winter and summer, making this the most lush and diverse of the deserts in the American Southwest. Most of the region is on hills and sloping, dissected plains. Average temperatures range from highs of 95°F in summer to lows of 46°F in winter, with an overall average of forty days with frosts below 32°F. Prolonged freezes can occur; temperatures have dipped to the single digits.

Lower Colorado Sonoran Desert (Palm Springs, CA; Phoenix and Yuma, AZ)

The Lower Colorado subdivision of the Sonoran Desert is characterized by large expanses of creosote bush and white bursage, with plants such as palo verde, ironwood, saguaro, and brittlebush lining some washes and slopes. Average rainfall is three to eight inches, falling mostly in winter. Over half the flora is composed of annuals. Most of the region is wide, flat valleys with small, sparsely vegetated mountain ranges. Average temperatures range from highs of 108°F in summer to lows of 45°F in winter. Frost is rare, with no more than ten days of frosts below 32°F in a given year. Temperatures have dipped to the low twenties in some areas.

Arizona Uplands Sonoran Desert. Illustration by Kim Duffek.

Desert and Semidesert Grasslands (Sierra Vista and Douglas, AZ; Albuquerque, Roswell, and Lordsburg, NM; Lubbock, Amarillo, Abilene, and west of Austin, TX)

Originally, Desert Grassland was characterized by perennial bunch grasses, including tobosa and grama grasses. In areas of heavy grazing, low-growing grasses such as curly mesquite grass now dominate, with invading cacti, shrubs, and forbs sometimes replacing the grasses. Other characteristic plants are yuccas, agaves, mesquites, and junipers. Average rainfall ranges from a mere eight inches in Albuquerque to nearly twenty-four inches in central Texas, distributed mostly in summer. Flat rolling plains make up much of this region. Average temperatures range from highs of 95°F in summer to lows of 23°F in winter. Over seventy-five days with frosts below 32°F are recorded.

Lower Colorado Sonoran Desert. Illustration by Kim Duffek.

Chihuahuan Desert (El Paso, TX; Carlsbad and Socorro, NM; San Simon, AZ)

The Chihuahuan Desert is a fairly high desert characterized by shrubs, such as creosote, coldenia, cenizo, and acacia, and small understory plants, punctuated by ocotillo and leaf succulents that include yucca, hechtia, and lechuguilla. Average rainfall is eight to twelve inches, distributed primarily in late spring and late summer. The region produces many wild plants that perform well in gardens with supplemental irrigation. Most of the region consists of rain shadow basins and slopes of the Basin and Range Formation with large expanses of outwash plain. Average temperatures range from highs of 98°F in summer to lows of 30°F in winter. More than sixty nights a year can drop below freezing in El Paso and more than that in other areas.

Desert Grasslands. Illustration by Kim Duffek.

Legend for Regional Tables

Native
- * = native to this bioregion
- 0 = native to Southwest deserts
- – = not native

Wildlife Habitat
- C = Cover
- F = Fruit
- I = Insects as food
- L = Leaves and twigs
- N = Nests
- P = Pollen and/or nectar

Chihuahuan Desert. Illustration by Kim Duffek.

Butterflies and Moths
    L = Larval food source
    A = Adult food source
    B = Both

Hummingbirds, Bees, and Bats
    * = Nectar source

Size H × W
    Height by width in feet

Flower Colors
    Bl = Blue
    Brn = Brown
    Gr = Green
    L = Lavender
    O = Orange
    Pi = Pink
    Pu = Purple
    R = Red
    V = Violet
    W = White
    Y = Yellow
    R-O (etc.) = Reddish Orange

Water Needs
    L = Low
    M = Medium
    H = High

Comments
    SG = Slow growth
    MG = Moderate growth
    FG = Fast growth
    CB/W = Can be cut back in winter for thicker growth
    CB/Sp = Can be cut back in spring for thicker growth
    CB/S = Can be cut back in summer for thicker growth
    LF = Larval food
    FS = Full sun
    PS = Partial shade
    Sh = Full shade
    W/S = Winter/Summer

Acknowledgments

The following people contributed their expertise to the regional plant tables.

Arizona Uplands Sonoran Desert
- Doug Larson, Arizona-Sonora Desert Museum
- Botany and Research Departments, Arizona-Sonora Desert Museum

Southern California Coastal Edge and Inland Valleys
- Michael Bostwick, Zoological Society of San Diego
- Sally Isaacson, Santa Barbara Botanic Garden, Santa Barbara
- Janica Jones, Los Angeles Zoo
- Margaret Robison, Theodore Payne Foundation, Sun Valley, CA
- Allison Shilling, California Native Plant Society, Perris

Chihuahuan Desert
- Daphne Richards, Texas Agricultural Extension Service, El Paso

Desert Grasslands
- Peter Gerlach, Spadefoot Nursery, Pearce, AZ

Lower Colorado Sonoran Desert
- Mike Bergan, Desert Water Agency, Palm Springs, CA
- Tim Gilliland, Alice Byrne School, Yuma, AZ
- Leigh Ann Hannan, Horticulturist, Yuma, AZ
- Dave Heveron, The Living Desert, Palm Desert, CA
- Shirley Waldrip, Desert Garden Nursery, Yuma, AZ

Mojave Desert
- Peter Duncombe, Desert Demonstration Gardens, Las Vegas, NV
- Susan Jones, Landscape Architecture Program, UNLV, Las Vegas, NV

Southern California Coastal Edge

Common Name	Scientific Name	Native	Wildlife Habitat	Humming-birds	Butter-flies	Bees	Moths	Bats
TREES								
Desert apricot	*Prunus fremontii*	*	CFNP	–	L	*	–	–
Holly-leaved cherry	*Prunus ilicifolia*	0	CFNP	–	L	*	–	–
Mexican elderberry	*Sambucus mexicana*	*	CFNP	–	A	*	–	–
Red silky oak	*Grevillea banksii*	–	CNP	*	–	–	–	–
Toyon	*Heteromeles arbutifolia*	0	CFIP	*	A	*	–	–
Wax myrtle	*Myrica californica*	*	CF	–	–	–	–	–
SHRUBS AND PERENNIALS								
Bearberry, Kinnikinnick	*Arctostaphylos uva-ursi*	*	F	*	A	*	L	–
Bicolor everlasting	*Gnaphalium bicolor*	*	FIP	–	B	–	–	–
Big sagebrush	*Artemisia tridentata*	*	F	–	L	–	–	–
Black sage	*Salvia mellifera*	*	F	*	A	*	–	–
Bladderpod	*Isomeris arborea*	*	F	*	L	*	–	–
Bush lupine	*Lupinus longifolius*	*	FLP	–	L	*	–	–
Bush monkey flower	*Mimulus (Diplacus) longiflorus*	*	P	*	A	–	–	–
Bush sunflower	*Encelia californica*	*	CFI	–	L	–	A	–
California buckwheat	*Eriogonum fasciculatum*	*	CFILNP	*	B	*	–	–
California figwort	*Scrophularia californica*	*	F	*	A	–	–	–
California sagebrush	*Artemesia californica*	*	C	–	L	–	–	–
Chamise	*Adenostoma fasciculatum*	0	CN	–	B	*	–	–
Conejo buckwheat	*Eriogonum crocatum*	*	FLP	–	B	–	–	–
Deerweed	*Lotus scoparius*	*	F	–	B	–	–	–
Dwarf sunflower	*Helianthus gracilentus*	0	FP	–	A	*	–	–
Fragrant sumac, Squawbush	*Rhus aromatica*	*	CN	–	A	*	–	–
Golden currant	*Ribes aureum*	–	FP	–	B	*	–	–
Goldeneye	*Viguiera deltoidea*	*	P	–	B	*	–	–
Golden yarrow	*Eriophyllum confertiflorum*	*	FP	–	A	–	–	–
Hummingbird fuchsia	*Epilobium canum ssp. canum*	*	P	*	A	–	–	–
Island bush snapdragon	*Galvezia speciosa*	0	CINP	*	–	*	–	–
Island ceanothus	*Ceanothus arboreus*	0	–	*	B	*	?	–
Laurel sumac	*Malosma laurina*	*	CF	–	–	*	L	–
Lemonade berry	*Malosma integrifolia*	*	CFNP	–	–	*	L	–
Narrow-leaved milkweed	*Asclepias fascicularis*	0	LP	–	B	–	–	–

Size HxW	Flowers	Water	Hardy to °F	Comments
13'x6'	W, Pi	L	0	MG; FS; LF for western tiger, two-tailed, and pale swallowtail butterflies
30'x15'	W	L	0–20 first year	MG; FS; black fruit messy; LF for western tiger, pale and two-tailed swallowtail, Lorquin's admiral, and coral hairstreak butterflies
20'x15'	Y-W	M-H	−10	FG, FS, showy flowers, birds very attracted to the fruit, give a few deep soakings in summer, regular water in winter
20'x12'	R	L-M	20	MG, FS, native to coastal Australia, cannot tolerate overwatering
20'x15'	W	L	0	SG, FS-PS, good garden plant
35'x10'	Gr, R	L	20	MG, FS coast—PS inland, tolerates wind but not salt spray
1'x8'	Pi-W	M	−15	MG, FS coast—Sh inland, slow to establish, withhold water in summer, LF for Walters' saturniid moth
3'x3'	Y-W	L	15	FG, FS, biennial or perennial herb, can be weedy, LF for American painted lady butterfly
8'x8'	Gr	L	0	SG, FS, very aromatic, short-lived, LF for Old World swallowtail and American lady butterflies
5'x6'	W, L	L	10	MG, FS-PS, fragrant flowers
4'x6'	Y	L	5	SG, FS, blooms almost continuously, LF for several white butterflies
4'x4'	Bl-Pu	L	27	FG, PS, flowers fragrant, LF for sooty hairstreak and several sulphur and blue butterflies
3'x2'	O, Y, R	L	15	MG, FS-PS, hybrids not as hardy
4'x4'	Y	L	28	FG, FS, LF for painted lady and dusky metalmark butterflies
5'x6'	W-Pi	L	5	MG, FS, tortoise food, important LF for many butterflies, esp. blues, coppers, and metalmarks
4'x4'	R	L	10	MG, FS, attractive perennial herb
5'x4'	Y	L	10	MG, FS, LF for painted lady butterfly
10'x8'	W	L	0	MG, FS, LF for painted lady butterfly
1'x3'	Y	L	20	MG-FG, FS, tortoise food, important LF for western green hairstreak, blues, and many other butterflies
3'x3'	Y	L	10	FG, FS-PS, important LF for coastal green hairstreak and many blue and duskywing butterflies
4'x4'	Y	L-M	10	FG, FS, seeds attract birds
5'x8'	W	L	0	FG, FS, backbone plant, colorful
6'x6'	Y-R	L	−40	MG, FS-PS, mountain species, not for hot deserts, LF for several copper, anglewing, and comma butterflies
3'x3'	Y	L	20	FG-MG, FS, LF for California patch butterfly
2'x1'	Y	L	5	FG, FS, seeds eaten by birds
3'x4'	R	L-M	−10	FG, FS-PS, spreads via underground roots
3'x5'	R	L	25	MG-FG, FS-PS, variety 'Firecracker' is smaller and more colorful
25'x15'	L	L	18	FG, FS-PS, avoid summer water, lives about 10 years, LF for California hairstreak and California tortoiseshell butterflies
12'x8'	Pi	L	32	MG, FS, LF for Walters' saturnid moth
6'x6'	Pi	L	28	MG, FS, sweet-tart berries eaten by birds, LF for Walters' saturniid moth
3'x3'	W	L-M	10	MG-FG, FS-PS, perennial herb, LF for monarch and queen butterflies

Common Name	Scientific Name	Native	Wildlife Habitat	Humming-birds	Butter-flies	Bees	Moths	Bats
Pitcher sage	Salvia spathacea	0	F	*	A	–	–	–
Snakeweed	Gutierrezia californica	0	FP	–	–	*	–	–
Spiny redberry	Rhamnus crocea	*	CFINP	–	B	*	–	–
Sugar bush	Rhus ovata	*	F	–	A	*	–	–
Tree mallow	Lavatera assurgentiflora	*	F	–	L	*	–	–
White sage	Salvia apiana	*	F	*	A	*	–	–
Wooly blue curls	Trichostemma lanatum	*	FP	*	A	*	–	–

GROUND COVERS AND VINES

Clematis	Clematis ligusticifolia	*	CIP	–	–	*	A	–
Coyote brush	Baccharis pilularis	*	CFP	–	A	*	–	–
Dutchman's pipe	Aristolochia species	0	FLP	–	L	–	–	–
Manroot, Wild cucumber	Marah macrocarpus	*	FLP	–	–	*	–	–
Snapdragon vine	Maurandya antirrhiniflora	0	P	*	–	–	–	–
Yarrow	Achillea millefolium	*	FIP	–	A	–	–	–

ANNUALS AND SHORT-LIVED PERENNIALS

California poppy	Eschscholtzia californica	*	FP	–	–	*	–	–
Chia	Salvia columbariae	*	FIP	–	–	*	–	–
Chinese houses	Collinsia heterophylla	*	FP	*	B	*	A	–
Desert lupine	Lupinus sparsiflorus	*	FLP	–	L	*	–	–
Foothill penstemon	Penstemon heterophyllus	0	FP	*	L	*	–	–
Groundsel	Senecio douglasii	*	FP	–	A	*	–	–
Royal penstemon	Penstemon spectabilis	*	FP	*	L	*	–	–
Succulent lupine, Arroyo lupine	Lupinus succulentus	*	FLP	–	L	*	–	–

ACCENT PLANTS

Alkali sacaton	Sporobolus airoides	*	CF	–	–	–	–	–
Candelabra aloe	Aloe candelabrum	–	FP	*	–	–	–	–
Chalky rock lettuce	Dudleya pulverulenta	*	P	*	A	–	–	–
Foxtail agave	Agave attenuata	–	FP	–	A	*	–	–
Giant wild rye	Elymus condensatus	*	FP	–	L	–	–	–
Lance-leaved dudleya	Dudleya lanceolata	*	P	*	L	–	–	–
Our Lord's candle	Hesperoyucca whipplei	*	CFNP	–	–	–	B	–
Prickly pear	Opuntia littoralis	*	FLP	–	–	*	–	–

Size HxW	Flowers	Water	Hardy to °F	Comments
1.5'x6'	R	L-M	0	FG, FS-PS, perennial herb, fragrant flowers
1'x1'	Y	L	20	FG, FS, neat-looking bush
4'x6'	Gr	L	10	MG-SG, FS coast—PS inland, spines, LF for Hermes copper butterfly
15'x10'	W	L	10	MG, FS, plant in winter in desert, sweet-tart berries eaten by birds
12'x5'	Pu	L	20	FG, FS, goldfinches love the seeds. LF for painted lady and west coast lady butterflies
5'x5'	W	L	12	MG, FS, silver foliage
3'x4'	Pu	L	0	FG, FS coast—PS inland, needs good drainage, sweet scent
5'x20'	W	M	-8	FG, FS-PS, shrubby vine, many flowers
3'x6'	Gr	L	10	FG; FS; lightly scented flowers; large, easy-to-grow ground cover
Varies	Pu-Br	L-M	Varies	MG, vines, flowers attract native flies, LF for pipevine and polydamas swallowtail butterflies
to 20'	Gr	L-M	20	FG, FS, untidy vine
to 10'	R, Pu	L-M	20	FG; FS-PS; delicate, beautiful hummingbird vine
1.5'x2'	W, Pi	L-M	-10	FG, FS-PS, ground cover, spreads by rhizome
2'x2'	Y	L	20	FG, FS, short-lived perennial
2'x2'	Bl	L	10	FG, FS, annual, seeds and seedlings eaten by birds
1'x1'	Y-Pu	M	10	FG, Sh, annual, LF for spring azure butterfly
1'x1.5'	L	L	5	FG; FS; annual; easy from seed; LF for sooty hairstreak, arrowhead blue, silvery blue, Perseus duskywing, several sulphur, Acmon, and Karner blue butterflies
2'x2'	Pu-Bl	L-M	0	FG; FS; long-lived penstemon; LF for common buckeye and Edith's, dotted, and variable checkerspot butterflies
3'x1'	Y	L	-6	FG, FS-PS, annual or short-lived perennial, weedy but attractive, leaves are toxic
3'x3'	Pu	L	0	FG; FS; can live about 10 years; LF for common buckeye and Edith's, dotted, and variable checkerspot butterflies
3'x3'	Bl	L	10	FG, FS, annual, LF for sooty hairstreak and several blue and sulphur butterflies
3'x3'	W	L-M	-15	FG-MG, FS-PS, gray-green leaves, tough plant
12'x8'	R, O	L	26	SG, FS, many good aloes for southern California, native to South Africa
2'x2'	R, Y	L	10	MG, FS-PS, delicate succulent, protect from mammals
4'x4'	Y-Gr	L	26	MG, PS, no spines or teeth on soft leaves, native to central Mexico
4'x3'	Y	L	0	MG, FS, LF for common ringlet and woodland skipper
2'x2'	R-Y	L	25	MG, FS coast—PS inland, LF for Moss's elfin and Sonoran blue butterflies
8'x2'	W	L	-10	MG, FS, pointy leaf tips, plant away from paths, dies after flower and seed production, reseeds, LF for Whipple yucca moth
3'x10'	O, R	L	20	MG; FS; spines, young pads, and fruit are tortoise food

Southern California Inland Valleys

Common Name	Scientific Name	Native	Wildlife Habitat	Humming-birds	Butter-flies	Bees	Moths	Bats
TREES								
Blue fan palms (varied)	*Brahea* spp.	0	CILNP	–	–	–	–	–
California buckeye	*Aesculus californica*	*	CFINP	–	–	*	–	–
California laurel, California bay, Oregon myrtle	*Umbellularia californica*	*	CFN	–	–	*	–	–
California sycamore	*Platanus racemosa*	*	CN	–	–	–	–	–
Catalina cherry, Hollyleaf cherry	*Prunus ilicifolia* spp. *lyonii*	0	CFIN	–	L	*	–	–
Coast live oak	*Quercus agrifolia*	*	CFILN	–	L	–	–	–
Desert willow	*Chilopsis linearis*	0	CILNP	*	A	?	L	–
Palo verde	*Parkinsonia* spp.	0	CFLNP	–	–	*	–	–
Toyon	*Heteromeles arbutifolia*	*	CFLN	*	A	*	–	–
Western redbud	*Cercis occidentalis*	*	CFILNP	*	A	*	–	–
SHRUBS AND PERENNIALS								
Anderson wolfberry	*Lycium andersonii*	*	CFINP	–	A	*	–	–
Bush anemone	*Carpenteria californica*	*	CILNP	*	A	*	A	–
Bush lupine	*Lupinus longifolius*	*	FLP	–	L	*	–	–
Butterfly weed	*Asclepias tuberosa*	0	CFILP	–	B	–	–	–
California buckwheat	*Eriogonum fasciculatum*	*	CFILNP	*	B	*	–	–
California holly grape	*Berberis pinnata*	*	CFINP	–	A	*	–	–
California sagebrush	*Artemisia californica*	*	CN	–	–	–	–	–
Canyon sunflower	*Venegasia carpesioides*	*	CFIP	*	A	*	–	–
Common butterfly bush, Summer lilac	*Buddleja davidii*	–	CILNP	*	–	*	A	–
Dock, Wild rhubarb	*Rumex hymenosepalus*	*	FP	–	L	–	–	–
Flannel bush	*Fremontodendron californicum*	*	CILNP	*	A	*	–	–
Greenbark ceanothus	*Ceanothus spinosus*	*	CFINP	–	B	–	–	–
Gregg's buckthorn	*Ceanothus greggii*	0	F	–	B	–	–	–
Island bush snapdragon	*Galvezia speciosa*	*	CINP	*	–	*	–	–
Little Sur manzanita	*Arctostaphylos edmundsii*	*	CFIN	*	–	–	B	–
Manzanita	*Arctostaphylos pungens*	*	L	*	A	–	L	–
Matilija poppy	*Romneya coulteri*	*	CILNP	*	A	*	–	–
Mexican bush sage	*Salvia leucantha*	–	CILNP	*	A	–	–	–
Mock locust	*Amorpha californica*	*	FIL	–	L	*	–	–
Mountain mahogany, Sweetbrush	*Cercocarpus betuloides*	*	CILN	–	L	*	A	–

Size HxW	Flowers	Water	Hardy to °F	Comments
30'x15'	Y-W	L	18	SG, FS, needs summer water in deserts, wind-pollinated
35'x35'	Y	H	10	MG, FS, toxic properties, leaf drop midsummer without water
75'x100'	Y	L	20	SG, FS-PS-Sh, leaf color yellow in autumn, prefers good soil
90'x50'	Gr	M	0	FG, FS, wind-pollinated, subject to anthracnose disease
45'x30'	W	L	20	MG; FS; edible fruits; LF for western tiger swallowtail, coral hairstreak, California hairstreak, and Lorquin's admiral butterflies
60'x70'	Y, Gr	L	10	FG-MG; FS; wind-pollinated; potential LF for California sister, several hairstreak, and duskywing butterflies
20'x20'	Pi, Pu	M	10	MG, FS, delicately scented flowers, LF for rustic sphinx moth
30'x30'	Y	L	15	MG-FG, FS, some with thorny branches
10'x10'	W	L	0	MG, FS-PS, conducive to fireblight
18'x18'	Pi, W	M-L	0	MG-SG, FS, fall foliage color, winter seed pods, edible fruits and flowers, good flowering in areas with less than 28°F lows, needs good drainage
6'x6'	Pi, Pu	L-M	5	SG, FS, birds and tortoises like orange-red edible fruit
6'x6'	W	L-M	20	SG, PS best, light pruning, fragrant flowers
4'x4'	Bl-Pu	L	27	FG; PS; fragrant flowers; LF for western and Queen Alexandria's sulphur, sooty hairstreak, Boisduval's blue, and Perseus duskywing butterflies
3'x2'	O, Y	M	-30	FG, FS-PS, herbaceous top freezes back at 32°F, good drainage needed, LF for queen and monarch butterflies
5'x6'	W, Pi	L	5	MG; FS-PS; good erosion-control plant; tortoise food; important LF for green hairstreaks, coppers, blues, and other butterflies
5'x5'	Y	L	10	SG, FS coast—PS deserts, berries for birds
5'x5'	Y-Gr	L	10	MG, FS, fragrant leaves, some ground-cover varieties
7'x7'	Y	L	20	MG-FG, PS
10'x10'	W, L, Pi, Pu	M	H	FG, FS-PS, will freeze to ground and resprout in spring, native to Asia
3'x3'	Br	L	H	FG, FS, herbaceous perennial, needs good drainage, LF for many copper butterflies
20'x20'	Y	L	0	FG, FS-PS, heavy bloomer, excellent show, short-lived, may cause dermatitis
20'x10'	Pu	L	10	FG, PS, generally not long-lived, avoid summer water, LF for California and hedgerow hairstreaks and California tortoiseshell butterflies
6'x6'	W	L-M	-5	MG, FS, LF for California hedgerow and western green hairstreak and California tortoiseshell butterflies
3'x5'	R	L	25	MG, FS coast—PS inland, needs good drainage, climbs through other shrubs
3'x6'	Pi-W	L	20	MG, FS-PS, needs good drainage, other species have taller form and more frost tolerance, LF for Walters' saturnia moth
5'x5'	W, Pi	M	-15	MG-SG, FS-PS, needs excellent drainage, LF for Walters' saturniid moth
8'x8'	W	L	0	FG, FS, CB/W, herbaceous, don't overwater, good soil binder
4'x4'	Pu	L	20	FG, FS-PS, CB/W, mostly herbaceous, native to Mexico, there are many good Salvias
10'x10'	R-Pu	L	0	MG, FS-PS, LF for silver-spotted skipper and California dogface butterflies
5'x12'	Gr-Y	L	18	MG, FS-PS, important browse for deer, LF for several hairstreak butterflies

Common Name	Scientific Name	Native	Wildlife Habitat	Humming-birds	Butter-flies	Bees	Moths	Bats
Mountain marigold	Tagetes palmeri	0	CILNP	–	A	*	–	–
New Mexico olive, Desert olive	Forestiera neomexicana	*	CFN	–	–	–	–	–
Pride of Madeira	Echium fatuosum	–	CILNP	–	–	*	–	–
Purple coneflower	Echinacea purpurea	0	FIP	–	A	*	A	–
Rockrose	Cistus purpurea hybrids	–	CILNP	*	A	*	A	–
Sea lavender	Limonium perezii	–	CIP	–	A	*	–	–
Senna	Senna purpusii	0	FIL	–	L	*	–	–
Toadflax	Linaria purpurea	–	IP	*	–	*	–	–
Wild lilac	Ceanothus sp. (many varieties)	*	CINP	–	B	–	–	–
Woods rose	Rosa woodsii ultramontana	–	FP	–	–	*	–	–
Yellow penstemon	Keckiella antirrhinoides	*	CFP	*	–	–	–	–

GROUND COVERS AND VINES

Common Name	Scientific Name	Native	Wildlife Habitat	Humming-birds	Butter-flies	Bees	Moths	Bats
Bougainvillea 'South Dakota Red'	Bougainvillea hybrid	–	CILNP	*	A	*	L	–
California fuchsia	Epilobium canum ssp. californicum	*	IP	*	A	–	–	–
Common yarrow	Achillea millefolium	*	FIP	–	A	–	–	–
Mexican evening primrose	Oenothera speciosa (berlandieri)	0	CILNP	–	A	*	B	–
Passion fruit	Passiflora edulis	–	CFIP	–	L	*	–	–
Trailing indigo bush	Dalea greggii	0	CFILP	*	B	–	–	–

ANNUALS AND SHORT-LIVED PERENNIALS

Common Name	Scientific Name	Native	Wildlife Habitat	Humming-birds	Butter-flies	Bees	Moths	Bats
California gold poppy	Eschscholtzia californica	*	FLP	–	–	*	–	–
Desert blue curls	Trichostema parishii	*	FP	–	–	*	–	–
Hooker evening primrose	Oenothera hookeri	–	FILP	–	–	–	B	–
Jewel flower	Streptanthus cordatus	0	FIL	*	L	–	–	–
Many-flowered snapdragon	Antirrhinum multiflorum	*	P	*	–	–	–	–
Owl's clover	Castilleja exerta	*	FP	–	–	*	–	–
Prickly poppy	Argemone munita	*	FP	–	–	*	–	–
Purple aster	Aster tanacetifolius, A. bigelovii	0	FP	–	B	*	–	–
Scarlet bugler	Penstemon centranthifolius	*	FP	*	L	–	–	–

ACCENT PLANTS

Common Name	Scientific Name	Native	Wildlife Habitat	Humming-birds	Butter-flies	Bees	Moths	Bats
Deergrass	Muhlenbergia rigens	0	CFI	–	L	–	–	–
Queen Victoria agave	Agave victoria-reginae	0	IP	A	–	*	–	*

Size HxW	Flowers	Water	Hardy to °F	Comments
3'x4'	Y	L–M	25	FG, FS–PS, herbaceous tops, may cause dermatitis, sometimes sold as T. lemmoni
9'x6'	Gr-Y	L	–10	FG, FS, fruit attracts wildlife
6'x6'	Pu	L–M	15	MG, FS, CB once a year, short life span, native to Canary Islands
4'x2'	O, Pu	M	32	FG, FS, herbaceous, long bloom from spring to first frost
4'x4'	Pi-W	L	15	FG, FS–PS, excellent in landscape, native to Mediterranean
3'x3'	Pu	L	28	FG–MG, FS coast—PS inland, native to Canary Islands
5'x5'	Y	L–M	28	MG, FS–PS, tortoise food, LF for several yellow and orange butterflies
3'x3'	Pu	M	28	FG, FS–PS, best in mass plantings, native to Italy
Varies	L	L	28	MG, FS, do not water much in summer, a large selection to choose from at specialty nurseries, LF for many hairstreak and pacuvius duskywing butterflies
6'x4'	Pi	L–M	–20	MG, PS, thicket-forming, mountain species
8'x10'	Y	L	0	MG, PS, good for erosion control
to 25'	R	L–M	28	FG, FS, shrubby vine, native to South America, LF for bougainvillea looper moth, caterpillars can decimate leaves
1.5'x4'	R-O	L–M	10	MG, PS, afternoon shade, CB/W, spreads via roots
1.5'x2'	W, Pi	L–M	–10	FG, FS–PS, many hybrids are available in many colors, ground cover, spreads by rhizome
1' high	Pi	L–M	H	FG, FS–PS, CB as necessary, ground cover, spreads by roots, can become dominant, flea beetles can denude it, tortoise food, LF for sphinx moths
to 30'	W-Pu	M	28	FG, FS–PS, vine, other good species and varieties, LF for zebra and many fritillary butterflies
1'x4'	Pu	L	15	MG, FS–PS, ground cover, avoid summer overwatering, LF for southern dogface and several blue butterflies
2'x2'	Y	L	20	FG, FS, short-lived perennial
3'x2'	Pu	L	–5	FG, FS–PS, short-lived perennial, aromatic
4'x2'	Y	L–M	–20	MG, FS–PS, CB/Sp, short-lived perennial, reseeds readily, LF for sphinx moths
2'x1'	Pu	L–M	H	FG, FS, short-lived perennial, LF for California marble and desert orange-tip butterflies
2'x5'	R	L	10	FG, FS, annual or short-lived perennial, must be in well-drained soil
1'x0.5'	Pu	L	H	FG, FS, annual, seeds sometimes hard to germinate
5'x2'	W	L	15	FG, FS, attractive and dramatic, annual to perennial, can reseed itself
1.5'x1'	Pu	L–M	H	FG, FS, annual or short-lived perennial, reseeds, LF for several crescent and checkerspot butterflies
2'x2'	R	L	12	FG, FS–PS deserts, short-lived perennial, LF for variable, Edith's and dotted checkerspot butterflies
4'x4'	W	L–M	–10	MG, FS–PS, many good grasses, wind pollinated, LF for common ringlet butterfly and several skippers
2'x2'	Y, R	L	H	SG; FS; native to NE Mexico; practically spineless; many good agaves available, although most have sharp leaf tips

Mojave Desert

Common Name	Scientific Name	Native	Wildlife Habitat	Humming-birds	Butter-flies	Bees	Moths	Bats
TREES								
Arizona ash	Fraxinus velutina	*	CNP	–	L	–	–	–
Smoke tree	Psorothamus spinosus	*	CFNP	–	–	*	–	–
Utah juniper	Juniperus osteosperma	*	CFN	–	–	–	–	–
SHRUBS AND PERENNIALS								
Antelope bitterbrush	Purshia tridentata	*	LP	–	–	*	–	–
Blackbush	Coleogyne ramosissima	*	FP	–	A	*	–	–
Blue dogbane	Amsonia brevifolia	*	P	–	–	–	*	–
Blue flax	Linum perenne lewisii	*	FP	–	A	*	–	–
California buckwheat	Eriogonum fasciculatum	*	CFIP	*	B	*	–	–
Cooper wolfberry	Lycium cooperi	*	CFINP	–	A	*	–	–
Currant leaf mallow	Sphaeralcea grossulariaefolia	*	FP	–	B	*	–	–
Desert almond	Prunus fasciculata	*	CFNP	–	L	*	–	–
Desert alyssum	Lepidium fremontii	*	FP	–	–	*	–	–
Desert holly	Atriplex hymenelytra	*	CFP	–	–	–	–	–
Desert peach	Prunus andersonii	*	CFNP	–	L	*	–	–
Desert plume	Stanleya pinnata	*	P	–	–	*	–	–
Desert sage	Salvia dorii v. dorii	*	FP	*	–	*	–	–
Desert saltbush	Atriplex polycarpa	*	CFP	–	–	–	–	–
Fernbush	Chamaebatiaria millefolium	*	CP	–	–	*	–	–
Fremont barberry, Desert mahonia	Berberis fremontii (Mahonia)	*	CFNP	–	–	*	–	–
Green encelia	Encelia virginensis	*	FP	–	–	*	–	–
Mojave aster	Machaerantha tortifolia	*	FP	–	B	*	–	–
Mormon tea	Ephedra nevadensis	*	FP	–	–	–	–	–
Mountain mahogany	Cercocarpus montanus	–	CILNP	–	L	*	–	–
Paper-bag bush, Bladder sage	Salazaria mexicana	*	P	–	–	*	–	–
Prairie sagebrush	Artemisia ludoviciana	*	F	–	L	–	–	–
Range ratany	Krameria parvifolia	*	P	–	–	*	–	–
Senna	Senna armata	*	L	–	L	*	–	–
Silver sagebrush	Artemisia cana	*	CF	–	L	–	–	–
Turpentine broom	Thamnosma montana	*	FP	–	–	*	–	–
Utah serviceberry	Amerlanchier utahensis	–	CFNP	–	A	–	–	–

Size HxW	Flowers	Water	Hardy to °F	Comments
30'x20'	Gr-Y	M	−10	MG; FS; heat tolerant; LF for western tiger, two-tailed, and pale swallowtail butterflies
20'x12'	Pu	L	25	SG–MG, FS, stunning in flower, hard to propagate, loves neglect
15'x12'	Gr	L	−10	SG, FS, needs good drainage and sun
10'x5'	W-Y	L	−18	MG, FS, similar to Apache plume
3'x3'	Y	L	5	MG, FS, good landscape potential
2'x2'	Pu	L	−10	Uncommon, very pretty perennial herb, propagated via cuttings
2'x2'	Bl	L	−30	FG, FS-PS-Sh, perennial herb good for wildflower gardens
3'x4'	W, Pi	L	0	MG; FS-PS; attractive; colorful; tortoise food; important LF for hairstreaks, coppers, blues, and other butterflies
3'x7'	W	L	5	SG, FS, spiny shrub, green fruit for birds and tortoises
0.5'x0.5'	O, R, Pu	L	15	FG-MG, FS, LF for several skippers and west coast lady butterfly
8'x4'	W	L	0	MG; FS; LF for western tiger, two-tailed, and pale swallowtail butterflies
1'x2'	Y	L	0	FG, FS, perennial wildflower, fragrant, other good *Lepidium* species
3'x3'	Y	L	20	MG, FS, very attractive, needs gypsum added to soil and good drainage
6'x3'	Pi	M	−16	MG; FS; LF for western tiger, two-tailed, and pale swallowtail butterflies
3'x3'	Y	L	−15	MG-FG, FS, highly adaptable
3'x3'	Bl	L	16	MG, FS, silver foliage, often used as border plant
4'x6'	Y	L	25	MG, FS, provides food for desert birds, helps reduce soil erosion
8'x4'	W	L	5	MG, FS, aromatic, needs good drainage
5'x5'	Y	L-M	−6	MG, FS-PS, worth searching for, colorful, dry red fruits
3'x2'	Y	L	15	MG-FG, FS, needs well-drained soil, neatly shaped shrub
1'x2'	Pu	L	15	FG, FS, good perennial, LF for field crescent butterfly
3'x3'	Y	L	0	SG, FS, very good landscape plant
6'x6'	W	L	5	MG, FS-PS, most adaptable mahogany, from higher elevation, LF for several hairstreak butterflies
3'x3'	Pu	L	12	MG, FS, needs good drainage, interesting fruit
2'x2'	Y-W	M	0	MG-FG, FS, good in wild lawns when cut short, fragrant silver foliage, LF for old world swallowtail and American lady butterflies
2'x2'	R-Pu	L	10	MG, FS, hard to establish, partially parasitic so grow next to *Ambrosia*, small spiny fruit
4'x4'	Y	L	22	FG, FS, worth looking for, tortoise food, LF for several sulphur butterflies
5'x5'	Y	L	−26	MG-FG, FS, good in wild lawns when cut short, fragrant silver foliage, LF for Old World swallowtail and American lady butterflies
3'x2'	Pu	L	H	MG, FS, very aromatic, unusual color
10'x15'	W	M	−20	MG, FS-PS, needs supplemental water and good soil, mountain species, fragrant flowers, edible fruit

Common Name	Scientific Name	Native	Wildlife Habitat	Humming-birds	Butter-flies	Bees	Moths	Bats
White bursage	Ambrosia dumosa	*	C	–	–	–	–	–
Winterfat	Ceratoides lanata	*	L	–	–	–	–	–
GROUND COVERS AND VINES								
Angelita daisy	Hymenoxys acaulis	*	FLP	–	A	*	–	–
Climbing snapdragon	Antirrhinum filipes	*	LP	*	B	–	–	–
Shadscale	Atriplex confertifolia	*	CFP	–	–	–	–	–
ANNUALS AND SHORT-LIVED PERENNIALS								
Beardtongue	Penstemon bicolor	*	FP	*	L	–	–	–
Desert anemone	Anemone tuberosa	*	P	–	–	*	–	–
Desert poppy	Eschscholtzia glyptosperma	*	FP	–	–	*	–	–
Mojave aster	Aster bigelovii	*	–	–	B	*	–	–
Nevada onion	Allium nevadensis	*	P	*	–	*	–	–
Palmer's penstemon	Penstemon palmeri	–	FP	*	L	–	–	–
ACCENTS								
Banana yucca	Yucca baccata	*	FIP	–	–	*	B	–
Beavertail prickly pear	Opuntia basilaris	*	FLP	–	–	*	–	–
Big galleta	Pleuraphis rigidus	*	FL	–	–	–	–	–
Blue fescue	Festuca ovina glauca	*	L	–	L	–	–	–
Diamond cholla	Opuntia ramosissima	*	FP	–	–	*	–	–
Joshua tree	Yucca brevifolia	*	FN	–	–	–	B	–
Mojave hedgehog	Echinocereus triglochidiatus mohavensis	*	FP	*	–	*	–	–
Mojave yucca	Yucca schidigera	*	FN	–	–	–	B	–
Nevada agave	Agave utahensis nevadensis	*	P	*	L	*	–	–
Pink pincushion	Coryphantha vivipara rosea	*	FP	–	–	*	–	–
Pygmy barrel cactus	Sclerocactus johnsonii	*	FP	–	–	*	–	–
Strawberry hedgehog	Echinocereus englemannii	*	FP	–	–	*	–	–
Switch grass	Panicum virgatum	*	C	–	–	–	–	–

Size HxW	Flowers	Water	Hardy to °F	Comments
2'x2'	Gr	L	10	FG–MG, FS, good for wild areas
2'x1.5'	W-Y	L	0	MG, FS, excellent for winter interest, quality wildlife forage, gray foliage
1'x1.5'	Y	M	0	FG, FS–PS, small perennial herb, group for better effect
3'x2'	Y	L	0	FG, PS, weak-stemmed vine, unusual, LF for common buckeye butterfly
2'x5'	Gr	L	20	MG, FS, ground cover, gray foliage
3'x2'	Pi	L	20	FG, FS, showy short-lived perennial, LF for several checkerspot butterflies
1.5'x1.5'	Pi, W	M	5	FG, FS, perennial from tuber, pretty, good container plant
0.5'x0.5'	Y	L	12	FG, FS, often lives several years, little sister to California poppy
3'x3'	Pu	L–M	8	FG, FS, short-lived perennial, good wildflower, LF for several crescent butterflies
1'x2'	Y	L	0	FG, FS, bulb, fragrant flowers
6'x3'	Pi	L	20	FG, FS, showy annual or short-lived perennial, from higher elevations, LF for several checkerspot butterflies
4'x4'	W	L	0	SG, FS–PS, best clumping yucca, bluish leaves, var. vespertina (night yucca) has larger flowers, LF for banana yucca moth
1'x3'	Pi, Pu	L	10	MG, FS–PS, avoid overwatering, spiny tiny glochids, fruits are food for tortoises, etc.
2'x3'	Gr	L	5	MG, FS, excellent grass for naturalistic landscape
1'x3'	Bl	M	0	FG, FS–PS, fine-leafed, distinct blue color, LF for satyr butterflies
2'x2'	Gr	L	0	MG, FS, several forms, small size, long spines
30'x15'	Gr-W	L	0	SG, FS, plant in winter, LF for Joshua tree yucca moth
2'x2'	R	L	0	MG, FS, attractive, uncommon, spines
12'x6'	W	L	12	SG, FS, good large yucca, LF for Mojave yucca moth
1'x2'	Y	L	0	MG, FS, good for small spaces, LF for Mojave giant skipper
0.5'x0.5'	Pu	L	0	MG, FS, small plant with showy flowers, sometimes sold as *Mammillaria vivipara*, spines
0.6'x0.3'	Pu, Gr-Y	L	10	MG, FS, very small, has spines
1'x0.3'	Pi	L	0	MG, FS–PS, very showy flowers, spines
7'x5'	Pi, W	L–M	-20	MG, FS, beautiful accent grass

Arizona Upland Desert

Common Name	Scientific Name	Native	Wildlife Habitat	Humming-birds	Butter-flies	Bees	Moths	Bats
TREES								
Blue palo verde	Parkinsonia florida	*	CFINP	–	–	*	–	–
Desert ironwood	Olneya tesota	*	CFINP	–	–	*	–	–
'Desert Museum' hybrid palo verde	Parkinsonia hybrid	–	CFINP	–	–	*	–	–
Desert willow	Chilopsis linearis	*	CINP	*	A	–	L	–
Texas ebony	Ebenopsis ebano	0	CFINP	–	A	*	?	–
Velvet mesquite	Prosopis velutina	*	CINP	–	B	*	–	–
Whitethorn acacia	Acacia constricta	*	CINP	–	L	*	–	–
SHRUBS AND PERENNIALS								
Autumn sage	Salvia greggii	0	IP	*	A	–	–	–
Baja fairyduster	Calliandra californica	0	FIP	*	B	*	–	–
Black dalea	Dalea frutescens	*	FI	–	B	–	–	–
Creosote	Larrea divaricata tridentata	*	CIP	–	–	*	–	–
Deer vetch	Lotus rigidus	*	FP	–	–	*	–	–
Desert broom	Baccharis sarothroides	*	CIP	–	A	*	L	–
Desert hackberry	Celtis pallida	*	CFILP	–	L	*	–	–
Desert honeysuckle	Anisacanthus thurberi	*	P	*	L	–	–	–
Desert lavender	Hyptis albida	*	F	*	A	*	–	–
Desert senna	Senna covesii	*	FIP	–	L	*	–	–
Desert zinnia	Zinnia acerosa	*	FP	–	A	*	–	–
Fairyduster	Calliandra eriophylla	*	FILP	*	B	*	–	–
Floss flower	Ageratum corymbosum	–	IP	–	A	–	–	–
Four-wing saltbush	Atriplex canescens	*	CFI	–	L	–	–	–
Gaura	Gaura lindhiemeri	0	IP	–	–	–	B	–
Globemallow	Sphaeralcea ambigua	*	CFIP	–	L	*	–	–
Graythorn	Ziziphus obtusifolia	*	CFN	–	A	*	–	–
Lantana cultivars	Lantana camara cultivars	–	FIP	*	A	–	–	–
Mexican red bird-of-paradise	Caesalpinia pulcherrima	–	FIP	*	A	*	–	–
Orange jacobinia	Justicia spicigera	0	IP	*	–	–	–	–
Paper flower	Psilostrophe cooperi	*	FP	–	–	–	–	–
Pine-leaf milkweed	Asclepias linaria	*	FILP	–	B	–	–	–
Pomegranate	Punica granatum	–	CFILN	–	–	*	–	–
Rabbitbrush	Ericameria (Chrysothamnus) nauseosa	0	FILP	–	B	*	–	–
Red jacobinia	Justicia candicans	*	IP	*	–	–	–	–
Sweetbush, Chuckwalla's delight	Bebbia juncea	*	FILP	–	B	*	–	–
Triangleleaf bursage	Ambrosia deltoidea	*	C	–	–	–	–	–

Size HxW	Flowers	Water	Hardy to °F	Comments
30'x30'	Y	L-M	15	MG, FS, thorns
30'x30'	Pu	L	15	SG, FS, sharp thorns
30'x30'	Y	L-M	15	FG, FS, no thorns
20'x20'	Pi, Pu	M	-10	MG, FS, delicately scented flowers, LF for rustic sphinx moth
20'x20'	W	L-M	20	SG, FS, very thorny, flowers scented, creates heavy shade, hummingbirds and verdins tend to nest in it
30'x30'	Y	L-M	0	FG, FS, LF for marina blue butterfly
15'x15'	Y	L	10	FG, FS, sharp thorns, LF for nise sulphur and isola blue butterflies
3'x3'	R, O, Pi, W	M	16	FG-MG, FS-PS, CB/W for thicker growth
4'x4'	R	L	26	MG, FS, CB/S, LF for marina blue butterfly
4'x5'	Pu	L	15	MG-FG, FS, CB/S, probably LF for southern dogface butterfly
10'x10'	Y	L	5	MG, FS, CB/S, goldfinches and house finches eat seeds
3'x2'	Y	L	5	FG, FS, good for revegetation
6'x8'	W	L	15	FG, FS-PS; plant males—females produce many weedy seeds
18'x18'	Gr	L	20	MG, FS, thorny shrub, tortoise food, berries for birds, LF for snout and leilia hackberry butterflies
6'x4'	O, R	L	25	MG; FS-PS; open, weeping habit; LF for elada checkerspot butterfly
6'x5'	L	L-M	20	MG-SG, FS, aromatic, attractive, do not overwater
1.5'x1.5'	Y	L	15	FG, FS, tortoise food, LF for sulphur butterflies
1'x1'	W	L	15	MG, FS, sometimes difficult to establish
3'x3'	Pi	L	15	MG, FS, CB/S for thicker growth, LF for marina blue and common blue butterflies
1.5'x 3.5'	Pu, W	M	0	FG, FS-PS, herbaceous shrub, native from Central America to Sonora, Mexico
8'x8'	Gr	L	10	MG, FS, LF for alpheus sootywing skipper
4'x4'	Pi-W	L-M	H	FG, FS, herbaceous shrub, CB/W for lush new growth, LF for white-lined sphinx moth
4'x4'	O, R, Pi, L, W	L	H	MG, FS, tortoise food, LF for communis checkered skipper
6'x8'	Gr-Y	M	15	MG, FS-PS, attracts wildlife, very thorny, can be used as a security barrier, berries poisonous to humans
3'x8'	O, R, Y, Pi	M	32	FG, FS, native to tropical America, CB/Sp if frost damaged, leaves can cause dermatitis
5'x8'	R-O	L-M	28	FG, FS, CB/Sp, prickly, native to West Indies
3'x4'	O	M	22	MG-FG, PS-FS, CB/W
2'x2'	Y	L	15	FG, FS, very attractive, easy from seed
3'x3'	W	L-M	10	MG, FS, LF for queen butterfly
10'x8'	R	L-M	10	MG, FS, birds love edible fruit, native to SE Europe and S Asia
4'x4'	Y	L	-20	FG, FS, fall flowers, LF for sagebrush checkerspot butterflies
4'x6'	R	L-M	26	MG, FS-PS, CB/S
2'x2'	Y	L	0	FG, FS, CB/Sp, can become weedy, LF for Wright's metalmark butterfly
2'x2'	Y-Gr	L	22	FG-MG, FS, good for wild areas, important nurse plant, pollen aggravates allergies, burrlike seeds

Common Name	Scientific Name	Native	Wildlife Habitat	Humming-birds	Butter-flies	Bees	Moths	Bats
Wolfberry	*Lycium* species	*	CFIP	*	A	*	?	–
Yellow bells	*Tecoma stans*	*	IP	*	–	*	–	–
Yellow evening primrose	*Calylophus hartwegii*	*	FLP	–	A	–	A	–
GROUND COVERS AND VINES								
Desert four o'clock	*Mirabilis multiflora*	*	FP	–	–	–	A	–
Fine-leaf verbena	*Verbena tenuisecta*	–	FIP	–	A	–	A	–
Native passion flower	*Passiflora arida*	*	FILP	–	L	*	–	–
Trailing four o'clock, Windmills	*Allionia incarnata*	*	P	–	A	*	–	–
Trailing lantana	*Lantana montevidensis*	–	FP	–	L	–	A	–
ANNUALS AND SHORT-LIVED PERENNIALS								
Baja lily	*Calochortus splendens*	*	P	–	–	*	–	–
Blue dicks	*Dichelostemma pulchellum*	*	FP	–	–	*	–	–
Cosmos	*Cosmos sulfureus* or cultivars	–	FIP	–	A	*	–	–
Golden fleece	*Thymophylla pentachaeta*	*	FIP	–	B	*	–	–
Gooding's verbena	*Glandularia goodingii*	*	FIP	–	A	–	A	–
Mexican poppy	*Eschscholtzia mexicana*	*	FP	–	–	*	–	–
Penstemon	*Penstemon* species	*	FP	*	L	–	–	–
Silverbells	*Streptanthus carinatus*	*	FIP	–	L	*	–	–
Tufted evening primrose	*Oenothera caespitosa*	*	FILP	–	–	*	B	–
ACCENT PLANTS								
Aloe	*Aloe* species	–	P	*	–	–	–	–
Desert milkweed	*Asclepias subulata*	*	P	–	B	–	–	–
Huachuca agave	*Agave parryi huachucensis*	*	IP	*	L	*	–	*
Indian rice grass	*Oryzopsis hymenoides*	*	F	–	–	–	–	–
Night-blooming hesperaloe	*Hesperaloe nocturna*	0	IP	–	–	–	A	*
Ocotillo	*Fouquieria splendens*	*	FP	*	–	–	–	–
Organ pipe cactus	*Stenocereus thurberi*	*	FP	–	–	–	A	*
Pincushion cactus	*Mammillaria* species	*	FIP	–	–	*	–	–
Prickly pear cactus	*Opuntia* spp.	*	CFILP	–	–	*	–	–
Red-flowered hesperaloe	*Hesperaloe parviflora*	0	IP	*	–	–	–	–
Saguaro	*Carnegiea gigantea*	*	CFNP	*	–	*	A	*
Slipper flower	*Pedilanthus macrocarpus*	*	P	*	–	–	–	–

Size HxW	Flowers	Water	Hardy to °F	Comments
8'x10'	Pu–W	L–M	H	MG, FS–PS, thorns, a number of good species are available, berries for birds and tortoises
6'x6'	Y	L–M	25	FG, FS–PS, CB/Sp if frost damaged
2'x2'	Y	L–M	15	MG, FS, CB/W for thicker growth
1'x3'	Pu	L	18	FG–MG, FS–PS, root perennial, stunning purple flowers
1'x3'	Pu	L–M	15	FG, FS–PS, ground cover, native to South America
to 20'	Pu, W	M	Root hardy	FG, FS, vine, LF for gulf fritillary butterfly
0.6'x3'	V	L	5	FG, FS, colorful ground cover
3'x3'	L–Pu, W	M	25	FG, FS–PS, CB/Sp if frost damaged, ground cover, native to South America, LF for melinus hairstreak butterfly
1'x1'	L	L	20	FG, FS, spring bloom, bulb, can be difficult to establish, needs well-drained soil, do not overwater
2'x1'	Bl	L	5	FG, FS, spring-blooming perennial bulb, needs well-drained soil, do not overwater
6'x2'	O, Y, R	M	32	FG, FS–PS, summer annual, CB/mid-S to renew growth
0.5'x0.5'	Y	L	18	FG, FS–PS, annual or short-lived perennial, LF for dainty sulfur butterfly
2'x4'	L–Pu	L–M	15	FG, FS–PS, annual or short-lived perennial, leaves can cause dermatitis
1'x1'	O	L–M	20	FG, FS–PS, annual
3'x1.5'	R, Pi, Bl	L–M	25	FG, FS–PS, CB flower stalks after flowering, annual or short-lived perennial, LF for anicia and arachne checkerspot butterfly
2'x1'	W	L–M	H	FG, FS, Winter/spring annual, LF for Sara and cethura orange-tip butterflies
2'x2'	W–Pi	M	12	FG, FS–PS, annual or short-lived perennial, needs good drainage, fragrant, tortoise food, LF for rustic sphinx moth
3'x3'	O, R, Y	L	25	FG, MG, SG, FS–PS, native mostly to Africa, some are small trees to 12'
3'x3'	W	L	H	FG, FS, frequented by pepsis wasps, LF for queen and monarch butterflies
3'x3'	Y	L	H	SG, FS–PS, LF for skippers
1'x 0.5'	W	L	−8	FG, FS, beautiful accent grass
4'x6'	W	L	10	MG, FS, graceful flower stalks to 10'
12'x10'	R–O	L	10	SG, FS, thorns, nursery-grown plants will have better roots than field-collected ones
10'x10'	W, Pi	L	25	SG, FS–PS, spines, fruits for animals, faster growth with moderate water in summer only
1'x1'	Pi, W, Y	L	H	SG, FS–PS, small spines, various species throughout the Southwest
Varies	Y, Pi, Pu	L	Varies	MG–FG, FS, tortoises eat fruit and young pads, most species are hardy to teens
3'x5'	R, Y	L	10	MG, FS, tall flower stalks
30'x10'	W	L	15	SG–MG, FS, protect from sun when young, fruit for animals, white-winged doves also pollinate it
3'x4'	Pi–R	L	25	MG, FS, interesting flowers, white sap can cause dermatitis

Lower Colorado Desert

Common Name	Scientific Name	Native	Wildlife Habitat	Humming-birds	Butter-flies	Bees	Moths	Bats
TREES								
Blue palo verde	Parkinsonia florida	*	CFINP	–	–	*	–	–
Desert fern, Feather tree	Lysiloma microphylla	0	CINP	–	B	*	?	–
Desert ironwood	Olneya tesota	*	CFINP	–	–	*	–	–
'Desert Museum' hybrid palo verde	Parkinsonia hybrid	–	CFINP	–	–	*	–	–
Desert willow	Chilopsis linearis	*	CINP	*	A	–	L	–
Foothills palo verde	Parkinsonia microphylla	*	CFINP	–	–	*	–	–
Sweet acacia	Acacia farnesiana	0	FINP	–	–	*	–	–
Texas ebony	Ebenopsis ebano	0	CFINP	–	A	*	?	–
Velvet mesquite	Prosopis velutina	*	CFINP	–	B	*	–	–
Western honey mesquite	Prosopis glandulosa var. torreyana	*	CFINP	–	B	*	–	–
SHRUBS AND PERENNIALS								
Arizona rosewood	Vauquelinia californica	0	CFIP	–	–	*	–	–
Baja fairyduster	Calliandra californica	0	FIP	*	B	*	–	–
Black dalea	Dalea frutescens	0	FI	–	B	–	–	–
Brittlebush	Encelia farinosa	*	FIP	–	–	*	–	–
Catclaw acacia	Acacia greggii	*	CFILNP	–	–	*	–	–
Chuparosa	Justicia californica	*	CFP	*	–	–	–	–
Creosote	Larrea divaricata	*	CFI	–	–	*	–	–
Desert hackberry	Celtis pallida	0	CFINP	–	L	–	–	–
Desert honeysuckle	Anisacanthus thurberi	0	FP	*	L	–	–	–
Desert lavender	Hyptis albida	*	FIN	–	–	*	–	–
Desert senna	Senna covesii	*	FIP	–	L	–	–	–
Dune buckwheat	Eriogonum deserticola	0	FIP	*	B	*	–	–
Elephant tree	Bursera microphylla	*	F	–	–	*	–	–
Fairyduster	Calliandra eriophylla	*	FILP	*	B	*	–	–
Fremont indigo bush	Dalea fremontii	0	LP	–	L	*	–	–
Globemallow	Sphaeralcea ambigua and relatives	*	FIP	–	L	*	–	–
Jojoba	Simmondsia chinensis	*	CF	–	–	–	–	–
Littleleaf cordia	Cordia parvifolia	0	CFNP	–	–	–	–	–
Mexican bird-of-paradise	Caesalpinia mexicana	–	FP	*	A	*	–	–
Quail bush	Atriplex lentiformis	*	CF	–	–	–	–	–
Ruellia	Ruellia peninsularis	0	CFIP	*	–	*	–	–
Shortleaf wolfberry	Lycium brevipes	*	CFINP	*	A	*	–	–
Texas ranger	Leucophyllum frutescens	0	CNP	–	A	*	–	–
Whitethorn acacia	Acacia constricta	*	FILNP	–	L	*	–	–

Size HxW	Flowers	Water	Hardy to °F	Comments
30'x30'	Y	L–M	15	MG, FS, many thorns
15'x18'	W	M	25	MG–FG, FS–PS, no thorns, LF for agarithe sulphur butterfly
30'x30'	Pu	L	15	SG, many thorns, edible seeds
30'x30'	Y	L–M	15	FG, FS, no thorns
20'x20'	Pi, Pu	L–M	−10	MG, FS, scented flowers, LF for rustic sphinx moth
20'x20'	Y	L	15	SG, FS, thorns
30'x20'	Y	L	10	FS, FG, sharp thorns, fragrant flowers
20'x20'	W	L–M	20	SG, FS, flowers scented, very thorny, hummingbirds and verdins tend to nest in it
10'x15'	Y	L–M	5 to 0	FG, FS, thorns, LF for marina blue butterfly
25'x30'	Y	L	0	FG, FS, thorns, suspected LF for Palmer's metalmark
15'x15'	W	L–M	15	SG–MG, FS–PS
6'x6'	R	L	25	MG–FG, FS–PS, CB/S for thicker growth, LF for marina blue butterfly
4'x5'	Pu	L	15	MG–FG, FS–PS, CB/S, probably LF for southern dogface butterfly
3'x4'	Y	L	28	MG–FG, FS–PS
10'x15'	Y	L	0	MG, FS–PS, fragrant flowers, curved thorns
4'x6'	R, Y	L	28	MG–FG, FS, yellow form is var. 'Julie'
6'x8'	Y	L	5	SG, FS, seeds attract goldfinches and other birds
18'x18'	Gr	L–M	20	SG, FS, thorny, tortoise food, birds eat berries, LF for snout and Leila hackberry butterflies
6'x4'	O, R	L	25	MG, FS–PS, LF for elada checkerspot butterfly
8'x10'	L	L	25	FG–MG, FS–PS, fragrant foliage
1.5'x1.5'	Y	L	15	MG, FS–PS, reseeds, LF for sulphur butterflies
2'x2'	Y	L	18	MG; FS; attractive; colorful; important LF for hairstreaks, coppers, blues, and other butterflies
6'x8'	W	L–M	30	MG, FS, can be as large as 18'x20' where protected from frost
3'x3'	Pi	L	15	MG, FS–PS, CB/S, LF for marina blue and common blue butterflies
4'x6'	Pu	L	23	MG–FG, FS, attractive, LF for southern dogface and Reakirt's blue butterflies
4'x4'	O, Pi, L, W, R	L	H	FG, FS, perennial shrubby herb, tortoise food, LF for communis checkered skipper
6'x10'	Y	L	20	SG–MG, FS–PS, male and female flowers on separate plants
8'x10'	W	L–M	18	MG, FS
15'x10'	Y	M	25	FG; FS; attracts big, gentle carpenter bees; native to Mexico
8'x12'	Gr	L	15	MG, FS, thorns, four-wing saltbush is a smaller alternative
4'x4'	Pu	L–M	26	MG, FS–PS, seedpods burst open when wet
9'x7'	L	L	5	MG, FS–PS, spiny shrub, red edible fruit
8'x8'	Pu, L, W	L	10	FG–MG, FS–PS, thin branches in winter, do not overwater, several varieties
10'x15'	Y	L	0	FG, FS, thorns, LF for isola blue butterfly

Common Name	Scientific Name	Native	Wildlife Habitat	Hummingbirds	Butterflies	Bees	Moths	Bats
Wolfberry, Lycium	*Lycium* species	*	CFIP	*	A	*	?	–
Yellow bells	*Tecoma stans*	0	IP	*	–	*	–	–

ANNUALS AND SHORT-LIVED PERENNIALS

Common Name	Scientific Name	Native	Wildlife Habitat	Hummingbirds	Butterflies	Bees	Moths	Bats
Arroyo lupine	*Lupinus succulentus*	*	FLP	*	L	*	–	–
Birdcage primrose	*Oenothera deltoidea*	*	FILP	–	–	–	B	–
Desert lily	*Hesperocallis undulata*	*	FP	–	–	–	A	–
Desert marigold	*Baileya multiradiata*	*	FIP	–	A	*	–	–
Desert tomato, Ground cherry	*Physalis crassifolia*	*	FP	–	–	*	–	–
Dune primrose	*Oenothera deltoidea*	*	FLP	–	–	*	A	–
Mohave aster	*Xylorhiza tortifolia*	*	FP	–	A	*	–	–
Sand verbena	*Abronia villosa*	*	FIP	–	B	–	A	–
Sundrops	*Camissionia brevipes*	*	P	–	–	–	A	–

NOTE: Penstemons, salvias, and hopbush (*Dodonea viscosa*) will grow, but are short-lived in this region.

ACCENT PLANTS

Common Name	Scientific Name	Native	Wildlife Habitat	Hummingbirds	Butterflies	Bees	Moths	Bats
Bamboo muhly	*Muhlenbergia dumosa*	*	FL	–	L	–	–	–
Bigelow's beargrass	*Nolina bigelovii*	*	CFP	–	–	*	–	–
Buckhorn cholla	*Opuntia acanthocarpa*	*	CFINP	–	–	*	L	–
Compass barrel	*Ferocactus cylindraceous*	*	FP	–	–	*	–	–
Desert agave	*Agave deserti*	*	FIP	*	–	*	–	*
Desert milkweed	*Asclepias subulata*	*	FILP	–	B	–	–	–
Desert spoon, Sotol	*Dasylirion wheeleri*	*	FIP	–	–	*	–	–
Fishhook cactus	*Mammillaria tetrancistra*	*	FP	–	–	*	–	–
Mexican tree ocotillo	*Fouquieria macdougalii*	0	P	*	–	–	–	–
Night-blooming cereus	*Peniocereus greggii*	*	FP	–	–	–	A	–
Ocotillo	*Fouquieria splendens*	*	FP	*	–	–	–	–
Organpipe cactus	*Stenocereus thurberi*	*	FIP	–	–	–	–	*
Prickly pear cactus	*Opuntia* species	*	CFILP	–	–	*	–	–
Red hesperaloe	*Hesperaloe parviflora*	0	FIP	*	–	–	–	–
Saguaro	*Carnegiea gigantea*	*	CFNP	*	–	*	A	*
Senita	*Pachycereus schottii*	*	FIP	–	–	–	B	–
Sideoats grama	*Bouteloua curtipendula*	*	FL	–	L	–	–	–

Size HxW	Flowers	Water	Hardy to °F	Comments
8'x10'	W, Pu	L-M	H	MG, FS-PS, thorns, fruit for birds
6'x6'	Y	L-M	25	MG-FG, FS, CB/S if frost damaged
4'x3'	Pu	L	5	FG; FS; annual; easy to grow from seed; LF for sooty hairstreak, arrowhead blue, silvery blue, Perseus duskywing, several sulphur, Acmon, and Karner blue butterflies
1'x1'	W	L	H	FG, FS, annual, LF for two-lined sphinx moth
3'x2'	W	L	8	SG, FS, bulb, by seed in deep sand, difficult to establish
1'x1'	Y	L	15	FG, FS, short-lived perennial or annual, reseeds readily
2'x2'	Y	L	28	FG, FS-PS, short-lived perennial, open habit, easy to grow from seed
1'x2'	W	L	10	FG, FS, annual, needs good drainage
.5'x.5'	L	L-M	20	FG, FS, short-lived perennial
1'x3'	Pi, Pu	L	H	FG; FS; annual; delicate scent in evenings; sticky, hairy leaves; hard to grow in other regions; LF for painted lady butterflies
1'x1'	Y	L	10	FG, FS, annual
4'x4'	Gr	L-M	10	MG, FS-PS, attractive, soft looking, tortoise food, LF for skippers
6'x6'	Y-W	L	10	SG, FS-PS, impressive, sometimes hard to find
4'x5'	R, Y	L	H, 10	SG-MG, FS, many spines, many other good species, plant away from paths, LF for moth species
10'x3'	Y	L	0	SG, FS, backbone plant, showy fruit, spines, plant away from paths
1.5'x2'	Y	L	22	MG, FS, plant away from paths, spine-tipped leaves can be nipped back, other good agaves available
2'x4'	Y	L	23	MG, FS, LF for monarch and queen butterflies
4'x6'	Y	L-M	0	MG, FS-PS, spine-toothed leaf edges, plant away from paths
1'x2'	Pi-Pu	L	10	MG, FS-PS, avoid overwatering, small spines, other good *Mammillaria* species available
6'x8'	R	L-M	28	MG-FG, FS, dense branches, thorns, plant away from paths
3'x3'	W	L	10	SG, FS-PS, sparse branches, found growing in open shrubs
10'x12'	R-O	L	10	SG, FS, thorns, plant away from paths, nursery-grown plants have better roots than field-collected ones
15'x20'	W, Pi	L	25	MG, FS, spines, plant away from paths, faster growth with moderate water in summer
Varies	Y, Pi	L	Varies	MG-FG, FS, spines, plant away from paths, most are hardy to below 20°F
3'x5'	R, Pi	L	10	SG-MG, FS-PS, other good hesperaloes are available
30'x10'	W	L	15	SG, FS, spines, plant away from paths, white-winged doves also pollinate it, needs sun protection when young
10'x10'	Pi	L	20	SG, FS, small spines, plant away from path, senita moth story similar to yucca moth
3'x3'	Pi	L	0	MG, FS, LF for several skipperlings and skippers

Desert Grasslands

Common Name	Scientific Name	Native	Wildlife Habitat	Hummingbirds	Butterflies	Bees	Moths	Bats
TREES								
Alligator bark juniper	Juniperus deppeana	*	CFN	–	L	–	–	–
American plum	Prunus americana	–	CFNP	–	L	*	–	–
Arizona ash	Fraxinus velutina	*	CNP	–	L	–	–	–
Arizona black walnut	Juglans major	0	CFN	–	–	–	–	–
Arizona cypress	Cupressus arizonica	0	CFN	–	–	–	–	–
Canyon hackberry, Netleaf hackberry	Celtis reticulata	*	CFN	–	L	–	–	–
Emory oak	Quercus emoryi	*	CLNS	–	L	–	–	–
Gambel oak	Quercus gambelii	*	CLNS	–	L	–	–	–
Mexican elderberry	Sambucus mexicana	0	CFNP	–	A	*	–	–
Native mesquite species	Prosopis velutina, torreyana, glandulosa	*	CFNP	–	–	*	–	–
New Mexico locust	Robinia neomexicana	0	P	–	L	*	–	–
One-seed juniper	Juniperus coahuilensis	0	CFN	–	L	–	–	–
Pinyon pine	Pinus edulis	0	CFN	–	–	–	–	–
Rocky mountain juniper	Juniperus scopulorum	0	CFN	–	–	–	–	–
Screwbean mesquite	Prosopis pubescens	0	CFNP	–	L	*	–	–
Shrub oak	Quercus turbinella	*	CLNS	–	L	–	–	–
Western black cherry	Prunus serotina rufula	0	CFNP	–	–	*	–	–
SHRUBS AND PERENNIALS								
Antelope horn	Asclepias asperula	*	LP	–	B	–	–	–
Apache plume	Fallugia paradoxa	*	P	–	A	*	–	–
Arizona rosewood	Vauquelinia californica	*	CFINP	–	A	*	A	–
Autumn sage	Salvia greggii	0	IP	*	A	–	–	–
Bee balm	Monarda menthaefolia	0	P	*	A	*	–	–
Butterfly weed	Asclepias tuberosa	0	LP	–	B	–	–	–
Chiltepin	Capsicum annuum	0	F	–	–	*	–	–
Cliffrose	Purshia mexicana	*	CFLP	–	L	*	–	–
Hummingbird bush	Zauschneria californica	0	P	*	–	–	–	–
Kidneywood	Eysenhardtia orthocarpa	*	FIP	–	B	*	–	–
Lobelia	Lobelia laxiflora	0	P	*	–	–	–	–
Mealy-cup sage	Salvia farinacea	0	PS	*	–	–	–	–
Mexican blue sage	Salvia chamaedryoides	0	P	*	–	*	–	–
New Mexico olive, Desert olive	Forestiera neomexicana	*	CFN	–	–	–	–	–
Pineleaf milkweed	Asclepias linarea	0	LP	–	B	–	–	–

Size HxW	Flowers	Water	Hardy to °F	Comments
40'x30'	–	L–M	0	FG, FS, animals attracted to fruit, LF for silva and olive hairstreak butterflies
20'x20'	W	L–M	H	MG; FS–PS; shrub or tree; edible fruit; spreads, creating thicket
30'x20'	Gr-Y	M	–10	FG; FS; heat tolerant; attractive tree; leaves and seeds create litter; LF for western tiger, two-tailed, and pale swallowtail butterflies
30'x30'	Y-Gr	M	5	SG, FS, shade tree, fruit is messy and staining
50'x50'	Y-W	M	0	MG, FS, evergreen, windbreak, interesting
30'x30'	Gr	M	5	SG, FS, drought hardy once established, tortoise food, fruit for birds, LF for snout, celtis and Clyton hackberry butterflies
30'x30'	Y-Gr	M	–10	MG; FS; evergreen; acorns; LF for araes skipper, juvinalis duskywing, quaderna hairstreak, and Arizona sister butterflies
25'x20'	Y-Gr	M	–10	MG, FS, deciduous, acorns, LF for Colorado hairstreak
20'x15'	Y-W	M–H	–10	FG, FS, showy flowers, birds attracted to the fruit, give a few deep soakings in summer, regular water in winter
25'x25'	Y	L–M	H	FG, FS, much of tree used by Native Americans, good source for honey
20'x15'	Pu-Pi	M	0	MG, FS, thorny, seeds, good barrier, LF for silver spotted skipper and funeralis duskywing butterflies
20'x15'	–	L–M	0	MG, FS, fruit for wildlife, LF for silva hairstreak butterfly
30'x20'	–	M	H	SG, FS–PS, evergreen, edible seeds
20'x20'	–	L–M	H	FG, FS–PS, attractive tree, fruit for wildlife
15'x10'	Y	L–M	0	MG, FS, interesting twisted seedpods
8'x8'	Y-Gr	M	12	MG, FS, evergreen, great small tree
25'x20'	W	L–M	H	MG, FS, attractive tree, animals eat the very small cherries
1'x2'	W	L	10	FG, FS, herbaceous, root perennial, LF for queen and monarch butterflies
6'x4'	W	L	0	SG, FS, holds interest in many seasons
15'x10'	W	L	15	SG, FS, spider mites can infest this plant but to little detriment
3'x3'	R, O, W, Pi	L–M	16	FG, FS–PS, CB/W, popular plant, blooms much of the year
2'x2'	Bl	M	0	MG, PS, great for butterflies
2'x1'	Y, O	L	0	FG, FS–PS, herbaceous, top freezes at 32°F, LF for queen and monarch butterflies
3'x2'	W	L–M	15	MG, FS–PS, may freeze out in teens, very hot fruit, LF for sphinx moths
6'x6'	Y	L	20	MG, FS, flowery and attractive, LF for desert elfin butterfly
1.5'x2'	R	M	5	FG, PS–Sh, fall bloom
10'x16'	W	L	5	MG, FS, fragrant flowers, LF for marine blue butterfly
1'x3'	R	L–M	10	MG–FG, FS–PS, herbaceous root perennial, flowers all summer
1'x1'	Bl	M	15	FG, PS, very beautiful blossoms, herbaceous, will reseed, ask for the native, not the cultivars
1'x2'	Bl	L–M	10	MG–FG, FS–PS, gray leaves, blue blossoms much of the year
9'x6'	Gr-W	L–M	–10	FG–MG, FS, fruit attracts wildlife
2'x1'	W	L	15	MG, FS–PS, LF for queen and monarch butterflies

Common Name	Scientific Name	Native	Wildlife Habitat	Humming-birds	Butter-flies	Bees	Moths	Bats
Rubberbrush, Mariola	Parthenium incanum	*	P	–	–	*	–	–
Scarlet betony	Stachys coccinea	0	FP	*	–	–	–	–
Smooth sumac	Rhus glabra	*	CFNP	–	–	*	–	–
Snakeweed	Gutierrezia sarothrae	*	FP	–	*	*	–	–
Wright buckwheat	Eriogonum wrightii	*	FIP	*	B	*	–	–
GROUND COVERS AND VINES								
Canyon grape	Vitis arizonica	0	FP	–	A	*	L	–
Common trumpet creeper	Campsis radicans	–	P	*	–	–	–	–
Indian root	Aristolochia watsonii	*	FLP	–	L	–	–	–
Passionflower vine	Passiflora mexicana	*	P	–	L	*	–	–
Snapdragon vine	Maurandya antirrhiniflora	*	P	*	–	–	–	–
Trumpet honeysuckle	Lonicera sempervirens	–	FP	*	A	–	–	–
White honeysuckle	Lonicera albiflora	*	FP	*	A	–	–	–
Woodbine	Parthenocissus inserta	*	F	–	–	*	–	–
ANNUALS AND SHORT-LIVED PERENNIALS								
Big penstemon	Penstemon pseudo-spectabilis	*	FP	*	L	–	–	–
Fendler's penstemon	Penstemon fendleri	*	FP	*	L	–	–	–
Hooker primrose	Oenothera hookeri	*	FILP	–	–	–	B	–
Thurber's penstemon	Penstemon thurberi	*	FP	*	L	–	–	–
Tufted evening primrose	Oenothera caespitosa	*	FILP	–	–	*	B	–
ACCENT PLANTS								
Banana yucca	Yucca baccata	*	FIP	–	–	*	B	–
Fendler's hedgehog	Echinocereus fendleri	*	FIP	–	–	*	–	–
Fishhook barrel cactus	Ferocactus wislizeni	*	FIP	–	–	*	–	–
Galleta grass	Hilaria jamesii	*	FL	–	–	–	–	–
Huachuca agave	Agave parryi huachucensis	*	IP	*	–	*	*	*
Ocotillo	Fouquieria splendens	*	FP	*	–	–	–	–
Palmer agave	Agave palmeri	*	IP	*	–	*	*	*
Parry agave	Agave parryi parryi	0	IP	*	–	*	*	*
Red hesperaloe	Hesperaloe parviflora	0	IP	*	–	–	–	–
Shin dagger	Agave schottii	*	IP	*	–	*	*	–
Soaptree yucca	Yucca elata	*	IP	–	–	–	B	–

Size HxW	Flowers	Water	Hardy to °F	Comments
2'x2'	W	L	0	MG, FS, good low shrub, fragrant foliage
1'x3'	R	M	5	FG, PS-Sh, herbaceous, better in shade
15'x15'	R	L-M	5	MG, FS, colorful, spreads by underground roots, prefers rich soil, lemonade-flavored berries
1.5'x2'	Y	L	0	MG, FS, santolina-like, aromatic, poisonous to livestock
3'x4'	R	L	10	MG; FS; elegant-looking white and pinkish flowers; tortoise food; important LF for hairstreaks, coppers, blues, and other butterflies
to 30'	W	M	0	FG, FS-PS-Sh, vine, slow to establish, tortoise food, fruit for birds, can take over, LF for ctenuchid moths
to 40'	O	M	0	FG, FS-PS, vine, huge fragrant flowers, suckering roots, native to Eastern United States
1'x1'	Pu	L	10	MG, FS-PS, odd flowers, hard to find but worth a search, LF for pipevine swallowtail butterfly
to 10'	Pu	L-M	10	FG, FS-PS-Sh, vine, LF for fritillary butterflies
to 10'	R, Pu	L-M	20	MG; FS-PS; delicate, beautiful hummingbird vine; tortoise forage
to 8'	R	M	0	MG-FG, FS-PS, twining vine, native to Eastern United States
6'x6'	W	M	0	MG-FG, FS, shrubby vine
to 40'	Gr	M	0	FG, FS-PS, red fall color, black fruit for the birds, deciduous
3'x2'	Pi	L	20	FG, FS-PS-Sh, showy short-lived perennial, LF for several checkerspot butterflies
2'x1'	Bl-Pu	L	H	FG, FS, short-lived perennial, LF for arachne and anicia checkerspot butterflies
4'x2'	Y	L-M	-20	MG, FS-PS, CB/W, short-lived perennial, can be weedy in wet places, LF for sphinx moths
2'x3'	Bl	L	0	FG, FS, showy short-lived perennial, LF for several checkerspot butterflies
1'x1.5'	W	M	5	MG-FG, FS-PS, fragrant short-lived perennial, javelina consume these plants, LF for sphinx moths
4'x4'	W	L	0	SG, FS-PS, best clumping yucca, bluish leaves
1'x3'	Pu	L	0	SG, FS, spiny, see claret cup in Chihuahuan section also
6'x2'	Y, O, R	L	0	SG, FS, stout hooklike spines, fruits attract birds and ground squirrels
3'x6'	Gr	L	5	FG, FS, good wild grass, highly durable
3'x3'	Y	L	10	SG, FS-PS, plant away from paths, sharp spines on leaf tips can be nipped off
12'x10'	R	L	10	MG, FS, thorns, nursery-grown plants will have better roots than field-collected ones
4'x4'	Y	L	10	MG-SG, FS, plant away from paths, sharp spines on leaf tips can be nipped off
2'x2'	Y	L	10	SG, FS-PS, plant away from paths, sharp spines on leaf tips can be nipped off
3'x5'	R, Y	L	10	MG-FG, FS-PS, flower spikes rise above plant, blooms at a young age
1'x1'	Y	L	10	SG, FS, makes small clumps but quick to flower, fragrant
8'x2'	W	L	H	SG, FS, LF for soaptree yucca moth

Chihuahuan Desert

Common Name	Scientific Name	Native	Wildlife Habitat	Humming-birds	Butter-flies	Bees	Moths	Bats
TREES								
Catclaw acacia	Acacia greggii	*	CIN	–	B	*	–	–
Desert willow	Chilopsis linearis	0	CFILNP	*	–	–	L	–
Screwbean mesquite, Tornillo	Prosopis pubescens	*	CFILNP	–	L	–	–	–
Texas ebony	Ebenopsis ebano	*	CFINP	–	B	*	–	–
Whitethorn acacia	Acacia constricta	*	FILNP	–	L	*	–	–
SHRUBS AND PERENNIALS								
Apache plume	Fallugia paradoxa	*	C	–	–	*	–	–
Arizona globe mallow	Sphaeralcea ambigua	0	FIP	–	L	*	–	–
Autumn sage	Salvia greggii	*	IP	*	A	–	–	–
Black dalea	Dalea frutescens	*	FLP	–	B	–	–	–
Blue mist	Eupatorium greggii	*	N	–	A	–	–	–
Canyon cassia	Senna wislizenii	*	FP	–	L	*	–	–
Cenizo, Texas Ranger	Leucophyllum frutescens	*	CNP	–	A	*	–	–
Chapparal sage	Salvia clevelandii	0	FP	*	–	–	–	–
Englemann daisy	Englemannia pinnatifida	–	F	–	A	–	–	–
Evergreen sumac	Rhus virens (R. chorio-phylla)	*	CFIN	–	–	*	–	–
Fairyduster	Calliandra eriophylla	0	FILP	*	–	–	–	–
Flame anisacanthus	Anisacanthus quadrifidus	*	LN	*	–	–	–	–
Henry sage	Salvia henryi	*	FP	*	–	–	–	–
Lantana 'New Gold', 'Sunset'	Lantana spp.	–	FIP	*	B	–	–	–
Littleleaf cordia	Cordia parvifolia	0	CLNP	*	–	–	–	–
Littleleaf sumac	Rhus microphylla	*	CFINP	–	–	*	–	–
Mealy-cup blue sage	Salvia farinacea	0	P	*	A	–	–	–
Mexican cliffrose	Purshia mexicana	0	CLNP	–	L	*	–	–
Paper flower	Psilostrophe tagetina	0	FLP	–	A	*	–	–
Prairie zinnia	Zinnia grandiflora	*	FIP	–	A	*	–	–
Red penstemon	Penstemon baccharifolius	*	FP	*	L	–	–	–
Shrub live oak	Quercus turbinella	0	CFLN	–	L	–	–	–
Southern sagebrush	Artemisia nova	–	F	–	L	–	–	–
Sundrops	Calylophus hartwegii	*	FLP	–	A	–	A	–
Sweetbush, Chuck-walla's delight	Bebbia juncea	0	FILP	–	B	*	–	–
Turpentine bush	Ericameria laricifolia	*	FIP	–	A	*	–	–
White beebrush	Aloysia gratissima	0	FIP	–	A	*	A	–
Wild buckwheat	Eriogonum wrightii	*	FLP	–	L	*	–	–
Wolfberry	Lycium berlandieri	*	CFINP	*	A	*	–	–

Size HxW	Flowers	Water	Hardy to °F	Comments
15'x25'	W-Y	L	0	MG, FS, thorny, small trees, fragrant flowers, LF for Mexican yellow butterfly
25'x30'	Pi, Pu	L-M	-10	MG, FS, delicately scented flowers, LF for rustic sphinx moths
15'x15'	Y	L-M	0	MG, FS, LF for tailed orange, Leda hairstreak, marine blue, and ceraunus blue butterflies
25'x20'	W	L	18	MG, FS, LF for coyote cloudywing skipper
10'x15'	Y	L	0	FG, FS, sharp thorns, LF for Mexican yellow and isola blue butterflies
5'x5'	W	L	0	MG, FS, light scent
4'x4'	O, R, L, Pi, W	L	H	FG, FS, tortoise food, LF for communis checkered skipper
3'x3'	R, Pi	L-M	16	FG-MG, FS-PS, CB/W for thicker growth, fragrant flowers
3'x4'	Pu	L	15	MG-FG, FS, other Daleas good too, LF for southern dogface and Reakirt's blue butterflies
1'x3'	Pu	L-M	Root hardy	FG, PS, perennial herb, spreads by rhizomes, dies to ground in winter
6'x6'	Y	L	10	FG, FS, blooms in fall, leafs out late in spring, tortoise food, LF sennae and nicippe sulphur butterflies
8'x8'	Pu, L, W	L	10	MG, FS, thin branches in winter, do not overwater, several varieties
5'x5'	Pu	L	16	MG, FS, requires good drainage
2'x3'	Y	L-M	10	FG, FS-PS, CB/Sp
5'x10'	W	L	5	SG, FS, excellent bird shelter and food source
3'x3'	Pi	L	15	MG, FS, spreads by rhizomes and seed
3'x4'	O, R	L	5	FG, FS, CB/S
2'x2'	R	L	15	FG, FS, CB/Sp
2'x2'	Y, O	M	28	FG, FS, cultivars do not become weedy, LF for gray hairstreak butterfly
8'x10'	W	L	18	FG, FS, showy in bloom
15'x15'	W	L-M	0	MG-SG, FS-PS, can be used as a shrub or small tree, red fall color, red lemonade-flavored berries, birds use for food and shelter
2'x2'	Pu	L-M	28	FG, FS-PS, perennial herb that dies back to ground in winter
5'x5'	W	L	-10	MG, FS, LF for desert elfin butterfly
2'x2'	Y	L	15	FG, FS, dried flowers persist on plant
0.5'x2'	Y	L	0	MG, FS, spreads by underground rhizomes
3'x2'	R	L	20	MG, FS, LF for several checkerspot butterflies
6'x12'	Gr	L	12	MG, FS-PS, LF for Ontario hairstreak
2'x2'	Y	L	0	SG, FS, silver foliage, mountain species, LF for Old World swallowtail and American lady butterflies
2'x2'	Y	L-M	15	MG, FS, CB/W for thicker growth
2'x2'	Y	L	0	FG, FS, CB/Sp, can become weedy, LF for Wright's metalmark butterfly
2'x3'	Y	L	0	MG, FS, CB/Sp, neat form, fall flowers
5'x8'	W	L	15	MG-SG, PS, fragrant flowers, can be weedy
2'x2'	W, Pi	L	0	MG, FS, tortoise food, LF for green hairstreak, several blue, and copper butterflies
8'x10'	Pu	L	15	MG, FS, very spiny, tortoises and birds love red fruits

Common Name	Scientific Name	Native	Wildlife Habitat	Humming-birds	Butter-flies	Bees	Moths	Bats
GROUND COVERS AND VINES								
Blackfoot daisy	Melampodium leucanthum	*	FP	–	A	*	A	–
Buffalo gourd	Cucurbita foetidissima	*	FP	–	–	*	–	–
Coral vine	Antigonon leptopus	0	FIP	*	A	*	–	–
Coyote melon	Cucurbita digitata	0	FP	–	–	*	–	–
Moss verbena	Verbena tenuisecta	–	FN	–	A	–	A	–
Prostrate dalea	Dalea greggii	*	FN	–	B	–	–	–
Yarrow	Achillea millefolium	–	IP	–	A	–	–	–
ANNUALS AND SHORT-LIVED PERENNIALS								
Butterweed, Groundsel	Senecio longi-lobus var. douglasii	*	FP	–	A	*	–	–
Chocolate flower	Berlandiera lyrata	*	FP	–	A	–	A	–
Desert bahia	Bahia absinthifolia	*	FLN	–	A	–	–	–
Desert marigold	Baileya multiradiata	*	FIP	–	A	*	–	–
Penstemon	Penstemon spp.	*	FP	*	–	*	A	–
Prickleleaf dogweed	Thymophylla acerosa	*	FIP	–	B	*	–	–
Tufted evening primrose	Oenothera caespitosa	0	FILP	–	–	*	B	–
ACCENT PLANTS								
Banana yucca	Yucca baccata	*	FIP	–	–	–	L	–
Beehive cactus	Coryphantha vivipara	*	FP	–	–	*	–	–
Blue grama	Bouteloua gracilis	*	FL	–	L	–	–	–
Claret cup cactus	Echinocereus triglochidiatus	*	FIP	*	–	–	–	–
Deer grass	Muhlenbergia rigens	*	CF	–	–	–	–	–
Giant cactus	Echinopsis terscheckii (Trichocereus)	–	FP	–	–	*	–	*
Lechuguilla	Agave lechuguilla	*	FP	*	–	–	–	*
Mojave mound cactus	Echinocereus triglochidiatus	*	FP	*	–	*	–	–
Ocotillo	Fouquieria splendens	*	FP	*	–	–	–	–
Prickly pear cactus	Opuntia spp.	*	CFILP	–	–	*	–	–
Red-flowered hesperaloe	Hesperaloe parviflora	0	FP	*	–	–	–	–

Size HxW	Flowers	Water	Hardy to °F	Comments
1'x1.5'	W	L	0	FG–MG, FS–PS, plant around walkways, ground cover, needs good drainage, light scent in evening
to 20'	Y-O	L	0	FG, FS, root perennial, trailing vine, gourd not edible
to 25'	Pi, R, W	M	25	FG, FS, vine, slow to establish, freezes to ground in winter, root hardy to 25°F
to 20'	Y	L	0	FG, FS, root perennial, trailing vine, fruit not edible
0.5'x6'	Pu	L–M	15	FG, FS–PS, long-blooming ground cover, native to South America
2'x6'	Pu	L	15	MG, FS, ground cover, LF for southern dogface and Reakirt's blue butterflies
1.5'x2'	W	M	–10	FG, PS, ground cover, spreads by rhizome
3'x1'	Y	L	–6	FG, FS–PS, annual or short-lived perennial, needs good drainage, reseeds
1'x1'	Y	L–M	–10	FG, FS, short-lived perennial, fragrant flowers, can be weedy
2'x2'	Y	L	15	FG, FS, perennial if given water or annual
1'x1'	Y	L	15	FG, FS, short-lived perennial or annual
1'x2'	R, Pi, Pu, W	L–M	Varies, < 20	FG–MG, FS, some PS, many good species, annual or short-lived perennial, mostly hummingbird flowers
1'x1'	Y	L	10	FG, FS, short-lived perennial, LF for dainty sulfur butterflies
2'x2'	W-Pi	L–M	12	FG, FS–PS, short-lived perennial, needs good drainage, fragrant, tortoise food, LF for sphinx moths
6'x10'	W	L	0	SG, FS–PS, plant away from paths, sharp-tipped leaves can be nipped back, LF for banana yucca moth
0.5'x 0.33'	Pi-Pu	L	0	MG, FS, small plant with showy flowers, spines, sometimes sold as *Mammillaria vivipara*
1.5'x0.1'	Gr	L	5	FG, FS, good meadow grass, LF for Uncas and Pahaska skipper and Ridings' satyr butterflies
1'x3'	R	L	0	SG, FS–PS, spines
3'x4'	W	L–M	10	MG, FS, CB/W
20'x10'	W	L–M	5	MG, FS, spiny, many large flowers several times per year, native to N. Argentina
2'x2'	Y, Pu	L	–10	SG, FS, plant away from paths, sharp-tipped leaves can be nipped back
1'x3'	R-O	L	0	MG, FS–PS, bright flowers, spines
12'x10'	R, O	L	10	MG, FS, thorns
varies	Y-Pi	L	Varies	MG–FG, FS, spines, tortoises eat fruits and young pads, most are hardy to teens
3'x3'	R, Y	L	10	MG, FS, tall flower spikes

REFERENCES AND ADDITIONAL READING

Chapter One

Ackerman, Diane. 2001. *Cultivating Delight: A Natural History of My Garden.* New York: HarperCollins.

Adams, Ansel. 1975. *The Role of the Artist in Conservation.* Berkeley: University of California College of Natural Resources, Department of Forestry and Conservation.

Allen, Marjory Gill (Baroness Allen of Hurtwood). 1968. *Planning for Play.* Cambridge: MIT Press.

Appleton, Jay. 1996. *The Experience of Landscape.* New York: John Wiley.

Beardsley, John. 1984. *Earthworks and Beyond: Contemporary Art in the Landscape.* New York: Cross River Press/Abbeville Press. (2nd ed., 1998.)

Bork, Dean R. 1983. "Grounds for Adventure." *Landscape Architecture* 73 (6): 66–69.

Carr, Judy F., and Chris Stevenson, eds. 1993. *Integrated Studies in the Middle Grades: "Dancing through Walls."* Teachers College, Columbia University. New York: Teachers College Press.

Cooper-Marcus, Clare. 2001. "For Children Only." *Landscape Architecture* 91 (12): 66–71, 85.

Dattner, Richard. 1969. *Design for Play.* New York: Van Nostrand Reinhold.

Dewey, John. 1938. *Experience and Education.* New York: Collier-Macmillan. (Reprint, 1970.)

Dramstad, Wenche E., James D. Olson, and Richard T. T. Forman. 1996. *Landscape Ecology Principles in Landscape Architecture and Land-Use Planning.* Washington, D.C.: Island Press and the American Society of Landscape Architects.

Ellis, Michael. 1973. *Why People Play.* London: Prentice-Hall International.

Eriksen, Aase. 1985. *Playground Design: Outdoor Environments for Learning and Development.* New York: Van Nostrand Reinhold.

Francis, Mark. 1995. "Childhood's Garden: Memory and Meaning of Gardens." *Children's Environments Quarterly* 12: 183–191.

Frost, Joe L., and Sue C. Wortham. 1988. "The Evolution of American Playgrounds." *Young Children* 43 (1): 19–28.

Gardner, Howard. 1993. *Multiple Intelligences: The Theory in Practice.* New York: Basic Books: A Division of HarperCollins.

———. 2000. *Intelligence Reframed: Multiple Intelligences for the 21st Century.* New York: Basic Books, Perseus Books Group.

Grant, Tim, and Gail Littlejohn. 2001. *Greening School Grounds: Creating Habitats for Learning.* Gabriola Island, British Columbia, Canada: New Society Publishers.

Hart, Roger. 1973. "Adventures in a Wooded Wonderland." *Natural History* 82 (9): 67–69.

———. 1979. *Children's Experience of Place.* New York: Irvington Publishers.

Johnson, Lauri Macmillan. 1988. "The Brook Knolls Cooperative Community: A Case Study for Resident Design of Public Open Space." *Landscape and Urban Planning* 17: 283–295.

———. 2002. "American Design on the Land," The University of Arizona, December 5. Unpublished text from class/workshop.

———. 2003. "Schoolyard Gardens for Integrated Learning," University of Texas, Arlington, October 23. Unpublished text from guest lecture/workshop.

———. 2004. "User Analysis in Landscape Architecture," School of Landscape Architecture, The University of Arizona, November 17. Unpublished text from guest lecture/workshop.

Lickona, Thomas. 1995. "Summing Up the Case for Values Education: Ten Good Reasons Why Schools Should Revive Moral Education." *Arizona School Board Association Journal* 25 (2): 8–9.

Lieberman, Gerald A., and Linda L. Hoody. 1998. *Closing the Achievement Gap: Using the Environment as an Integrating Context for Learning.* State Education and Environment Roundtable, 16486 Bernardo Center Drive, Suite 328, San Diego, CA 92128.

Moore, Robin C. 1993. *Plants for Play: A Plant Selection Guide for Children's Outdoor Environments.* Berkeley, CA: MIG Communications.

Moore, Robin C., and Herb H. Wong. 1997. *Natural Learning: The Life History of an Environmental Schoolyard.* Berkeley, CA: MIG Communications.

Nabhan, Gary, and Stephen Trimble. 1994. *The Geography of Childhood: Why Children Need Wild Places.* Boston: Beacon Press.

Nicholson, Simon. 1976. "How Not to Cheat Children: The Theory of Loose Parts." University Extension, University of California, Davis. Handout.

Page, Robert R., Cathy A. Gilbert, and Susan A. Dolan. 1998. *A Guide to Cultural Landscape Reports: Contents, Process, and Techniques.* U.S. Department of the Interior, National Park Service. Cultural Resource Stewardship and Partnership, Park Historic Structures and Cultural Landscape Program, Washington, D.C.

Pregill, Philip, and Nancy Volkman. 1999. *Landscapes in History: Design and Planning in the Eastern and Western Traditions.* 2nd ed. New York: John Wiley and Sons.

Rosenthal, Ann T. 2003. "Teaching Systems Thinking and Practice through Environmental Art." *Ethics and the Environment* 8 (1): 153–168.

Schicker, Lisa. 1987. "Design Criteria for Children and Wildlife in Residential Developments." In *Integrating Man and Nature in the Metropolitan Environment: Proceedings: National Symposium on Urban Wildlife,* ed. Lowell W. Adams and Daniel L. Leedy, 99–105. Columbia, MD: National Institute for Urban Wildlife.

Sebba, Rachel. 1991. "The Landscapes of Childhood: The Reflection of Children's Environment in Adult Memories and in Children's Attitudes." *Environment and Behavior* 23: 395.

Skelding, Mark, Martin Kemple, and Joseph Kiefer. 2001. *Living Traditions, A Teacher's Guide: Teaching Local History Using State and National Learning Standards.* Montpelier, VT: Common Roots Press.

Tufts, Craig. 1993. *The Backyard Naturalist.* Washington, D.C.: National Wildlife Federation.

Twain, Mark (Samuel Langhorne Clemens). 1876. *The Adventures of Tom Sawyer.* Hartford, CT: The American Publishing Company.

Vasiloff, Heidi. 1998. "Schoolyard Wildlife Habitats—Building for the Future." *Arizona Wildlife Views* 40 (6): 6–7.

Weston, Arthur. 1962. *The Making of American Physical Fitness.* New York: Appleton-Century-Crofts.

Wilson, Ruth. 1995. "Let Nature Be Your Teacher." *Day Care and Early Education* 22 (3): 31–34.

———. 1997. "The Wonders of Nature: Honoring Children's Way of Knowing." *Early Childhood News* 9 (2): 6–9, 16–19.

Additional Sources

Ackerman, Diane. 1995. *The Rarest of the Rare.* New York: Random House.

Adams, Eileen. 1990. *Learning through Landscapes: A Report on the Use, Design, Management and Development of School Grounds.* Winchester, U.K.: Learning through Landscapes Trust.

———. 1991. "Back to Basics: Aesthetic Experience." *Children's Environment Quarterly* (New York) 8: 2.

Arizona Native Plant Society. 1990–1996. Desert Butterfly Gardening; Desert Shrubs; Desert Groundcovers and Vines; Desert Grasses; Desert Accent Plants; and Desert Trees. Tucson, AZ. Brochures.

Brett, Arlene, Eugene Provenzo, and Robin Moore. 1993. "Child's Play." *The American School Board Journal* 180 (12): 22–25.

Brown, David E., Charles E. Lowe, and Charles P. Pase. 1982. "Biotic Communities of the American Southwest—United States and Mexico." *Desert Plants* 4: 1–4.

Carmen, Sam. 1992. *Guidelines and Features for Outdoor Classrooms.* Indianapolis, IN: Indiana Department of Natural Resources, Division of Forestry.

Carr, John N. 1992. *Arizona Wildlife Viewing Guide.* Helena and Billings, MT: Falcon Press.

Cockrum, E. Lendell. 1982. *Mammals of the Southwest.* Tucson: University of Arizona Press.

Coffee, Stephen R., and Mary S. Rivkin. 1990. "Make the Most of Your Schoolyard." *Principal* 79 (2): 31–35.

Dubos, René. 1980. *The Wooing of Earth: New Perspectives on Man's Use of Nature.* New York: Charles Scribner's Sons.

Engel-Wilson, Carolyn. 1992. *Landscaping for Desert Wildlife.* Phoenix: Arizona Game and Fish Department.

Forman, Richard T. T., and Michel Godron. 1986. *Landscape Ecology.* New York: John Wiley and Sons.

Friedberg, M. Paul. 1970. *Play and Interplay: A Manifesto for New Design in Urban Recreational Environment.* New York: Macmillan.

Gardner, Howard. 1991. *The Unschooled Mind: How Children Think and How Schools Should Teach.* New York: Basic Books, HarperCollins.

Guy, Linda A., Cathy Cromell, and Lucy K. Bradley. 1996. *Success with School Gardens: How to Create a Learning Oasis in the Desert.* Phoenix: Arizona Master Gardener Press.

Hart, Roger. 1979. *Children's Experience of Place.* New York: Irvington Publishers.

———. 1992. "Children's Participation: from Tokenism to Citizenship." Innocenti Essays, No. 4. Florence, Italy: UNICEF Centre.

———. 1997. *Children's Participation: The Theory and Practice of Involving Young Citizens in Community Development and Environmental Care.* New York: UNICEF; and London: Earthscan.

Hart, Roger, Robin C. Moore, Clare Cooper Marcus, Audrey Penn Rodgers, and Paul Arnold. 1974. "The Children's Landscape." *Landscape Architecture* 65 (5): 354–380, 415–417.

Hoffa, Robert L. 1996. *Coexisting with Urban Wildlife.* Prescott, AZ: Sharlot Hall Museum Press.

Hoffmeister, Donald F. 1986. *Mammals of Arizona.* Tucson: University of Arizona Press.

Kirby, Mary Ann. "Nature as Refuge in Children's Environments." *Children's Environments Quarterly: Children and Vegetation* 6 (1): 7–12.

Kovalik, Susan J., and Karen Olsen. 1994. *Integrated Thematic Instruction: The Model.* Kent, WA: Susan Kovalik and Associates.

Moore, Robin. 1986a. *Children's Domain—Play and Place in Child Development.* London: Croom Helm.

Moore, Robin. 1986b. "The Power of Nature." *Children's Environments Quarterly* 3 (3): 52–69.

Moore, Robin. 1989. "Before and After Asphalt: Diversity as an Ecological Measure of Quality in Children's Outdoor Environments." In *The Ecological Context of Children's Play,* ed. Marianne N. Bloch and Anthony D. Pellegrini, 191–213. Greenwich, CT: Ablex Publishing.

Moore, Robin C., Susan M. Goltsman, and Daniel S. Iacofano. 1992. *Play for All Guidelines.* Berkeley, CA: MIG Communications.

Moore, Robin, and Herb Wong H. 1984. "Animals on the Washington Environmental Yard." *Children's Environments Quarterly* 1 (3): 43–51.

Olds, Anita. 1989. "Nature as Healer." *Children's Environments Quarterly: Children and Vegetation* 6 (1): 27–32.

Ryan, Deborah E. 1990. "Playing with Public Art." *Landscape Architecture* 80 (9): 76–78.

Schneekloth, Lynda H. 1989. "Where Did You Go? The Forest. What Did You See? Nothing." *Children's Environments Quarterly: Children and Vegetation* 6 (1): 7–12.

Stine, Sharon. 1997. *Landscapes for Learning: Creating Outdoor Environments for Children and Youth.* New York: John Wiley and Sons.

Sutton-Smith, Brian. 1990. "School Playground as Festival." *Children's Environments Quarterly* 7 (2): 3–7.

Tuan, Yi-Fu. 1978. "Children and the Natural Environment." In *Children and the Environment,* ed. Irwin Altman and Joachim F. Wohlwill, 5–32. New York: Plenum Press.

Tufts, Craig, and Peter Loewer. 1995. *Gardening for Wildlife: How to Create a Beautiful Habitat for Birds, Butterflies, and Other Wildlife.* Emmaus, PA: Rodale Press.

Wilson, Edward O., ed. 1988. *Biodiversity.* Washington, D.C.: National Academy Press.

Chapter Two

Crowe, Sylvia. 1958. *Garden Design.* New York: Hearthside Press.

Duell, Prentice. 1919. *Mission Architecture as Exemplified in San Xavier del Bac; Including a Complete List of the Missions of the Southwest.* Tucson, AZ: Archaeological and Historical Society.

Hogarth, William. 1772. *The Analysis of Beauty (Written with a View of Fixing the Fluctuating Ideas of Taste).* London: Printed by W. Strahan for Mrs. Hogarth.

Johnson, Lauri Macmillan. 2001. "Design Fundamentals." In *Encyclopedia of Gardens: History and Design,* ed. Candice Shoemaker, Vol. 1, A–F, 355–375. Chicago: Fitzroy Dearborn Publishers.

Leszczynski, Nancy. 1999. *Planting the Landscape: a Professional Approach to Garden Design.* New York: John Wiley & Sons.

McHarg, Ian L. 1969. *Design with Nature.* Garden City, NY: Doubleday.

Additional Sources

Birnbaum, Charles A., ed. 1999. *Preserving Modern Landscape Architecture: Papers from the Wave Hill National Park Service Conference.* Cambridge, MA: Spacemaker Press.

Birnbaum, Charles A., and Robin Karson, eds. 2000. *Pioneers of American Landscape Design.* New York: McGraw Hill.

Carr, Ethan. 1998. *Wilderness by Design: Landscape Architecture and the National Park Service.* Lincoln: University of Nebraska Press.

Crandell, Gina, and Heidi Landecker, eds. 1998. *Designed Landscape Forum 1.* Washington, D.C.: Spacemaker Press.

Francis, Mark, and Randolph Hester. 1990. *The Meaning of Gardens: Idea, Place, and Action.* Cambridge: MIT Press.

Frankel, Felice, and Jory Johnson. 1991. *Modern Landscape Architecture: Redefining the Garden.* New York: Abbeville Press.

Haskell, Barbara. 1999. *The American Century: Art and Culture, 1900-1950.* New York: Whitney Museum of American Art.

Hunt, John Dixon, and Peter Willis, eds. 1975. *The Genius of the Place: The English Landscape Garden, 1620-1820.* New York: Harper and Row; London: Elek.

Jellicoe, Geoffrey, and Susan Jellicoe. 1975. *The Landscape of Man: Shaping the Environment from Prehistory to the Present Day.* New York: Viking Press; London: Thames and Hudson. Rev. and enlarged ed., New York and London: Thames and Hudson, 1987; 3rd ed., New York: Thames and Hudson, 1995.

Jencks, Charles. 1987. *Post-Modernism: The New Classicism in Art and Architecture.* New York: Rizzoli; London: Academy Editions.

Kassler, Elizabeth B. 1964. *Modern Gardens and the Landscape.* New York: Museum of Modern Art. Rev. ed., 1984.

Kostof, Spiro. 1987. *America by Design.* New York: Oxford University Press.

Landecker, Heidi, ed. 1997. *Martha Schwartz: Transfiguration of the Commonplace.* Washington, D.C.: Spacemaker Press.

Lippard, Lucy R. 1983. *Overlay: Contemporary Art and the Art of Prehistory.* New York: Pantheon.

Lyall, Sutherland. 1991. *Designing the New Landscape.* New York: Van Nostrand Reinhold; London: Thames and Hudson.

Moore, Charles Willard, William J. Mitchell, and William Turnbull, Jr. 1988. *The Poetics of Gardens.* Cambridge: MIT Press.

Mosser, Monique, and George Teyssot. 1990. *L'Architettura dei giardini d'Occidente: Dal Rinascimento al Novecento.* Milan: Electa. Translated as *The History of Garden Design: The Western Tradition from the Renaissance to the Present Day.* London: Thames and Hudson, 1991.

Newton, Norman T. 1971. *Design on the Land: The Development of Landscape Architecture.* Cambridge: Harvard University Press.

Scott, Robert Gillam. 1980. *Design Fundamentals.* Huntington, NY: Robert E. Krieger Publishing.

Simo, Melanie. 1999. *100 Years of Landscape Architecture: Some Patterns of a Century.* Washington, D.C.: American Society of Landscape Architects Press.

Simo, Melanie, and David Dillon. 1997. *Sasaki Associates Integrated Environments.* Washington, D.C.: Spacemaker Press.

Thacker, Christopher. 1979. *The History of Gardens.* Berkeley: University of California Press; London: Croom Helm.

Tishler, William H., ed. 1989. *American Landscape Architecture: Designers and Places.* Washington, D.C.: The Preservation Press, National Trust for Historic Preservation.

Treib, Marc, ed. 1993. *Modern Landscape Architecture: A Critical Review.* Cambridge: MIT Press.

Walker, Peter, and Melanie Simo. 1994. *Invisible Gardens: The Search for Modernism in the American Landscape.* Cambridge: MIT Press.

Wilkinson, Elizabeth, and Marjorie Henderson. 1985. *The House of Boughs: A Sourcebook of Garden Designs, Structures, and Suppliers.* New York: Viking Press.

Chapter Three

Caudill, William W. 1973. *The "Analysis Card" Technique.* Pullman: Washington State University at Pullman. Handout.

Garden Conservancy, The. 1996. "Roberto Burle Marx: Legend and Legacy." Symposium presented by The Garden Conservancy and co-sponsored by The Americas Society and Longwood Gardens, March 1996, New York, NY, and Kennett Square, PA. Brochure.

Kiefer, Joseph, and Martin Kemple. 1998. *Digging Deeper: Integrating Youth Gardens into Schools and Communities.* Philadelphia, PA: American Community Gardening Association.

Lynch, Kevin, and Gary Hack. 1984. *Site Planning.* 3rd ed. Cambridge: MIT Press.

Page, Robert R., Cathy A. Gilbert, and Susan A. Dolan. 1998. *A Guide to Cultural Landscape Reports: Contents, Process, and Techniques.* Washington, D.C.: U.S. Department of the Interior, National Park Service; Cultural Resource Stewardship and Partnership, Park Historic Structures and Cultural Landscape Program.

Rutledge, Albert J. 1971. *Anatomy of a Park: The Essentials of Recreation Area Planning and Design.* New York: McGraw-Hill.

Silko, Leslie Marmon. 1995. "Interior and Exterior Landscapes: The Pueblo Migration Stories." In *Landscapes in America,* ed. George F. Thompson, 155–170. Austin: University of Texas Press.

Simonds, John Ormsbee. 1983. *Landscape Architecture: A Manual of Site Planning and Design.* New York: McGraw-Hill.

Additional Sources

Birnbaum, Charles A., ed. 1996. *The Secretary of the Interior's Standards for the Treatment of Historic Properties, with Guidelines for the Treatment of Cultural Landscapes.* Washington, D.C.: U.S. Department of the Interior, National Park Service, Cultural Resource Stewardship and Partnerships, Heritage Preservation Services, Historic Landscape Initiative.

Booth, Norman K. 1983. *Basic Elements of Landscape Architecture.* New York: Elsevier Science Publishing.

Booth, Norman K., and James E. Hiss. 1991. *Residential Landscape Architecture: Design Process for the Private Residence.* Englewood Cliffs, NJ: Prentice Hall.

Hester, Randolph T. 1984. *Planning Neighborhood Space With People.* 2nd ed. New York: Van Nostrand Reinhold.

Laurie, Michael. 1986. *An Introduction to Landscape Architecture.* 2nd ed. New York: Elsevier Science Publishing.

Melnick, Robert Z. 1981. "Capturing the Cultural Landscape." *Landscape Architecture* (January): 56–60.

Peña, William. 1987. *Problem Seeking: An Architectural Programming Primer.* 3rd ed. Washington, D.C.: AIA Press.

Chapter Four

Dubos, René. 1972. *A God Within.* New York: Charles Scribner's Sons.
McHarg, Ian L. 1969. *Design with Nature.* Garden City, NY: Doubleday.

Additional Sources

White, Edward T. 1983. *Site Analysis Diagramming Information for Architectural Design.* Tallahassee, FL: Architectural Media.

Chapter Five

Americans with Disabilities Act Design Guidelines. Effective in 1990. U.S. Department of Justice. http://www.azcentral.com/ (site visited June 6, 2004).

Duffield, Mary Rose, and Warren Jones. 2001. *Plants for Dry Climates: How to Select, Grow, and Enjoy.* Cambridge, MA: Perseus Publishing.

Kaplan, Rachel, and Stephen Kaplan. 1998. *With People in Mind: Design and Management of Everyday Nature.* Washington D.C.: Island Press.

Livingston, Margaret. 2001. "Xeriscape." In *Encyclopedia of Gardens: History and Design,* ed. Candice A. Shoemaker, Vol. 3, P–Z, 1455–1457. Chicago: Fitzroy Dearborn Publishers.

McPherson, Gregory, and Charles Sacamano. 1989. *Southwestern Landscaping That Saves Energy and Water.* Tucson, AZ: Cooperative Extension, University of Arizona.

Mielke, Judy. 1993. *Native Plants for Southwestern Landscapes.* Austin: University of Texas Press.

Moore, Robin C., and Herb H. Wong. 1997. *Natural Learning: The Life History of an Environmental Schoolyard.* Berkeley, CA: MIG Communications.

Nabhan, Gary Paul. 1985. *Gathering the Desert.* Tucson: University of Arizona Press.

Safety Guidelines. 1991. Washington, D.C.: U.S. Consumer Product Safety Commission (CPSC).

Schaefer, Renee Suzanne. 2003. "Defining Success in Schoolyard Design in Tucson, Arizona: Evaluating Schoolyards Utilizing Assessment, Staff Perceptions, and Achievement Test Scores." Master's thesis, School of Landscape Architecture, The University of Arizona, Tucson.

Steen, Athena Swentzell, Bill Steen, and David Bainbridge. 1994. *The Straw Bale House.* White River Junction, VT: Chelsea Green Publishing.

Thompson, Donna, and Susan Hudson. 2000. *National Action Plan for the Prevention of Playground Injuries.* Cedar Falls: National Program for Playground Safety, School of Health, Physical Education, and Leisure Services (HPELS), University of Northern Iowa.

Titman, Wendy. 1994. *Special Places, Special People: The Hidden Curriculum of School Grounds.* WWFUK (World Wide Fund for Nature)/Learning through Landscapes. Surrey, UK: Panda House.

Whyte, William H. 1980. *The Social Life of Small Urban Spaces.* Washington, D.C.: The Conservation Foundation.

Additional Sources

David, Al. 1987. *Garden Ponds: A Complete Introduction.* Neptune City, NJ: T.F.H. Publications.

Ellefson, Connie Lockhart, Thomas L. Stephens, and Douglas Welsh. 1992. *Xeriscape Gardening: Water Conservation for the American Landscape.* New York: Macmillan.

Elmore, Francis H. 1976. *Shrubs and Trees of the Southwest Uplands.* Tucson, AZ: Southwest Parks and Monuments Association.

Harris, Charles W., and Nicholas T. Dines, eds. 1998. *Time-Saver Standards for Landscape Architecture.* 2nd ed. New York: McGraw-Hill.

Johnson, Eric A., and Scott Millard. 1993. *The Low-Water Flower Gardener.* Tucson, AZ: Ironwood Press.

Lancaster, Brad. 2006. *Rainwater Harvesting for Drylands.* Vol. 1, *Guiding Principles to Welcome Rain into Your Life and Landscape.* Tucson, AZ: Rainsource Press.

Moody, Mary. 1994. *Creating Water Gardens.* Sydney, Australia: Lansdown Publishing.

Mutel, Cornelia Fleischer, and John C. Emerick. 1984. *From Grassland to Glacier: The Natural History of Colorado.* Boulder, CO: Johnson Books.

Nash, Helen. 1996. *The Complete Pond Builder.* New York: Sterling Publishing.

Peace, Tom. 2000. *Sunbelt Gardening: Success in Hot-Weather Climates.* Golden, CO: Fulcrum.

Robinette, Gary O. 1984. *Water Conservation in Landscape Design and Management.* New York: Van Nostrand Reinhold.

Robinson, Peter. 1987. *Pool and Waterside Gardening.* London: Hamlyn Publishing Group.

———. 1999. *Water-Wise Gardening.* New York: Dorling Kindersley.

Schuler, Carol. 1993. *Low-Water-Use Plants: For California and the Southwest.* Tucson, AZ: Fischer Books.

Stadelmann, Peter. 1992. *Water Gardens.* Hauppauge, NY: Barrons Educational Series.

Sunset Books and Sunset Magazine, eds. 1988. *Sunset Western Garden Book.* Menlo Park, CA: Sunset Publishing.

Walker, Theodore D. 1978. *Site Design and Construction Detailing.* Mesa, AZ: PDA Publishing.

———. 1985. *Planting Design.* Mesa, AZ: PDA Publishing.

Wasowski, Sally, and Andy Wasowski. 1991. *Native Texas Plants: Landscaping Region by Region.* Houston, TX: Gulf Publishing.

———. 1995. *Native Gardens for Dry Climates.* New York: Potter.

Winger, David, ed. 1998. *Xeriscape Color Guide: 100 Water-Wise Plants for Gardens and Landscapes.* Golden, CO: Fulcrum.

Chapter Six

Williams, Ted. 2001. "Out of Control." *Audubon Magazine* (September–October): 38–47.

Additional Reading and Sources

Sources of information useful for developing the wildlife habitat garden and curriculum to accompany its use as a teaching tool are diverse. The sources below are good places to begin.

Societies and Institutions

Arizona Native Plant Society, P.O. Box 41206, Sun Station, Tucson, AZ 85717, www.aznps.org (accessed August 8, 2007).

Arizona-Sonora Desert Museum, 2021 N. Kinney Rd., Tucson, AZ 85743-8918, (520)883-1380, www.desertmuseum.org (accessed August 8, 2007).

Balboa Park, City of San Diego, 2125 Park Blvd., San Diego, CA 92101-4792, www.balboapark.org (accessed August 11, 2007).

Boyce Thompson Arboretum, 37615 U.S. Hwy. 60, Superior, AZ 85273, (520)689-2723, www.ag.arizona.edu/BTA (accessed August 11, 2007).

Butterflies across the Americas, National Council of State Garden Clubs, Inc., 4401 Magnolia Ave., St. Louis, MO 63110-3492, (314)776-7574, Fax: (314)776-5108.

California Native Plant Society, 18550 Country Pine Rd., Perris, CA 92570, www.cnps.org (accessed August 11. 2007).

Council for Environmental Education, 5555 Morningside Drive, Houston, TX 77005-3216, (713)520-1936.

Desert Botanical Gardens, 1201 N. Galvin Parkway, Phoenix, AZ 85008, (480)941-1225, www.dbg.org (accessed August 11, 2007).

Desert Demonstration Gardens, 3701 S. Valley View Blvd., Las Vegas, NV 89153, (702)258-3205, www.springspreserve.org (accessed August 11, 2007).

Desert Water Agency, 1200 Gene Autry Trail South, Palm Springs, CA 92264, (760)323-4971, www.dwa.org (accessed August 11, 2007).

El Paso Native Plant Society, 7760 Maya Ave., El Paso, TX 79912.

Lady Bird Johnson Wildflower Center, 4801 La Crosse Ave., Austin, TX 78739-1702, (512)292-4200, www.wildflower.org (accessed August 11, 2007).

The Living Desert, 47900 Portola Ave, Palm Desert, CA 92260, www.livingdesert.org (accessed August 11, 2007).

Los Angeles Zoo Native Garden, 5336 Crystal Springs Dr., Los Angeles, CA 90027, (323)644-6400, www.lazoo.org (accessed August 11, 2007).

Native Plant Society of New Mexico, P.O. Box 5917, Santa Fe, NM 87502, www.npsnm.unm.edu (accessed August 11, 2007).

Native Plant Society of Texas, 117 W. 7th St., Suite 3, Georgetown, TX 78626, www.npsot.org (accessed August 11, 2007).

Nevada Mojave Native Plant Society, 8180 Placid Dr., Las Vegas, NV 98123.

New Mexico State University Cooperative Extension, Box 30003, MSC 3AE, Las Cruces, NM 88003, www.cahe.nmsu.edu/ces (accessed August 11, 2007).

Project SEED-Student Environmental Demonstration Gardens, 811 W. 16th St., Yuma, AZ 85364, (520)329-7996.

Project WILD, 5430 Grosvenor Lane, Suite 230, Bethesda, MD 20814-2142, (301)493-5447.

Quail Botanical Gardens, P.O. Box 230005, Encitas, CA 92023-0005, (760)436-3036.

San Diego Zoo, Education Department, P.O. Box 120551, San Diego, CA 92112-0551, (619)234-3153, www.sandiegozoo.org (accessed August 11, 2007).

Texas A&M University Cooperative Extension Service, 1030 N. Zaragosa Rd., Suite A, El Paso, TX 79907, (915)859-7725, http://aggie-horticulture.tamu.edu (accessed August 11, 2007).

The Theodore Payne Foundation, 10459 Tuxford St., Sun Valley, CA 91352, (818)768-1802, www.theodorepayne.org/home.html (accessed August 11, 2007).

University of Arizona Cooperative Extension, Tucson: (520)626-5161, Phoenix: (602)470-8086, http://ag.arizona.edu/extension (accessed August 11, 2007).

University of California Cooperative Extension, 2 Coral Circle, Monterrey Park, CA 91755, (323)838-8330, http://celosangeles.ucdavis.edu (accessed August 11, 2007).

Yuma Conservation Garden, 2520 E. 32nd St., Yuma, AZ 85365, (520)317-1935.

Publications

Desert Butterfly Gardening. 1996. Tucson: Arizona Native Plant Society and Sonoran Arthropod Studies Institute.

Desert Plants. 1990–1997. Tucson: Arizona Native Plant Society.

Duffield, Mary Rose, and Warren D. Jones. 1981. *Plants for Dry Climates*. Los Angeles: Price Stern Sloan.

Foss, Diana M., and Ronald K. Jones. 1999. *Creating a School Habitat*. Austin: Texas Parks and Wildlife Department.

Glassberg, Jeffrey. 2001. *Butterflies through Binoculars: The West*. New York: Oxford University Press.

Growing Ideas: A Journal of Garden-Based Learning. National Gardening Association, 1100 Dorset Street, South Burlington, VT 05403, www.kidsgardening.com (accessed December 3, 2004).

Holmes, Roger, and Rita Buchanan. 1992. *Taylor's Guide to Gardening in the Southwest*. Taylor's Weekend Gardening Guides. Boston: Houghton Mifflin.

How to Attract Hummingbirds and Butterflies. 1991. San Ramon, CA: Ortho Books.

Johnson, Eric A. and Scott Millard. 1992. *The Low-Water Flower Gardener*. Natural Garden Series. Tucson, AZ: Ironwood Press.

Krebbs, Karen. 2002. *Hummingbirds, Beauty in Flight*. Lincolnwood, IL: Publications International.

Kress, Stephen. 1985. *The Audubon Society Guide to Attracting Birds*. New York: Charles Scribner's Sons.

Labadie, Emile L. 1978. *Native Plants for Use in the California Landscape.* Sierra City, CA: Sierra City Press.

Landis, Betsey. 2001. *Southern California Native Plants for School Gardens.* Sacramento: California Native Plant Society.

Landscaping for Desert Wildlife. 1999. Phoenix: Arizona Game and Fish Department.

Lavies, Bianca. *Compost Critters.* 1993. New York: Dutton Children's Books.

Lenz, Lee W., and John Dourly. 1981. *California Native Trees and Shrubs.* Claremont, CA: Rancho Santa Ana Botanic Garden.

Logsdon, Gene. 1983. *Wildlife in Your Garden, or Dealing with Deer, Rabbits, Raccoons, Moles, Crows, Sparrows, and Other of Nature's Creatures.* Emmaus, PA: Rodale Press.

MacMahon, James A. 1985. *Deserts.* Audubon Society Nature Guides. New York: Knopf.

McKinley, Michael. *How to Attract Birds.* 1983. San Francisco, CA: Ortho Books.

Mielke, Judy. 1993. *Native Plants for Southwestern Landscapes.* Austin: University of Texas Press.

Millard, Scott. 1989. *Gardening in Dry Climates.* San Ramon, CA: Ortho Books.

Miller, George O. 1991. *Landscaping with Native Plants of Texas and the Southwest.* Stillwater, MN: Voyageur Press.

Perry, Bob. 1992. *Landscape Plants for Western Regions.* Claremont, CA: Land Design.

Phillips, Judith. 1987. *Southwestern Landscaping with Native Plants.* Santa Fe: Museum of New Mexico Press.

Phillips, Steven J., and Patricia Wentworth Comus, eds. 2000. *A Natural History of the Sonoran Desert.* Tucson: Arizona-Sonora Desert Museum.

Schneck, Marcus. 1992. *Your Backyard Wildlife Garden: How to Attract and Identify Wildlife in Your Yard.* Emmaus, PA: Rodale Press.

Schuler, Carol. 1993. *Low-Water-Use Plants for California and the Southwest.* Tucson, AZ: Fisher Books.

Science and Children. National Science Teachers Association, 1840 Wilson Blvd., Arlington, VA 22210-3000, http://www.nsta.org (accessed August 11, 2007).

Squire, Ann. 1996. *101 Questions and Answers about Backyard Wildlife.* New York: Walker and Company.

Stebbins, Robert C. 1966. *Field Guide to Western Reptiles and Amphibians.* Peterson Field Guide Series. Boston: Houghton Mifflin.

Tufts, Craig, and Peter Loewer. 1995. *The National Wildlife Federation's Guide to Gardening for Wildlife.* Emmaus, PA: Rodale Press.

Tuttle, Merlin D. 1987. *America's Neighborhood Bats.* Austin: University of Texas Press.

Tuttle, Merlin D., and Donna L. Hensley. 1993. *Bat House Builder's Handbook.* Austin: University of Texas Press.

Wasowski, Sally, and Andy Wasowski. 2002. *Native Texas Plants: Landscaping Region by Region.* Houston: Gulf.

Waterwise Gardening. 1989. Menlo Park, CA: Sunset.

WILD *School Sites: A Guide to Preparing for Habitat Improvement Projects on School Grounds.* 1993. Houston: Council for Environmental Education.

Internet Sources

BATS

"The Adventures of Echo the Bat" interactive program, http://science.hq.nasa.gov/kids/imagers/echohome.html (accessed August 11, 2007).

Bat Conservation International, www.batcon.org (accessed August 11, 2007).

Journey North Bats, www.learner.org/jnorth/www/critters/bat (accessed August 11, 2007).

Thematic resource, http://www.cccoe.k12.ca.us/bats/ (accessed August 11, 2007).

BEES

Bees, http://www.cyberbee.net (accessed August 11, 2007).
Cactus Bees, http://desertdiscovery.arizona.edu/bees.html (accessed August 11, 2007).
Elementary Lessons on Africanized Honey Bees, http://ag.arizona.edu/pubs/insects/ahb/ahbhome.html (accessed August 11, 2007).
Planting Bee Gardens, GEARS Tucson, http://gears.tucson.ars.ag.gov/book/index.html (accessed August 11, 2007).

BUTTERFLIES

Butterflies of North America, www.npwrc.usgs.gov/resource/distr/lepid/bflyusa/bflyusa.htm (accessed August 11, 2007).
Butterfly links, http://entowww.tamu.edu/extension (accessed August 11, 2007).
Butterfly University, www.butterflies.com (accessed August 11, 2007).

HUMMINGBIRDS

Journey North: Unpave the Way for Hummingbirds, www.learner.org/jnorth/unpave/hummer.html (accessed August 11, 2007).
Wild Birds Unlimited: Facts and Supplies, www.wbu.com/edu/hummer.htm (accessed August 11, 2007).

INSECTS

Elementary Lessons on Insects, http://insected.arizona.edu/home.html (accessed August 11, 2007).

MOTHS

Moths of North America, www.butterfliesandmoths.org (accessed August 11, 2007).

NATURAL SCIENCE

Arizona-Sonora Desert Museum, www.desertmuseum.org (accessed August 11, 2007).
Four to Explore, www.42explore.com (accessed August 11, 2007).
Globe Program, http://archive.globe.gov/globe_html.html (accessed August 11, 2007).
Science Spot, http://sciencespot.net (accessed August 11, 2007).
Teaching about Ecosystems, www.eartheducation.org (accessed August 11, 2007).

WILDLIFE GARDENS

California plants, www.laspilitas.com (accessed August 11, 2007).
National Wildlife Federation, Backyard Wildlife Habitat, www.nwf.org/backyardwildlifehabitat (accessed August 11, 2007).
References for low deserts, http://ag.arizona.edu/maricopa/garden/html/library/ref-anml.htm (accessed August 11, 2007).
Step-by-step guide to starting a school garden, http://aggie-horticulture.tamu.edu/kinder/steps.html (accessed August 11, 2007).
Texas Wildscapes, www.tpwd.state.tx.us/huntwild/wild/wildscapes (accessed August 11, 2007).

WORM COMPOSTING

Composting with worms, cityfarmer.org/wormcomp61.html (accessed August 11, 2007).
Vermicomposting (worm composting), www.mastercomposter.com (accessed August 11, 2007).

Plant Nurseries with a Good Selection of Native Plants

ARIZONA

Arid Zone Trees, P.O. Box 167, Queen Creek, AZ 85242, (602)987-9094.
Arizona Cactus Sales, 1619 S. Arizona Ave., Chandler, AZ 85248, (480)963-1061.

B & B Cactus Farm, 11550 E. Speedway, Tucson, AZ 85748, (520)721-4687.

Bach's Greenhouse Cactus Nursery, 8602 N. Thornydale, Tucson, AZ 85742, (520)744-3333.

Civano Nursery, 5301 S. Houghton Rd., Tucson, AZ 85747, (520)546-9200, *www.civano nursery.com* (accessed August 11, 2007).

Desert Gardens Nursery, 14312 S. Avenue 1E, Yuma, AZ 85365, (520)344-8712.

Desert Survivors, 1020 W. Starr Pass, Tucson, AZ 85713, (520)791-9309, www.desert survivors.org (accessed August 11, 2007).

Desert Way Nursery, 2321 N. Grand Dr., Apache Junction, AZ 85220, (480)982-8632.

Diamond JK Nursery, HC1, Box 389, Elgin, AZ 85611, (520)455-9262.

Mesquite Valley Growers, 8005 E. Speedway, Tucson, AZ 85710, (520)721-8600.

Native Seeds/SEARCH, 526 N. 4th Ave., Tucson, AZ 85705, (520)622-5561.

Silverbell Nursery, 2730 N. Silverbell Rd., Tucson, AZ 85745, (520)622-3907.

Southwest Desert Growers, 4027 E. Sagebrush, Sierra Vista, AZ 85650, (520)803-0063.

Spadefoot Nursery, HC1, Box 347C, Pearce, AZ 85625, (520)824-3247, E-mail: spade foot@vtc.net.

Tohono Chul Park, 7366 N. Paseo del Norte, Tucson, AZ 85704, (520)544-7922.

Wild Seed, Inc., P.O. Box 27751, Tempe, AZ 85285, (602)276-3536, Fax: (602)276-3524.

CALIFORNIA

Albright Seed Company, 487 Dawson Drive, Bay 5S, Camarillo, CA 93012, (800)423-8112, (805)484-0551, Fax: (805)987-9021, www.albrightseed.com (accessed August 11, 2007).

Green Desert Nursery, 79-301 Avenue 40, Bermuda Dunes, CA 92203, (760)360-6937.

Mockingbird Nurseries, 1670 Jackson St., Riverside, CA 92504, by appointment: (909)780-3571.

Pilitas Nursery, Las, 8331 Nelson Way, Escondido, CA 92026, (760)749-5930.

Tree of Life Nursery, 3321 Ortega Hwy., San Juan Capistrano, CA 92693. Open to public Fridays 9–4, (714)728-0685, www.TreeOfLifeNursery.com (accessed August 11, 2007).

NEVADA

Hoosier Desert Nursery, Native Mojave Plants, Las Vegas, NV, (702)943-1111.

Turner Greenhouses, Wholesale Cactus and Succulents, Las Vegas, NV, (702)645-2032.

NEW MEXICO

Crownsville Nursery (cactus and succulent nursery), P.O. Box 797, Crownsville, NM 21032, (410)849-3143.

Mesa Garden, P.O. Box 72, Belen, NM 87002, (505)864-3131, *http://www.mesagarden.com* (accessed August 11, 2007).

Plants of the Southwest, Albuquerque Retail Store: (505)344-8830; Santa Fe Retail Store: (505)438-8888; Mail Order Catalog: (800)788-7333, www.plantsofthesouthwest.com (accessed August 11, 2007).

Santa Ana Garden Center, The Pueblo of Santa Ana, 157 Jemez Dam Road, Bernalillo, NM 87004, (505)867-1322.

TEXAS

Barton Springs Nursery, 3601 Bee Caves Rd., Austin, TX 78746-5313, (512)328-6655.

Bolton Works and Country Landscapes, 333 W. Hwy. 290, P.O. Box 1100, Dripping Springs, TX 78620, (512)894-4234, E-mail: dnorman@wimberley-tx.com.

Desertland Nursery, 11306 Gateway East, El Paso, TX 79922, (915)858-1130, E-mail: desertland@worldnet.att.net.

Dodds Family Nursery and Florist, 515 W. Main St, Fredericksburg, TX 78624-3129, (830)997-9571.

Keller's Goin' Native, P.O. Box 486, Karnes City, TX 78118-0486, (830)780-4506.

Native American Seed, 127 N. 16th St, Junction, TX 76849, 1-800-728-4043, http://www.seedsource.com (accessed August 11, 2007).

Native Ornamentals, 110 S. 6th St., Mertzon, TX 76941, (915)835-2021.

Natives of Texas Nursery, 6520 Medina Hwy., Kerrville, TX 78028, (830)896-2169, http://nativesoftexas.com (accessed August 11, 2007).

Texas Ornamental Service, 9531 FM 1105, Jarrell, TX 76537, (512)746-5006.

Wichita Valley, 5314 Southwest Parkway, Wichita Falls, TX, (940)696-3082, http://www.fallsonline.com/wichitavalley (accessed August 11, 2007).

Wildseed Farms, P.O. Box 3000, 425 Wildflower Hills, Fredericksburg, TX 78624-3000, 1-800-848-0078, http://www.wildseedfarms.com (accessed August 11, 2007).

Find Nurseries

Nurseries by state (substitute state abbreviation), findnurseries.com (accessed August 11, 2007).

Wildlife Habitat Council, 8737 Colesville Rd., Suite 800, Silver Spring, MD 20910, phone: (301)588-8994, Fax: (301)588-4629, www.wildlifehc.org/managementtools/backyard stateresources.cfm (accessed August 11, 2007).